Appraising Foreign Investment
in Developing Countries

APPRAISING FOREIGN INVESTMENT IN DEVELOPING COUNTRIES

by

Deepak Lal

in collaboration with Martin Cave,
Paul Hare and Jeffrey Thompson

HEINEMANN LONDON

Heinemann Educational Books Ltd

LONDON EDINBURGH MELBOURNE AUCKLAND
TORONTO HONG KONG SINGAPORE
KUALA LUMPUR IBADAN NAIROBI
JOHANNESBURG LUSAKA
NEW DELHI

ISBN 0 435 84460 1

332.673091724

330.52 LAL

87740

Published by Heinemann Educational Books Ltd
48 Charles Street, London W1X 8AH
IBM set by Preface Limited, Salisbury, Wilts.
Printed in Great Britain by
William Clowes and Sons
London, Colchester, Beccles

Preface

This study is the product of a project on foreign investment in developing countries, financed by a grant from the Economic and Social Research Committee of the U.K.'s Overseas Development Administration. It took two years to execute and was based at Queen Elizabeth House, Oxford. It consisted of two stages. The first involved the preparation of guidelines for appraising foreign investment in developing countries, and this stage was completed in June 1971, and the revised Guidelines form Part II of this book. In the second stage of the project these Guidelines were then used to evaluate a number of foreign investment projects in Kenya and India. The data for these studies was gathered by Martin Cave and Jeffrey Thompson in Kenya and Paul Harc in India during the summer of 1971. Additional information was obtained in two visits I paid to the countries concerned. The choice of countries as well as the projects evaluated were determined by the willingness of firms to provide us with the data, as well as the restrictions imposed by my familiarity with the various economies, government approval to carry out the necessary research, as well as the availability of research workers. The results of these case studies form Parts III and IV of the book. These parts are based substantially on the work of my three research associates, and the specific parts of the book for which each of them is responsible are acknowledged in the appropriate places in the text.

We have accumulated a large number of debts in completing this study. Rather than give a two-page list of names we should like to make a blanket acknowledgment of our indebtedness to the numerous academics, businessmen and officials in India, Kenya and England, without whose help this study would not have been possible.

Oxford and London   Deepak Lal

Contents

PART FOUR: ASPECTS OF FOREIGN INVESTMENT
           IN KENYA

PART FIVE: PASSION, POLITICS AND POWER

Introduction

Private overseas investment (POI) is a burgeoning field of research, as well as a source of divergent passions at the moment. To launch yet another study of POI therefore requires some justification. This will also provide a useful introduction to this book.

As the title suggests, this book is essentially concerned with appraising POI in developing countries from the host country's point of view. More specifically it is aimed at providing decision-makers in developing countries with the necessary tools to determine the social net benefit to them from the operation, or in some cases divestment, of particular acts of POI. As such, our chief aim is in many ways markedly different from those of other studies in this field,[1] which have concentrated on either one or more of the following aspects: the determinants of POI; the theoretical integration of POI into standard economic theory; historical, country and/or industry studies of the essential development, features and effects of POI; the effects of past POI on various economic magnitudes in the investing and host countries; delineation of the tensions between host governments and foreign investors. All these aspects are however relevant in devising policies towards POI in developing countries, as well as in determining the limits of the bargaining process which, as we shall repeatedly emphasise in this book, is at the heart of the problem of appraising POI from the host country's point of view. Therefore the first part of the book will present a selective summary of the above aspects which may

1. See the following: C. Kindleberger, ed., *The International Corporation* (MIT, 1970); C. Kindleberger, *American Business Abroad* (Yale, 1969); Vernon, *Sovereignty at Bay* (Basic Books, New York, 1971); J. Dunning, ed., *The Multinational Enterprise* (Allen and Unwin, 1971); P. Ady, ed., *Private Foreign Investment and the Developing World* (Praeger, 1971).

be relevant in providing decision-makers in developing countries with available information on general features of POI which they may need to keep in mind when appraising particular acts of foreign investment.

The main aim of the book however is to provide 'planners' in developing countries with simple decision rules for deciding whether or not it is socially profitable to allow particular foreign investments, and/or to force the divestment/nationalisation of existing foreign investments in their country. This immediately suggests that the relevant decision rules must be designed to deal with discrete acts of foreign investment, and that in general it will not be of much use for policy-makers to be told that POI on average in the past has increased national welfare by Rs.X, or it can be taken that Rs X of POI leads to a Rs.Y improvement/worsening in the host country's balance of payments. This is apart from the practical problem of deriving suitable ways of measuring these 'ex post' effects of POI, for as the existing literature has repeatedly emphasised the answers are crucially dependent on what assumptions are made about the 'alternative position', that is the situation as it would have existed in the absence of POI. Whilst some assumptions about the 'alternative' position remain necessary for 'ex ante' appraisal of POI, these, as I shall argue in Part II, are relatively more tractable. Clearly, therefore, the relevant methodology for our purposes is cost-benefit analysis.

The existing literature on cost-benefit analysis has however confined itself mainly to providing decision rules for evaluating *domestic* investments. It needs to be extended to cover *foreign* investments by incorporation of the special cost and benefits which are associated with POI. This is done in the Guidelines of Part II. These Guidelines form an extension of the *OECD Manual of Industrial Project Analysis in Developing Countries, Vol. II; Social Cost Benefit Analysis* by I. M. D. Little and J. A. Mirrlees. The basic evaluation procedures of the *Manual* have been adopted because it helps to separate clearly the effects on potential social welfare which can be ascribed to POI *per se*, and those which are the result of general governmental policy, as for instance, the existence of a highly differentiated and varying effective protective structure in most developing countries. As will be clear from the discussion in Part I of this book and the case studies in Parts III and IV, the degree of effective protection provided is an important determinant of the social and private profitability of particular acts of POI, and more importantly it is in determining the degree of effective protection granted to particular foreign investments that most of the bargaining power of developing countries, and the distribution of the potential gains between the investor and the host country, lies. An extension of the OECD Manual method for evaluating POI therefore provides a simple and important tool in determining the potential social net benefit of particular foreign investments, as well as providing the essential information required for attempts to maximise the share of the social profit which accrues to the host country in the bargaining process with the foreign investor. Part II of the book is devoted to this task.

The case studies of particular foreign investments in India and Kenya which form Parts III and IV of the book, show how the Guidelines can be applied in practice, as well as demonstrating the micro-economics of foreign investment in the, admittedly, small sample of cases studies. These case studies should therefore also be of more general interest to all those interested in the micro-economics of development. They provide as well some empirical evidence on various general aspects of the motivation, and effects of POI in developing countries, which have been the chief concern of other researches on POI.

Finally, it is obvious that a study of POI is, par excellence, a subject in political economy. Whilst economists are perhaps advisedly told to stick to their last, many of those writing on POI have not been able to do so,[1] and in any case it would be myopic to ignore what, in the eyes of many people, is the major problem connected with POI — its effects on national sovereignty and power. Part V deals with these aspects of politics and power, in a highly selective, though — it is hoped — neither too shallow nor too polemical a manner.

1. See, for instance, Kindleberger, op. cit., Johnson in Part II of Kindleberger, ed., op. cit., Part V of Dunning, ed., op. cit., and Ady, ed., op. cit. Also see K. Boulding and T. Mukherjee, *Economic Imperialism* (Michigan, 1972).

Abbreviations

AER	*American Economic Review*
ARI	Accounting Rate of Interest
CDC	Commonwealth Development Corporation
CRI	Consumption Rate of Interest
CRIB	Commission for Regulating International Business
CSIR	Council for Scientific and Industrial Research (India)
DAC	Development Assistance Committee
DFCK	Development Finance Company of Kenya
EAC	East African Cables Ltd.
GDP	Gross Domestic Product
GNP	Gross National Product
HDPE	High density polyethylene
IBRD	International Bank for Reconstruction and Development
ICDC	Industrial and Commercial Development Corporation (Kenya)
ICICI	Industrial Credit and Investment Corporation of India
ICO	An international canning organisation
ICOR	Incremental capital-output ratio
IDBI	Industrial Development Bank of India
IFCI	Industrial Finance Corporation of India
IRR	Internal Rate of Return
JPE	*Journal of Political Economy*
KIE	Kenya Industrial Estates Ltd.
KTDC	Kenya Tourist Development Corporation
LDC	Less developed countries
LHS	Left hand side
LM	Little-Mirrlees
MSC	Marginal social cost
MSV	Marginal social value
NCAER	National Council of Applied Economic Research (India)
NCC	National Construction Corporation (Kenya)
NDC	National Development Corporation (Tanzania)
NOCIL	National Organic Chemical Industries Ltd. (India)
NPV	Net Present Value
NSB	Net Social Benefit
OECD	Organisation for Economic Co-operation and Development
PIL	Polyolefins Industries Ltd. (India)
POI	Private Overseas Investment (Investor(s))
QJE	*Quarterly Journal of Economics*
R & D	Research and Development

RHS	Right hand side
SCF	Standard conversion factor
SER	Shadow exchange rate
SL	A safari lodge
SWR	Shadow Wage Rate
UDC	Uganda Development Corporation
UNIDO	United Nations Industrial Development Organisation
VMP	Value marginal product

PART ONE

Foreign Investment in Developing Countries

A General Review

This part provides a highly selective summary of the dimensions, determinants and effects of foreign investment in developing countries, its aim being to provide planners with an overall view of the features of foreign investment, which will help to put in perspective the specific guidelines and case studies which follow in subsequent parts. Though based entirely on secondary sources, it is by no means a complete review of the literature on foreign investment.

I.1 DIMENSIONS

This chapter provides a selective summary of the available evidence on the dimensions of the existing stock and recent flows of foreign investment to developing countries. It delineates the regional and sectoral composition of the stock and the flows, and assesses the relative importance for developing countries of POI flows compared with other flows of foreign capital to developing countries.

Figs. I.1 and I.2, illustrate the available estimates for the *stock* of POI at the end of 1970 in developing countries, by region, sector and country of ownership. The following characteristics of this stock are notable. First, Latin America dominates in terms of its relative share of the total stock of POI, as well as the stock of POI in each sector, in developing countries. Secondly, the U.S.A. is the largest owner of the POI stock in developing countries, and its holdings are heavily concentrated in Latin America, though it is the largest owner of the POI stock in every region except Africa and Asia. Thirdly, the U.K., which is the second largest owner of the aggregate developing country POI stock, has the largest share of the regional capital stocks in Africa and Asia, though its holdings of POI in developing countries are fairly

1

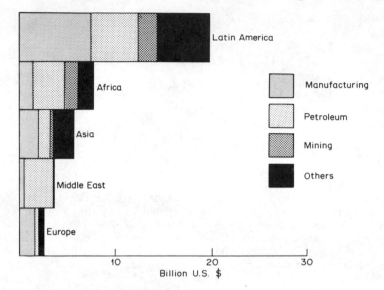

Figure I.1

REGIONAL AND SECTORAL DISTRIBUTION OF THE
STOCK OF POI IN DEVELOPING COUNTRIES — END
1970. Source: Table I.1.

diversified by region. Fourthly, France's overseas investments
are heavily concentrated in Africa, and it is the third largest
owner of the developing country POI stock. Fifthly, 33% of
the total POI stock is in petroleum and 31% in manufacturing. Sixthly, if investments in mining and agriculture are
added to those in petroleum 'nearly half of the estimated
stock of foreign private investment is in sectors which provide
raw materials for the OECD countries'.[1] These characteristics
are important in explaining the host country reaction to POI
as we shall see in Part V.

The total stock of POI in developing countries at the end
of 1967, according to recent estimates made by the OECD

1. *Development Assistance Review* (OECD, Paris, 1971), p. 90.

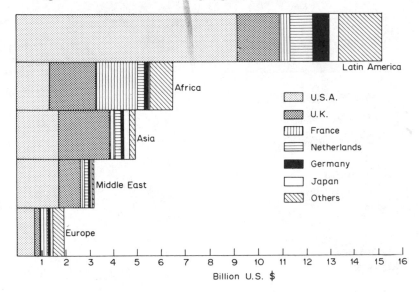

Figure I.2

STOCK OF FOREIGN CAPITAL IN DEVELOPING
COUNTRIES END 1967 BY REGION AND CAPITAL
EXPORTING COUNTRY. Source: Table I.2.

secretariat,[1] represented 25% of the total POI stock in the
world, and accounted for about 7% of the total output of
developing countries, and about 20% of the output of their
industrial sectors.

The structure of recent POI *flows* to developing countries,
by capital-exporting country, recipient region and sector, is

1. 'Anatomy of Foreign Private Investment in Developing Countries' by M. R.
Emerson, of the OECD Economics and Statistics Dept., presented at a conference
on private foreign investment, OECD Development Centre, Paris, June 8, 1972,
and which forms Appendix A of a study by Reuber et al., on foreign investment
in developing countries for the OECD Development Centre: G. L. Reuber, H.
Crookell, M. Emerson and G. Gallais-Hamonno, *Private Foreign Investment in
Development* (Clarendon Press, Oxford, 1973). The Emerson paper will be
referred to hereafter as Emerson, op. cit., and the Reuber study as a whole as
Reuber et al.

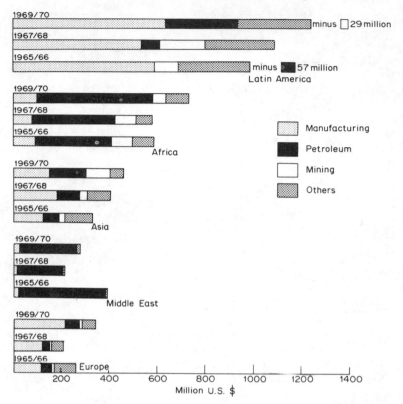

Figure I.3

REGIONAL AND SECTORAL DISTRIBUTION OF TOTAL
DAC INVESTMENT FLOWS IN DEVELOPING
COUNTRIES, 1965–1970 (Average Annual Flows)
Source: Table I.6.

illustrated by Figs. 1.3 and 1.4. These highlight the following
points. First, there has been a marked increase in POI flows
from the U.K., Netherlands, Germany and Japan, whilst
flows from the U.S.A., though quantitatively the largest from
any single DAC country, stagnated during the period
1967-70. Secondly, in terms of regions, Latin America has
accounted for the largest share of POI flows, though Africa

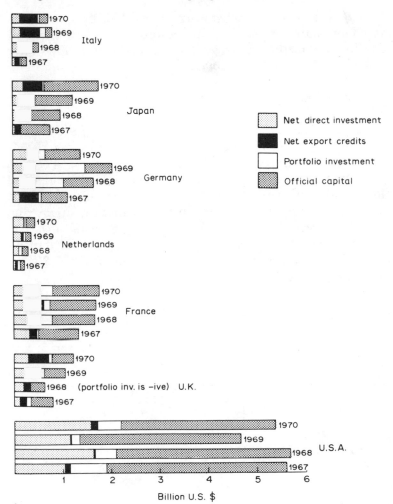

Net direct investment

Net export credits

Portfolio investment

Official capital

Figure I.4
CAPITAL   EXPORTS   TO   DEVELOPING   COUNTRIES
FROM SELECTED DAC COUNTRIES, 1967–1970.
Source: Table I.4.

has also been receiving substantial flows. Thirdly, petroleum and manufacturing continue to absorb the largest share of POI flows. Fourthly, most of the manufacturing flows have been to Latin America, though both Asia and Europe have received substantial flows during the period. Fifthly, petroleum flows though substantial have been declining to the Middle East, but are larger and growing more rapidly to Africa. They are concentrated on Africa south of the Sahara, with Nigeria receiving the largest share. Sixthly, there has been large-scale growth in the flows in the mining sector in Asia, which are concentrated in Indonesia, the Philippines and Papua and New Guinea. There is, however, disinvestment proceeding in the mining sector in Latin America, largely due to the takeover of U.S. copper mines by the Chileans. The table below (Table 1) summarises the percentage distribution of the flow of total DAC direct investment in 1965-70, by region and sector.

Table 1: Percentage Distribution of the Flow of DAC Direct Investment in Developing Countries, 1965–70

	1965–66	(percentages) 1967–68	1969–70
A. *By Region*			
Europe	10	8	11
Africa	23	23	24
Latin America	36	43	39
Middle East	15	8	9
Asia	13	16	15
B. *By Sector*			
Petroleum	29	29	40
Mining	8	12	4
Manufacturing	37	37	37
Other	23	21	17

Source: Computed from data in Appendix Table I.6.

It might also be interesting to see how these flows of POI in recent years relate to the existing stock of POI in different regions and sectors. In Table 2 below, we have computed the annual compound *rates of growth* of the POI stock by region and sector during the period 1967-70, in developing countries.

Table 2: Annual Compound Growth Rates of POI Stock in Developing Countries by Region and Sector, 1967—70

			Sector: (percentages)		
Region	Petroleum	Mining	Manufacturing	Other	Total
Europe	9.97	0.00	7.72	7.72	7.72
Africa	8.01	2.28	2.60	4.46	5.07
Latin America	1.96	1.64	4.77	3.23	3.23
Middle East	4.46	0.00	0.00	0.00	3.85
Asia	5.67	9.97	6.27	1.64	4.46
Total	4.47	2.60	5.07	3.23	4.16

This table highlights the importance of recent capital flows to Europe, Africa and Asia, and into the manufacturing sector as a whole. The case studies of the manufacturing sectors in Kenya and India, in Parts III and IV of this book, may therefore be of more than transient interest.

Finally, Figs. 1.4 and 1.5, provide the dimensions of the relative importance of *direct investment flows in the total flow of foreign capital* from DAC countries to developing countries. The following features may be noted. First, after stagnating in the late fifties and early sixties, there has been a marked upward trend in POI flows to developing countries since 1964, though even in 1969, the level of POI flows was only marginally higher than in 1957. Secondly, both in terms of absolute size and in terms of their rate of growth over the period 1956-72, POI flows have been substantially smaller in magnitude than official aid flows, as can be seen from Table 3 below. The view that POI flows can be expected substantially to replace foreign aid flows as a source of capital to developing countries,[1] therefore needs to be treated with a great deal of circumspection on the basis of past trends.

1. This view seems to be held to some extent by the U.K. Government. See SID and ODI: *Britain's Role in the Second Development Decade* (London, 1972).

Table 3: Levels and Annual Compound Rates of Growth of Capital Flows from DAC Countries to Developing Countries, 1956—72

	Level (billion US $)		Growth Rate (percentage)
	1956 (1)	1972 (2)	1956—72 (3)
Official Flows	3.260	10.195 (55)[c]	7.386
Net Direct Inv.	2.350	4.306 (23)	3.858
Portfolio Inv.[a]	0.601[b]	2.695 (14)	10.521
Export Credits	0.458	1.429 (8)	7.371
Total	6.258	18.625 (100)	7.054

Source: Columns (1) and (2), Pt. Appendix Table I.5; column (3) computed from previous columns.
Note: a. includes both multilateral and bilateral portfolio investment.
      b. the 1957 figure has been used, as the figure for 1956 was unduly low (see Stat. Appendix to Pt. I, Table I.5). The growth rate in column 3 is for 1957—72.
      c. percentages of column total.

Thirdly, a large part of the POI flow has been from retained earnings. Thus the OECD study cited earlier,[1] estimated that in 1968-70 net new POI inflows averaged 3.4 billion US $ per annum, while reinvested earnings were about 1.5 billion US $ per annum. The study also estimated that the net POI inflows in 1970 formed 8% of net capital formation in developing countries (net new POI flows accounting for 5.6% and reinvested earnings for 2.4% of net capital formation). Fourthly, there has been an extremely rapid growth in export credits during this period. This source of external capital is particularly important in the composition of capital flows from the U.K. and Italy. There has however been a rapid rise in this source of capital from the U.K., Japan and Italy, whilst the export credits extended by Germany have been shrinking in the period 1967-70. Given the baneful effects of export credits compared to other forms of external capital on developing countries, this trend is not very heartening, and underlines the growing mercantilism in the attitudes of many

1. Reuber et al., op. cit., Appendix A.

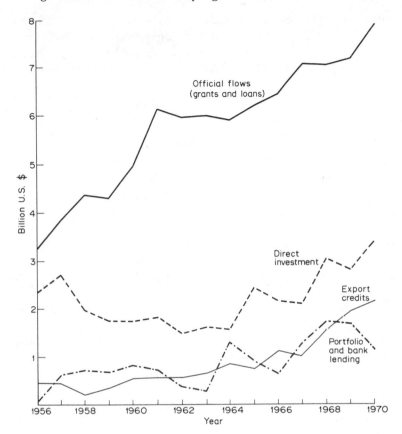

Figure I.5
CAPITAL FLOWS FROM DAC COUNTRIES TO
DEVELOPING COUNTRIES.
Source: Table I.5.

developed countries. Finally, it may be noted that portfolio
investment has been growing more rapidly than direct
investment during the period 1957-70, though the overall
level of capital obtained through bond issues was about a
third of that obtained through direct investment. From
Appendix Tables I.4 and I.5, it can be seen that in the period

1960-70, between two-thirds to three-quarters of all the bonds issued to provide capital for developing countries were issued by international agencies, particularly the IBRD and the IDB. However, the number of developing countries able to raise capital by issuing their own bonds in DAC countries has been rising.[1] In 1971, eleven developing countries floated bonds, Israel, Spain and Mexico being the main borrowers who accounted for over four-fifths of the bonds issued by developing countries, but with India appearing on the list for the first time, with a small issue by a private firm.[2] The OECD *Development Assistance Review 1971* predicted that 'portfolio and other lending especially in the form of bond issues and bank lending ... may well expand its share of overall flows during the Second Development Decade.' Moreover the 1972 OECD *Development Cooperation Review* noted that 'a striking development in the past year has been the increase in private bank lending of Euro-currencies to developing countries. These transactions consist of bank credits financed by a group of banks from several countries, including to a limited extent non-DAC members.' Its estimates for the total gross amounts involved ranged from $1.2 billion to $3–4 billion in the year ending 30th April 1972. The data compiled by the OECD for Euro-currency loans to developing countries in 1971 and 1972 is given in Table 1.7 in the Appendix. The borrowers were 'generally among the more advanced developing countries such as Venezuela, Mexico, Argentina, etc., but the list includes a few countries with GNP per capita under $300 but disposing of exportable natural resources — Zaire, Algeria and Zambia. Little information is published about the interest rates on these

1. *The Development Assistance Review 1971*, op. cit., states that during the period 1960–1970:

   'The main borrowers were Mexico, Israel and Argentina, who are now well established in the market. Thirteen more countries are approaching the same category having made several issues of bonds: Jamaica (9 issues), Venezuela (7 issues), Brazil, Spain, the Philippines, Peru (6 issues each), Ivory Coast, Gabon, Malaysia, Colombia (5 each), and the Netherlands Antilles, Panama, Trinidad and Tobago (4 each). Finally 14 countries have made one or two issues, including five smaller countries in Latin America, two Francophone African countries and two European developing countries' (pp. 92–3).

2. *Development Cooperation 1972 Review* (OECD, Paris, 1972).

loans, but it appears that in most cases, depending on the credit standing of the borrower, they are costing ¾ to 1½ per cent above the six-month Euro-dollar deposit ratio, which has varied between 5.8 per cent and 9.6 per cent in 1970-71.'[1] It may also be noted that the Reuber study cited earlier also found that international companies have acted as important financial intermediaries in enabling private borrowing by developing countries in developed country capital markets. They estimate that 'it appears that from 1965 to 1968 roughly three-quarters of net LDC borrowing was done via other governments, about one-eighth via international agencies, and close to one-tenth through private firms and agencies.'[2] Thus whilst portfolio investment has often been considered to be an alternative source of obtaining development capital to direct investment, the two may increasingly be complementary.

Statistical Appendix

Table I.1. *Regional and Sectoral Distribution of the Stock of Foreign Direct Investment in Developing Countries at end 1970* (billion US $)

	Latin America	Europe	Africa	Middle East	Asia	Total
Petroleum	4.8	0.4	3.3	3.2	1.3	13.0
Mining	2.1	0.1	1.4	—	0.4	3.9
Manufacturing	7.5	1.5	1.3	0.2	1.8	12.3
Other	5.4	0.5	1.6	0.1	2.1	9.7
Total	19.8	2.5	7.6	3.5	5.6	38.9

Source: See Table 1.2, Reuber et al., op. cit., p. 4.

1. *Development Cooperation Review* 1972, op. cit., p. 64.
2. Reuber et al., op. cit., p. 55.

Table 1.2 Stock of Direct Investment in Developing Countries by Capital-Exporting Country, Region and Sector, at end 1967 (million US $)

	Regions						Sectors			
	Latin America	Europe	Africa	Middle East	Asia	Total	Petroleum	Mining	Manufacturing	Other
United States	9,160	750	1,370	1,780	1,780	17,450	6,600	2,050	4,730	4,060
United Kingdom	1,710	230	1,950	840	2,070	6,740	2,090	580	1,580	2,490
France	470	290	1,730	160	280	2,920	850	420	920	730
Netherlands	930	100	320	170	260	1,790	1,340	20	320	160
Germany	710	180	140	20	70	1,200	40	50	1,020	90
Canada	810	20	60	10	70	1,110	20	210	200	680
Italy	400	180	250	30	30	880	190	20	590	80
Japan	390	x	10	90	200	700	80	60	430	140
Belgium	120	80	480	x	20	690	20	100	370	210
Switzerland	270	80	20	10	20	410	–	10	210	200
Sweden	70	10	80	–	20	200	–	70	110	10
Portugal	10	30	90	–	–	120	20	30	50	30
Australia	–	x	–	–	100	100	10	20	30	50
Denmark	20	10	x	–	x	30	–	–	20	10
Norway	10	x	x	–	–	10	–	–	10	x
Austria	10	x	–	–	–	10	–	x	10	x
Total	15,160	1,950	6,510	3,110	4,900	34,350	11,260	3,640	10,570	8,880

Source: Table A.8, Reuber et al., op cit, p. 283.
Totals may not add because all figures have been rounded to the nearest $10 million, amounts less than $5 million being shown as 'x'.

Table 1.3 *Estimate of Investment by DAC Members in Developing Countries end 1967, Accumulated Stock* (billion US $)

	Petro-leum	Mining	Manufac-turing	Other	Total
Europe	0.3	0.1	1.2	0.4	2.0
Africa	2.6	1.3	1.2	1.4	6.5
Latin America and Caribbean	4.5	2.0	6.5	4.9	17.9
Middle East	2.8	—	0.2	0.1	3.1
Asia and Oceania	1.1	0.3	1.5	2.0	4.9
Total	11.3	3.6	10.6	8.8	34.3

Note: Figures do not add to totals because of rounding. The stock of investment is understood to mean the net book value to the direct investor of affiliates (subsidiaries, branches and associates) in developing countries.
Source: Table VI.3, *Development Assistance Review 1971*, OECD.

Table I.4 Capital Flows from DAC Countries to Developing Countries (million US $)

Country	Total Net Direct Investment						Total Net Export Credits						Portfolio Investment (Bilateral and Multilateral)					
	1967	1968	1969	1970	1971	1972	1967	1968	1969	1970	1971	1972	1967	1968	1969	1970	1971	1972
1 U.S.A.	1,060.0	1,624.0	1,257.0	1,742.0	2,010.0	1,976.0	61.7	34.6	−49.0	126.0	169.0	334.3	800.7	457.4	251.0	570.0	585.0	1,049.7
2 U.K.	162.0	216.0	353.5	321.2	321.6	372.6	113.4	141.4	265.8	436.4	583.1	535.4	68.0	−26.4	98.4	(33.6)	−92.5	−94.9
3 France	370.7	349.2	268.4	235.1	170.4	230.6	138.3	240.6	380.0	303.7	222.0	271.0	6.8	256.6	102.9	290.5	98.4	226.2
4 Netherlands	57.5	89.3	165.9	211.7	297.7	249.8	7.0	−11.8	25.4	2.4	5.3	67.8	50.2	63.6	28.1	26.5	73.3	5.4
5 Germany	169.3	192.0	233.6	317.5	358.1	558.8	363.1	255.2	244.5	187.2	412.2	−61.6	61.6	621.1	1,022.6	173.5	138.2	136.2
6 Japan	66.4	90.8	144.1	261.5	222.4	204.0	103.8	260.7	299.6	386.9	494.0	190.6	−0.1	0.0	8.0	21.0	259.2	857.7
7 Italy	66.9	118.4	125.4	123.4	213.7	245.1	54.1	270.2	450.1	327.9	311.3	−11.9	10.4	12.3	135.0	48.9	35.6	161.7
8 Switzerland	46.2	79.2	47.9	55.4	65.7	73.1	60.0	106.4	48.2	22.3	82.5	−19.2	23.9	37.3	−0.9	23.2	119.2	35.7
9 Belgium	20.2	7.0	19.7	45.7	28.5	57.7	28.4	114.7	100.0	114.8	77.1	81.1	17.0	15.3	19.0	12.4	52.9	47.7

Table I.4 (continued)

Country	Total Net Private Capital Flows						Total Net Official Capital Flows					
	1967	1968	1969	1970	1971	1972	1967	1968	1969	1970	1971	1972
1 U.S.A.	922.4	2,116.0	1,459.0	2,438.0	2,764.0	3,360.0	3,723.0	3,607.0	3,257.0	3,218.0	3,504.0	3,545.0
2 U.K.	343.4	331.0	717.7	791.6	811.8	813.1	498.0	429.0	428.5	453.4	573.8	625.0
3 France	515.8	846.4	751.13	829.3	490.8	727.8	825.5	873.9	958.7	999.0	1,125.5	1,337.1
4 Netherlands	114.7	141.1	219.4	240.6	376.3	323.0	113.5	134.4	149.8	210.8	218.9	312.0
5 Germany	593.8	1,068.3	1,500.7	678.2	908.5	633.4	546.8	595.2	527.6	731.1	898.4	956.8
6 Japan	170.1	351.5	451.7	669.4	975.6	1,252.3	627.4	678.3	811.4	1,151.6	1,161.8	1,467.5
7 Italy	131.4	400.9	710.5	500.2	560.6	394.9	55.9	149.5	137.2	176.7	304.3	247.0
8 Switzerland	130.1	222.9	95.2	100.9	203.6	89.6	4.1	18.5	23.8	25.4	27.6	67.4
9 Belgium	65.6	137.0	138.7	172.9	158.5	186.5	98.8	106.0	118.6	120.9	146.9	206.6

Table 1.4 (continued)

Country	1967 NI	1967 RE	1968 NI	1968 RE	1969 NI	1969 RE	1970 NI	1970 RE	1971 NI	1971 RE
U.S.A.	790.0	270	1,142.0	482	750.0	507.0	1,141.0	608.0	1,565.0	645.0
Germany	98.3	71	109.0	83	132.8	100.8	183.6	133.9	200.5	157.6
Italy	51.9	15	102.4	16	125.4	–	123.4	NA	NA	NA
Switzerland	37.2	9	39.2	40	NA	NA	NA	NA	NA	NA
Belgium	10.2	10	5.0	2	8.8	10.9	36.6	9.1	11.4	17.1
Japan	NA	NA	NA	NA	NA	NA	261.5	–	222.4	–

Notes:
NI – net new investment
RE – reinvested earnings
NA – not available
– – nil or negligible
( ) – OECD Secretariat estimate

Source: *Development Assistance Review* (OECD, Paris), 1969, 1970, 1971, 1972, 1973.

Table I.5 *Private Capital Flows and Official Grants and Loans from DAC Countries to Developing Countries, 1956–1972* (million US $)

		Private Capital Flows (Net)				
Year	Total	Direct Invest- ment	Portfolio & Bank Lending	Export Credits	Official Flows (Grants & net loans)	Total
1956	2998	2350	190	458	3260	6258
1957	3779	2724	601	454	3856	7635
1958	2917	1970	733	214	4387	7304
1959	2820	1782	691	347	4311	7131
1960	3150	1767	837	546	4965	8115
1961	3106	1829	704	573	6143	9249
1962	2453	1495	386	572	5984	8437
1963	2557	1603	296	660	6015	8572
1964	3729	1572	1298	859	5916	9645
1965	4121	2468	902	751	6199	10320
1966	3959	2179	655	1124	6431	10390
1967	4381	2105	1269	1007	7060	11441
1968	6377	3043	1738	1596	7047	13424
1969	6587	2910	1630	2047	7192	13779
1970	7019	3557	1251	2211	7984	15003
1971	8215	3874	1617	2724	9030	17245
1972	8430	4306	2695	1429	10195	18625

Source: *Development Cooperation Review 1973* (OECD, Dec 1973) and earlier editions of the same.

1. Excludes grants by voluntary private agencies for which figures were not available till 1970. The OECD's estimate for this item was $855 m in 1970 and $890 m in 1971.

Table I.6 Regional and Sectoral Distribution of Total DAC Direct Investment in Developing Countries, 1965–1970, Average Annual Flows (million US $)

	Year	Petro-leum[1]	Mining	Manufac-turing	Other	Total
Europe	1965–1966	44	10	124	90	268
	1967–1968	19	3	130	55	207
	1969–1970	60	5	224	59	348
Africa	1965–1966	328	85	89	84	586
	1967–1968	352	85	80	65	582
	1969–1970	487	58	95	99	739
Latin America and Caribbean	1965–1966	−57	99	591	292	925
	1967–1968	73	180	540	297	1,090
	1969–1970	295	−29	643	306	1,215
Middle East	1965–1966	374	1	12	5	392
	1967–1968	198	—	7	14	219
	1969–1970	243	—	24	15	282
Asia and Oceania	1965–1966	62	28	129	117	336
	1967–1968	92	37	185	99	413
	1969–1970	155	104	147	68	474
Total	1965–1966	751	223	945	588	2,507
	1967–1968	734	305	942	530	2,511
	1969–1970	1,240	138	1,133	547	3,058

1. Including natural gas.
Source: Table VI.2, *Development Assistance Review 1971*, OECD.

Table I.7 *Euro-Currency Loans to Developing Countries,*
1971 and 1972 (million US $)

Country	1971	1972
Algeria	120.0	275.0
Argentina	50.0	263.7
Brazil	212.0	577.3
Brunei	—	27.5
Colombia	—	90.0
Dominican Republic	—	4.0
Dubai	—	18.3
Gabon	10.0	25.0
Greece	60.0	330.0
Guinea	—	40.0
Hong-Kong	—	20.0
Indonesia	—	97.6
Iran	224.0	461.4
Israel	—	10.0
Ivory Coast	22.0	—
Kenya	—	15.0
Malaysia	—	76.1
Mauritania	8.0	—
Mexico	140.0	508.8
Nicaragua	10.0	15.0
Panama	16.0	40.0
Peru	—	209.4
Philippines	—	61.3
South Korea	40.0	30.0
Spain	420.0	253.1
Swaziland	—	3.2
Venezuela	78.3	258.5
Yugoslavia	10.0	255.0
Zaire	55.0	90.0
Zambia	—	25.0
Total developing countries	1,475.3	4,080.2
Other countries	2,645.0	3,771.0
Total	4,120.3	7,851.2

Source: *Development Cooperation Review* OECD 1973, p. 53

I.2 DETERMINANTS

Why do firms invest abroad? The answer to this question is of relevance in appraising foreign investment in developing countries for two reasons. First, it will determine the areas into which foreign investment is likely to flow, and secondly, it will determine the minimum acceptable terms on which the foreign investor will be likely to come to the host country. Both these factors will be important in the bargaining process which determines the distribution of the potential gains from a particular act of POI between the host country and the foreign investor.

There is a rapidly growing literature on the determinants of POI, and this chapter provides a highly selective summary of the available evidence on why firms invest abroad.[1]

Theoretically, there seems to be an emerging consensus that the theory of direct investment is an integral part of the theory of industrial organisation, in particular of the theory of monopolistic competition. For in a world characterised by universal perfect competition there would be no direct investment, as the foreigner would always be at a disadvantage compared with local competitors (actual or potential) in the host country, because of the costs of overcoming economic and/or cultural/social 'distance'. The foreigner must therefore possess some advantage which makes it possible for him to overcome these costs and earn a higher rate of return on the particular investment than local competitors in the host country. This naturally suggests that if there are market imperfections, in either product or factor markets or internal and/or external economies in production, such that the foreigner is at an advantage because of the former and/or because of his ability to internalise the latter compared with local competitors, then this would provide a rationale for foreign investment occurring. A succinct summary of the monopolistic advantages which could lead to direct foreign investment is provided by Kindleberger.

---

1. See Kindleberger, op. cit.; Kindleberger, ed., op. cit.; Vernon, op. cit.; Dunning, ed., op. cit.; Reuber et al., op. cit.; and R. E. Caves, 'International Corporations: The Industrial Economics of Foreign Investment', *Economica*, Feb. 1971.

These are:

1. departures from perfect competition in goods markets, including product differentiation, special marketing skills, retail price maintenance, administered pricing, etc.;

2. departures from perfect competition in factor markets, including the existence of patented or unavailable technology, of discrimination in access to capital, of differences in skills of managers organised into firms rather than hired in competitive markets;

3. internal and external economies of scale, the latter being taken advantage of by vertical integration;

4. government limitations on output or entry.[1]

Furthermore we can try and delineate which particular type of monopolistic advantage is likely to account for POI in different sectors in developing countries. Considering first the sectors producing raw materials, namely, mining, petroleum and agriculture, the main monopolistic advantage which is likely to explain POI in these sectors are internal and external economies of scale. International companies with investments in these sectors would be those whose operations are 'backward vertical (or cost oriented)', in terms of a classification suggested by Dunning.[2] This would include both enterprises whose direct investment 'represents the extension of the *purchasing* function of the investing firm and is undertaken to obtain cheaper and more reliable supplies of raw materials or processed goods for the investing company';[3] and for those firms who are mainly in the extractive industries, with the aim of supplying their output to world markets. As investments in mining, petroleum, and the production of agricultural raw materials account for about half the PQI stock in developing countries (ch. I.1), factor No. 3, viz. the existence of internal and external economies of scale in these sectors, is likely to be one of the most important determinants of POI in developing countries.

Manufacturing accounts for the bulk of the remaining stock of POI in developing countries, and also for a substantial share of new POI inflows. All four sources of

1. Kindleberger, op. cit., p. 14.
2. J. Dunning, 'The Multinational Enterprise: The Background' in Dunning, ed., op. cit., pp. 21–22.
3. Ibid.

monopolistic advantage are likely to be important, but there is some evidence to suggest that some of these factors are more important than others in explaining the flow of POI into the manufacturing sector in developing countries. The dominant model in the literature for explaining POI in manufacturing is the product cycle model evolved by Vernon, Huffbauer and Hirsch.[1] According to this model, advanced country (mainly U.S.) enterprises generate new technology-intensive products and processes given their relatively more abundant supply of technological and skilled manpower. These countries, and especially the U.S., then have a comparative advantage in the production and initial export of 'knowledge' intensive products; the 'knowledge' being protected as the property of the innovating firm through patents. Initially, given the absolute advantage of the innovating country in producing these 'knowledge' intensive products, foreign markets are serviced by exports. However, with the erosion of the 'patent' by imitative adaptation by other developed-country producers, the innovating firm's export position is threatened, and to counter this it may establish overseas subsidiaries to exploit what remains of its advantage. It may thus still retain its oligopolistic advantage for some time, but will eventually find that its original lead is completely eroded. At this stage it may decide to find a very much lower cost production site for the product where its competitors would not easily be able to follow. It is the last stage in the process which may account for the spread of some international companies producing 'high technology' products from developed to developing countries. Thus it is in the last stage of the product cycle, when traditional relative factor cost considerations become important, that international companies may invest in developing countries with cheap labour, to give rise to 'wage-gap' trade in 'high technology' products, as compared with the 'technology-gap'

---

1. R. Vernon, 'International Investment and International Trade in the Product Cycle', *Quarterly Journal of Economics,* 1966; G. Huffbauer, *Synthetic Materials and the Theory of International Trade* (London, Duckworth, 1965); S. Hirsch, *Location of Industry and International Competitiveness* (OUP, Oxford, 1967).

trade which characterises the first stage of the product cycle. There are already an increasing number of cases in which international companies are shifting the location of their plants to developing countries, to take advantage of their relatively cheaper labour.[1]

However, the product cycle is not likely to explain a large part of POI in developing countries. In particular, more recently one of the major forms of direct investment has been through the growth of the vertical division of labour by multinational corporations, the location decisions for various parts of the vertically integrated process being determined by relative factor prices.[2] Moreover, quite a substantial part of POI in the manufacturing sector in developing countries is in 'simple technology' products, where the processes of production are fairly uncomplicated and relatively easy to learn; for example, soap, textiles, cement, tobacco. The chief explanation for POI in 'simple technology' products is competitive imperfections mainly arising 'from import restrictions and/or high transport costs and from the economies of experience and/or scale possessed by the investing company over its local competitors'.[3] In this 'simple technology' area too, what needs to be explained is why foreign firms decide to invest in the host country rather than servicing these foreign markets by exports. The basic explanation seems to be the reaction of an oligopolistic international firm faced by the prospect of

1. Thus the DAC Review 1971 states: 'increased possibilities for the export of manufactured products from developing countries may well provide interesting openings for private investment. During the 1970s more Hong Kong- or Singapore-type centres of growth will hopefully begin to get established' (p. 100).
2. Whilst G. Helliner, 'Manufactured Exports and Multinational Firms: Their Impact Upon Economic Development' (mimeo), April 1972, notes that: 'the greatest expansion will be ... in labour-intensive processing, assembly and component manufacturing activities within vertically integrated international industries, it is already common practice in many American electronics, machinery, and transport equipment firms to ship parts to low wage countries for labour-intensive assembly or processing, following which the semi-finished product is re-exported for finishing or sale elsewhere; and this phenomenon appears to be increasing rapidly in importance. In many cases, this form of manufacturing for export is undertaken within an 'export processing zone' or similar enclave in the less developed countries'. An important example of such an export processing zone which is already functioning is Taiwan.
3. Dunning, op. cit. Note that these 'simple technology' products do not necessarily have low capital to labour ratios, their chief characteristics being the stability of the existing technology, and the relative ease in acquiring it.

losing its traditional export markets as a result of the imposition of import controls by the host country and/or the strategic decisions of its oligopolistic competitors. Such 'defensive' investment is thus part of the international firm's strategic decision-making in an oligopolistic market.

In a survey of 80 international firms with operations in developing countries, a study by Reuber et al. for the OECD[1] found that what they termed market development investments 'tended to be essentially defensive of markets built up by exporting, while export-oriented investments were often undertaken to defend existing global markets from low-priced international competition. In either case the corporate initiative usually reflected a direct threat to existing operations. With market development investments the threat, often indirect, came from the observed tendency of LDC governments to block or hinder imports as markets grow. With the export-oriented type, the threat came more often from other multinational companies'. The third category of investments in the Reuber sample were classified as 'government-initiated',[2] for which obviously, the protection offered in domestic host country markets would be an important determinant of POI flows.

This suggests, therefore, that given that POI in developing countries is often defensive in nature, and does not conform to the usual picture of multinational companies 'being engaged in a continuous survey of the world's resources and markets in search of global efficiency and expansion',[3] the bargaining power of developing countries when facing particular foreign investors may be much greater than they and many outside observers have credited them with in the past.

1. Reuber et al. op. cit.; Market-development investments were defined as those with the 'distinguishing features: (i) that the output of the product is intended primarily for consumption in the host country and (ii) that the investment is made primarily in response to underlying economic considerations such as the size of the local market and its long run potential, local production costs, and so on' p. 74.

2. Reuber et al., op. cit., 'export-oriented' is self-explanatory, whilst 'government-initiated' investments were defined as those which occur mainly in response to government subsidies of one kind or another that on balance are sufficiently large to make the investment attractive to the investors irrespective of underlying demand and cost conditions (chapter 4).

3. Reuber et al., op. cit.

Moreover this 'defensive' model of POI in developing countries also implies that the main bargaining counter that the host country possesses is its ability to restrict the entry to the host country markets of the particular foreign investor's oligopolistic rivals. These restrictions of entry may be in the form of import and/or investment controls, both of which are common in many developing countries.

That the restriction of entry of oligopolistic rivals may be the chief 'incentive' to lure foreign firms to host developing countries is also borne out to some extent by attempts to assess the importance of the traditionally conceived incentives, in the forms of implicit or explicit fiscal subsidies, in the foreign firm's investment decision.[1] Thus H. J. Robinson[2] in a study of the motivation of private foreign investment found that whereas governments attached the highest importance to tax concessions as an inducement to foreign firms to invest in their countries, this factor did not even figure in the foreign investors' response to the factors to which they attached most importance in making investment decisions. For the foreign firms, the important factors, in decreasing degree of importance were: effective development planning and execution, liberal capital and profit repatriation, non-discrimination against foreign ownership and control, uniform treatment of home and foreign enterprises, and minimum 'red tape'. The Reuber study, cited earlier, found that for its sample of foreign firms, the conclusion about the relative importance of various concessions to investors in the foreign firm's investment decision was that: 'protection of the domestic LDC markets stands out in importance, as one would expect, for market-development and government-initiated projects. Financial and other incentives by contrast, are relatively more important in our sample for export-oriented firms. . . . The survey evidence also indicates that

1. In fact there is evidence to suggest that domestic investment in developed countries is not greatly influenced by fiscal incentives. See for the U.K.: National Economic Development Council, *Investment Appraisal* (HMSO, London, 1967), and for Canada, J. F. Helliwell, *Public Policies and Private Investment* (OUP, Oxford, 1968).
2. H. J. Robinson, 'The Motivation and Flow of Private Foreign Investment', *International Development Centre*, Stanford Research Institute, California, 1961, cited in Reuber et al., op. cit., p. 132.

incentives have had some effect on decisions about where to locate projects among the LDCs, the most important of these seem to be tariffs and quotas on competing imports, concessions in imports of inputs and tax concessions'.[1] It seems likely therefore that the main area in which the bargaining process in manufacturing should take place is in determining the nature and size of the effective protection offered to the foreign investor by the host country. As the degree of effective protection offered will also be an important determinant of the net social benefits of the foreign investor's operations in the host country, the whole bargaining process from the host country's viewpoint can be reduced to determining the degrees of effective protection, within which the minimum acceptable social profit to the host country and private profit to the foreign investor lies, and trying to obtain the best terms which maximise the potential social gains to the host country. The Guidelines of Part II, are expressly addressed to providing decision-makers in developing countries with the necessary tools to undertake this task.

Meanwhile in forming some judgment on what the likely minimum acceptable private rate of return to foreign investors would be, it may be useful to summarise the evidence which exists on the planning rates of return sought by foreign investors. The evidence obtained from their sample by the Reuber study is given in Table 4 below.

Whilst these rates of return give some indication of foreign investors' expectations, namely about 15%, these planning rates of return seem higher than the realised rates of return on both U.K. and U.S. foreign investment. Thus the Reddaway report[2] found the average realised rates of return on U.K. investment in different sectors and regions, given in Table 5 below. The average rates of return on all U.K. foreign investment was 8.5% for all industries excluding oil, for the nine-year period 1956-64, and 13% for oil, whilst the annual average post-tax rate of return on U.K. investments in LDCs

---

1. Reuber et al., op. cit., p. 127.
2. W. B. Reddaway, *Effects of U.K. Direct Overseas Investment — An Interim Report* (Cambridge, 1967).

Table 4 Planning Rates of Return
After-tax Cut-off Rate of Return for New Projects

Home Country	Other Developed Countries	Developing Countries
A *Home Country of Investor*		
Europe	12.7	7.9	13.7
North America	18.4	18.4	20.6
Japan	13.0	10.5	10.5
Total	14.5	14.8	15.4
B. *Type of Investment*		
Export-oriented	18.7	20.4	20.4
Market-develop.	12.2	11.8	13.6
Import-displacing	13.9	11.5	12.1
Total	14.5	14.8	15.4

Source: Reuber et al., op. cit., Table 4.8, p. 98.

Table 5 Post-Tax Profitability of U.K. Foreign Investment
(annual average, 1956—64)

A. *By Industry*	Per Cent	
Mining	13.7	
Building Materials	13.5	(these figures relate to
Food, Drink, Tobacco and		U.K. investment in these
Household Products	8.8	sectors in *both* LDCs and
Chemicals	7.9	developed countries)
Textiles	7.7	
Paper	7.7	
Metals and Metal products	7.4	
Electrical Engineering	5.4	
Vehicles and Components	5.0	
Non-electrical Eng.	4.5	
Total, excluding Oil	8.5	
Oil	13.0	

Source: Reddaway, op. cit., Table IV.2.

Table 5 (continued)

B. *By Developing Country*	*Per Cent Post-Tax Profitability*	*Percentage Change in Operating Assets* (annual averages, 1956—64)
Malaysia	26.9	113.8
India	8.6	113.9
Ghana	10.6	−0.8
Brazil	5.3	43.2
Jamaica	8.4	115.9
Nigeria	4.7	44.7
Argentina	1.6	135.9
World	8.5	

Source: Reddaway, op. cit., Tables IV.5 and 6.

varied from a high of 26.9% for Malaysia to a low of 1.6% for Argentina. Nor did the relatively low return on investment in Argentina discourage the flow of U.K. foreign investment to this area, for during the same period (1956-64) net operating assets of U.K. companies increased by 135.9%, whilst in Malaysia where the highest post-tax rate of return was achieved they rose by 113.8%. This tends to support the conclusion of the Reuber study that whilst profitability is an important determinant of POI, profitability is broadly conceived by the foreign investors, with variations in short-run profits being set against long-run strategic considerations.

Moreover DAC estimates[1] of realised post-tax rates of return on U.S. and U.K. overseas investment, in manufacturing and other industries in areas of heavy concentration of investments, are between 8 and 12 per cent, with the overall weighted average rate of return after tax on the book value of U.K. and U.S. foreign investments in developing countries being estimated at 9.7%. Finally, a recent study by Steuer[2] gives some estimates of rates of return earned on foreign investments in the U.K. These are summarised in Table 6:

1. Cited by Needleman in Ady, ed., op. cit., p. 80.
2. M. D. Steuer et al., *The Impact of Foreign Direct Investment on the United Kingdom* (Dept. of Trade and Industry, HMSO, London, 1973).

Table 6 Average Rates of Return[a] *on Foreign Investment in the U.K.*
(Per cent)

A. *By Source*[b]	Year	1965	1966	1967	1968
U.S.A.		12.5	11.0	9.2	10.5
E.E.C.		9.9	6.9	5.6	6.3
Total		10.6	9.5	8.1	9.3

B. *By Industry*	Year	1965	1966
1. Food, Drink and Tobacco		12.3	9.8
2. Chemicals and Allied Industries		17.2	13.2
3. Metal Manufacture		6.5	4.4
4. Mechanical Engineering		13.1	10.1
5. Electrical Engineering		10.3	9.6
6. Vehicles		10.9	4.4
7. Other Manufactures		9.6	7.8

Source: (A) Table 10.XX and (B) Table 10.XXII in M. D. Steuer et al., *The Impact of Foreign Direct Investment on the United Kingdom* (Dept. of Trade and Industry, HMSO, 1973).
Notes (a) after U.K. tax; (b) excludes oil, insurance and banking.

Thus the realised post-tax rates of return on POI in developing countries, of about 9% are much lower than the planned rates of about 15%. This range then will probably correspond to the upper and lower limit of the expected private rate of return of foreign investors.

The expected rate of return is obviously in part dependent on the planning horizon, and *ceteris paribus*, if the foreign investor and host country have different planning horizons, the perceived rates of return of the two parties would differ. The Reuber study provides some data on the planning horizon of foreign investors. It concluded that: 'although the survey evidence is somewhat incomplete on this point, it suggests a planning horizon of some 7 years on average for export-oriented projects compared to 11 to 12 years for locally oriented projects. If one considers the national origin of the investor, European and North American investors evidently plan over some 9 to 12 years compared with a time horizon that is about half as long for Japanese investors'.[1]

I.3 EFFECTS

The problem of determining the effects of POI on host developing countries is bedevilled by the question: What would the alternative situation have been in the absence of POI? Some assumptions about the 'alternative situation' are inevitable if applied work in this field is to proceed at all. However, as it is impossible to 'prove' the validity of the particular *ceteris paribus* assumptions made by different researchers, there is naturally room for widely divergent views on this question, as is amply illustrated by the existing literature.[2] Nevertheless in this chapter we summarise the possible effects of POI on host developing countries which have been suggested in the literature, as well as the results obtained from our Case Studies in Parts III and IV.

At a theoretical level, there are the effects suggested by the theory of trade and welfare. Here the welfare effects of POI have been derived by treating the foreign investment inflow as an addition to the host country's capital stock, and an improvement in its technology.[3] Symmetrically, with the argument for an optimum tariff on foreign trade in goods, based on terms of trade effects, there is a case for an optimum tax on capital imports, if capital imports affect the terms of trade,[4] adverse changes in the terms of trade in both cases being able in principle to lead to 'immiserising

1. Reuber et al., op. cit., p. 99.
2. See for example, I. M. D. Little, 'On Measuring the Value of Private Direct Overseas Investment' and R. Vernon, 'United States Enterprise in Less Developed Countries: Evaluation of Cost and Benefit' in G. Ranis, ed., *The Gap Between Rich and Poor Nations* (London, Macmillan, 1972). Also see P. Streeten, 'Costs and Benefits of Multinational Enterprises in Less Developed Countries' in Dunning, ed., op. cit.
3. See H. G. Johnson, 'The Efficiency and Welfare Implications of the International Corporation' in Kindleberger, ed., op. cit.
4. See M. Kemp, *The Pure Theory of International Trade and Investment* (Prentice Hall, 1969), Part III, and R. W. Jones, 'International Capital Movements and the Theory of Tariffs and Trade', *Quarterly Journal of Economics*, Feb. 1967.

growth'.[1] This case is however not likely to be of much practical significance.

Disregarding the above possibility of 'immiserising growth', the presumptive benefits from POI can be briefly summarised. First, and most importantly, in developing countries with surplus labour and a savings constraint, there is the direct benefit given by the difference between the wages actually paid to the local labour employed by the foreign firm, and the social opportunity cost of this labour to the host country. Also, if the foreign capital is associated with domestic capital, any return the latter receives, which is in excess of what it could earn elsewhere in the economy, is also a net benefit to the host country. Secondly, and equally importantly, are the implicit and explicit taxes paid by the foreign investor to the host country. Thirdly, and more debatably, there are the effects due to the 'technical progress' (widely conceived to include the introduction of better management and marketing techniques, the implanting of new skills, as well as the introduction of new technology) which POI is supposed to bring. As the possession of superior 'knowledge' is claimed to be one of the chief attributes of international firms, and the maximisation of the rents obtainable from this 'knowledge' the main motivation for foreign investment, the gains from 'technical progress' to the host country depend crucially on its ability to squeeze some of these potential rents from the foreign investor for itself. This would occur if there are genuine external economies generated as a result of the operation of the foreign firm, and/or if part of the potential rents to the foreigner's superior 'knowledge' are passed on to host country nationals in the form of lower product and/or higher factor prices. Finally, there are the benefits given by the present value of the *net* capital inflow (taking account of the initial capital inflow, retained earnings, and the outflows on account of dividends, royalties, fees, interest, and repatriation of capital) over the lifetime of the investment. From the time stream of

1. See J. Bhagwati, 'Immiserising Growth: A Geometrical Note', *Review of Economic Studies*, June 1958.

these net benefits of POI to the host country, their internal rate of return (IRR) can be determined. This will represent the rate of return to the host country from the operation of the foreign firm.

The next question then is whether this rate of return is acceptable, and hence, whether the foreign investment is in the country's interest. It is here that the significance of assumptions regarding the 'alternative situation' becomes all-important. We postpone consideration of this problem to Part II.

So far, it will be noted that we have not said anything about the balance of payments effects of POI, even though this has been the main area in which empirical work on host country effects of POI in both developed and developing countries has been carried out.[1] This is for two reasons. First, what we have presented above represents the real income net benefits from POI, and their direct impact on the host country's welfare are obvious. No such normative significance can be claimed for any computed balance of payments effects of POI. In fact, secondly, the balance of payments effects are even more crucially dependent on making further *ceteris paribus* assumptions. For, from the absorption approach to the balance of payments, it is well known that the change in the balance of payments following foreign investment, which leads to a rise in the host country's real income, will depend upon the extent to which expenditure rises (or is allowed to rise by the government) following the real income increase. If expenditure remains unchanged at the pre-POI level, the whole of the real income rise associated with the foreign investment will appear as a balance of payments surplus. On the other hand, if expenditure is allowed to rise, by the full amount of (more than) the real income rise, there will be no change (a worsening) in the balance of payments following the foreign investment. The computed balance of payments effect will therefore depend

---

1. See Reddaway, op. cit.; G. C. Hufbauer and F. M. Adler, *Overseas Manufacturing Investment and the Balance of Payments* (U.S. Treasury Dept., Washington, D.C., 1968); and the series of studies by Needleman et al., for UNCTAD (mimeo).

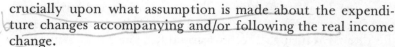

crucially upon what assumption is made about the expenditure changes accompanying and/or following the real income change.

Some other writers have identified other indirect effects of POI which are even more intangible, and difficult to compute.[1] A large number of these are really a variant of the political effects which we shall be discussing in greater detail in Part V. There are however various indirect economic effects which have been suggested, which need to be noted. The first concerns the effects of POI on indigenous enterprise. This is really part of the problem of assessing the external effects of POI, in this case the external economies or diseconomies resulting from the POI's operation in encouraging/discouraging the emergence or development of domestic entrepreneurship. Evidence on this point is extremely hard to come by, and even if it were available would be extremely hard to quantify. However, it may be worthwhile to see to what extent a domestic alternative to fostering/ encouraging the development of indigenous entrepreneurship in countries where it is notably lacking, is feasible. To this end a case study of an industrial estate in Kenya, whose aim is to develop indigenous African entrepreneurship, is included as an appendix to Part IV. Its conclusions are not very encouraging about the feasibility and desirability of fostering domestic entrepreneurship by this means. This does not of course tell us anything about the externalities associated with foreign enterprise in this area, but it does suggest that in countries where there is a shortage of domestic entrepreneurs, it may not be possible to foster them through government policy, and therefore at least until the spontaneous emergence of such entrepreneurs (albeit through processes which are not as yet understood), reliance on foreign enterprise may be unavoidable. Even if it could be established that the presence of foreign enterprise lengthened the time-lag involved in the emergence of local entrepreneurs in these countries, as long as there would be a time-lag in their emergence even *without* the presence of the inhibiting

---

1. See Streeten, 'Costs and Benefits . . .', op. cit., and 'New Approaches to Private Overseas Investment' in Ady, ed., op. cit.

foreigners, it would seem to be more desirable to maximise the certain current gains from foreign enterprise, rather than wait for the uncertain future gains from the development of indigenous entreprise.

The second set of indirect effects which have been suggested as being associated with POI in developing countries, are deleterious external effects on income distribution and consumption patterns.[1] Considering income distribution first, the fact that POI often pays wages to both its skilled and unskilled workers and indigenous managers above comparable wages in domestic enterprise, is taken to imply that the government's task of moving to a more equitable income distribution is made that much more difficult. In this situation, however, there are two different factors pulling in opposite directions in their effects on the host country's welfare. For as we argued above, one of the important indirect taxes on POI, and hence benefits to the host country, is given by the differences between the social opportunity costs of the factors employed and the actual wages paid to them by the foreign firm. From this viewpoint the higher wages paid by POI are a benefit to the host country. Clearly, the way out would be to let the foreign company pay the higher wages, but the recipients should be taxed at higher rates in the interests of a better income distribution. The government might not however be able to enforce the desired income-distribution directly, and might then, as a second-best measure, try to influence income distribution indirectly, through choosing investment projects with more desirable distributional effects. It should then weight the distributional effects of projects, and choose those (both domestically and foreign financed) whose social profitability, taking account of distributional factors, is highest. In Part II, a method for deriving distributional weights, given a basic policy value-judgment, is described, and has been used in our case studies in Parts III and IV.[2]

---

1. See Streeten, op. cit., and Frances Stewart's comments in Ady, ed., op. cit., pp. 68–73.
2. POI may however also raise the wages of *other* employees, and then the marginal cost to the country in raising all other wages will be an extra cost to add to the wage bill of the POI. I owe this point to David Newbery.

There is another strand to this distributional argument which may be noted. This suggests that POI, particularly in the manufacturing sector, produces consumer goods for the rich, as given the pattern of demand generated by the existing income distribution, the production of such goods is more privately profitable than the production of mass consumption goods, which would yield a higher level of social welfare. It is further argued that the obvious remedy — a direct attack on the inequitable income-distribution — is not feasible, presumably for political reasons, and hence at least the distribution of *consumption* should be sought to be made more equitable by the *indirect* means of controlling the relative *supply* of different types of consumer goods. This argument seems schizophrenic for two reasons. First, it assumes that the rich who are politically powerful enough to prevent their incomes and hence their consumption from being cut by direct means, would lamely acquiesce in the same result being achieved by a back-door method. Secondly, it assumes that a government which is powerless to impose an effective income-redistribution programme is powerful enough to impose an effective production control programme.

The next set of external effects is concerned with consumption. The first is the demonstration effect on the local populace of the consumption pattern of expatriate managers, etc. who usually come as part of the POI package. There is obviously something in this argument, but given the fairly rapid dissemination of knowledge of the relatively higher consumption pattern in developed countries through the mass-media all around the world, it is difficult to evaluate the extent to which the presence of expatriates worsens the situation.

The second concerns the quality of the products, particularly of consumer goods produced by foreign firms in developing countries. It is claimed that, unnecessarily, higher quality standards are maintained than are appropriate to satisfy the wants of consumers in developing countries, and implicitly therefore that the resources embodied in maintaining the higher quality are a waste from the developing country's viewpoint. This argument is fallacious. If there are lower cost substitutes available, with relatively high-price elasticities of demand, and consumers in developing countries do not derive any additional satisfaction from the higher quality characteristics of the more expensive product, profit maximising firms will produce the lower-cost and cheaper substitute in the developing country. If consumers in developing countries too, however, prefer the higher quality product to the cheaper lower quality substitute, then it is not for us to say that they should really only prefer the cheaper lower quality goods! Not surprisingly, this particular argument then quickly slides over to the earlier income distribution argument, when it is suggested that it is only the 'rich' who prefer the higher quality goods, and if income distribution were more equal there would not be any demand for these goods. But this argument, as we have already noted, requires direct means to alter the distribution of income, and not the control of the relative supply of different consumer goods.

There is one other issue concerning the measurement of the effects of POI which needs to be discussed. This is whether it is meaningful to look at the inflow and outflows on the capital account of the balance of payments associated with the foreign investment as a measure of the real income or balance of payments effect of POI. It seems to me that what has been missing in the discussion on this issue[1] is the recognition of the simple point that if *the internal rate of return* of the time stream of capital flows associated with the project is calculated, then *it can be* meaningfully compared with the appropriate social opportunity cost of capital in the host country. This comparison would be valid, under one limiting case of the 'alternative situation', namely that the only difference between the POI and a domestic alternative was in the forms of financing the project.[2] Then the IRR of

1. See Pearson Commission, *Partners in Development* (Pall Mall, 1969); Vernon, *Sovereignty at Bay*, op. cit.; Streeten, 'New Approaches ...', op. cit.; Little, 'On Measuring the Value ...', op. cit.
2. I have presented an analysis of the desirability of foreign borrowing making this assumption elsewhere. See Lal, 'When is Foreign Borrowing Desirable?', *Bulletin of the Oxford University Institute of Economics and Statistics*, August 1971. This analysis also takes into account the various structural characteristics which, it has been suggested, are important in developing countries, and it derives a simple algorithm for assessing the desirability of foreign borrowing, when the domestic and foreign alternatives only differ in the alternative forms of financing.

the capital flows associated with the POI alternative will give
the 'costs' of foreign financing, and as long as' the social
opportunity costs of domestic financing are equal to or
greater than this IRR, the foreign alternative will be more
desirable (on real income, and given the link between real
income and potential balance of payments effects suggested
earlier, also on balance of payments grounds), unless the
differential 'productivity' effects of the domestic alternative
are sufficiently greater than those for the foreign alternative
to counteract the relative cheapness of foreign as compared
with domestic capital. This last factor is unlikely, however, to
be relevant for most POI projects in developing countries, as
it is likely that one of the main gains from POI will be
differential 'productivity' effects which are greater than those
of any domestic alternative. As it is unlikely that it will be
possible to quantify these *differential* 'productivity' effects
with any degree of precision, it will be important to
determine whether or not the IRR of the expected or actual
capital flows associated with the foreign investment is greater
or less than the social opportunity cost of capital to the host
country. For if it is lower, then there would be a *prima facie*
case in favour of the POI project, and it will be chiefly for
cases where the IRR of the capital flows is higher than the
social opportunity cost of capital, that it will be necessary to
form further judgments on the differential 'productivity'
effects of POI as compared with the domestic alternative.
The framework of the Guidelines in Part II enables both
these questions to be answered.

PART TWO

Guidelines for Appraising Foreign Investment in Developing Countries

The Guidelines developed in this part are designed to provide the essential tools to help planners in developing countries decide on the desirability of particular foreign investments in their country. They can also be used to assess the 'ex post' effects of past POI, as has been done in the case studies in Parts III and IV of the book. These Guidelines are essentially complementary with the OECD's *Manual of Industrial Project Analysis in Developing Countries. Vol. II: Social Cost Benefit Analysis* by I. M. D. Little and J. A. Mirrlees. The same methods for evaluating the 'shadow' prices of produced goods and services are advocated. However in certain other important respects — the valuation of labour, income-distribution, technology and foreign financing — the Guidelines go beyond the *Manual*, and are to that extent an essential extension of its methods for evaluating the effects of POI on the host country.

Chapter II.1 sets out the preliminary considerations involved in delineating and estimating the various costs-benefits of POI to the host country, including a discussion of the problem of taking into account the alternatives to POI. Chapter II.2 gives a highly condensed version of the *Manual's* methods of shadow pricing produced inputs and outputs[1] whilst an Appendix provides a justification of the method and a comparison with those alternative methods which use a shadow exchange rate. Chapter II.3 deals with the problems of valuing unskilled and skilled labour, including the problems involved in 'training' and the development of skills. Chapter II.4 deals with the problem of taking account of the differential effects (if any) of POI on technical progress in the host country — the issues relating to the so-called 'transfer of technology' problem. Chapter II.5 deals with linkage effects and other externalities, Chapter II.6 with income distribution (both intra-temporal and inter-temporal) and the choice of a discount rate. Chapter II.7 discusses the implications of foreign financing in terms of the transfer

---

1. For a critical discussion of the *Manual's* methods see the symposium in the *Bulletin of the Oxford Institute of Economics and Statistics*, February 1972, and D. Lal, *Methods of Project Analysis — A Review* (World Bank Occasional Papers, Johns Hopkins, Baltimore, 1974).

problem and costs of alternative methods of financing the project. Chapter II.8 deals with uncertainty, and the problems connected with making estimates of the 'alternative situation'. Chapter II.9, brings the various components of the framework together, and is specifically concerned with the bargaining aspects of POI.

II.1 PRELIMINARIES

Our objective in these Guidelines is to provide policy-makers with decision rules for accepting or rejecting particular POI projects (subject to qualifications associated with the game-theoretic 'bargaining' aspects of the decision which are discussed in Chapter II.9).

Formally, policy-makers may be considered to be faced by the problem of maximising a specified social welfare function subject to given resource and transformation constraints. A POI project, say to produce good X, will then have to be evaluated in terms of its impact on social welfare, taking into account the opportunity costs of all the domestic resources which will be absorbed by the project. These opportunity costs and relative benefits of POI production of good X will depend upon the alternatives to that investment. The following alternatives have been considered relevant:[1]

(1) a domestic firm makes the good X
(2) the good X is imported
(3) to do without the good for the time being
(4) another foreign firm may be allowed to make the investment

In case (1), it will be necessary to compare the *relative social opportunity costs* of producing the good by the two alternative forms of financing, the social value of the good being the same whatever the form of financing. There may however in addition to the differential costs, also be some differential benefits due to different external economies generated by foreign and domestic firms producing the same good, as well as differing gestation lags, and levels of output by the two forms of financing.

In case (2), the value of the good will be given by its CIF price, and the evaluation of a project to produce it through POI will then be identical to that of any other investment

1. See Streeten, 'Costs and Benefits ...', op. cit.; and A. K. Sen, 'Cost-Benefit Analysis of Foreign Investment', OECD/UNCTAD (mimeo) 1970.

project on the lines of the OECD *Manual*, with the addition of considerations regarding the 'transfer problem' aspect of the capital inflows and outflows.

Case (3) will be identical with case (2), if we value the output of the project in terms of its CIF price, on the lines of the *Manual*, for the marginal social value of the good (tradeable) will, when it is produced, be given by its CIF price.

Case (4) is chiefly concerned with the 'bargaining' problem to be discussed in Chapter II.9. But even in the presence of game-theoretic considerations, foreign firm A's operations should be evaluated in the same way as foreign firm B's operations, and the one which makes the highest contribution to domestic social welfare should be accepted.

Thus essentially there are only two relevant alternatives for our purposes — cases (1) and (2). They differ to the extent that in case (1), we are interested in estimating the *differential* net social benefits of domestic and foreign firms' operations, whereas in case (2), we would be only doing the standard cost-benefit type of analysis of the foreign firm's operations. But it is obvious that in order to estimate the differential effects in case (1), we would still have to do the standard cost-benefit analysis of the foreign firm as in case (2). Thus the latter case is really subsumed under case (1), and no extra information is required. Hence the exercise reduces to delineating, estimating and comparing the cost-benefits of producing a particular good X, either by domestic or foreign financial arrangements, including different mixes of the two.

The index we shall use to help decide whether or not to accept foreign investment will then be the one which is normally used in investment appraisal, that is the net present value (NPV) criterion, or when more convenient the internal rate of return (IRR) of the project. However, we still need a numeraire in which the social welfare effects of the different investments can be expressed. To allow complementary use of the *Manual*, we shall adopt its convention of taking savings valued in foreign exchange as our numeraire.[1] This may seem

---

1. More precisely, the *Manual's* numeraire is 'uncommitted social income expressed in foreign exchange.'

odd, as normally changes in social welfare are identified with a weighted sum of changes in intertemporal consumption flows resulting from the project, which are moreover expressed in terms of the domestic currency. However the *Manual* numeraire is just an inversion of the more conventional numeraire – present consumption in domestic currency, for the general problem in any form of project analysis is to make commensurable present consumption and future consumption (given by current savings) and domestic and foreign resources. As long as we use the same relative prices for making the conversions, it does not matter which of the two relevant 'commodities' (present consumption or savings/ domestic resources or foreign resources) we take as our numeraire.

The next problem then is to decide on the set of relative prices by which the inputs and outputs of a particular project are to be multiplied, discounted to some base date, and summed to yield the NPV of the project. In evaluating particular investments from the social viewpoint, these prices should reflect social costs and benefits, so that the final value is the social net present value of the project. The next section discusses how these 'shadow' prices are to be derived when private and social costs and values diverge.

But assuming that we can assign these 'shadow' prices, the criterion for acceptance in case (1) would be whether the social rate of return (IRR) to the host country of the POI project is greater than that of its domestic rival (assuming that both IRRs are greater than or equal to the relevant social discount rate for the economy).

In case (2), we compare the net present value of the costs of producing the goods through POI, with the NPV of the costs of importing the good. Let the former be C_p, the latter C_m, and let the output of the good be x_n in each period, during the T years of the life of the project, and p_n be the import price. We then have:

$$C_p = \sum_{n=0}^{T} C_n (1 + r_n)^{-n} \qquad (I.1)$$

(where r_n is the relevant discount rate for the economy in period n and C_n are the costs incurred in year n) and

$$C_m = \sum_{n=0}^{T} p_n \cdot x_n (1 + r_n)^{-n} \tag{I.2}$$

and our criterion for acceptance is

$$C_p \leqslant C_m$$

or $\quad C_m - C_p \geqslant 0 \tag{I.3}$

that is

$$\sum_{n=0}^{T} \cdot (p_n \cdot x_n - C_n)(1 + r_n)^{-n} \geqslant 0 \tag{I.4}$$

But as the LHS of the above expression is nothing else but the NPV of the project when the 'shadow' price of the output is the CIF price (the *Manual* shadow price), we have for case 2 the standard cost-benefit rule that the POI project is accepted when it has a positive NPV with 'shadow' pricing of the inputs and outputs.

The first stage in appraising a POI project must therefore be the same as with any other social cost benefit analysis of an investment project, for there is *always* (except for non-tradeables) the opportunity (alternative) of importing the good the POI project will produce. The second stage is to see whether the alternative 1, or some combination with POI, is better than the POI project being considered. If there is no difference in the technology and the various external effects of POI and domestic firms, then the only source of any difference in their respective social rates of return will be due to the differential social costs of the two forms of *financing* the project. The delineation of these differences and discussion of the ways of taking them into account is postponed till Chapter II.7.

However, one of the major themes in the writing on POI[1] is that POI possesses certain technical and skill components which are specific to that form of financing, and which lead to differences in productivity of the POI and domestic firms

---

1. See Kindleberger, op. cit.; Vernon, op. cit.; Caves, op. cit.; Kindleberger, ed., op. cit.; Dunning, ed., op. cit.

in producing the same good. Furthermore it is claimed that POI is associated with various external economies/diseconomies which do not accrue (or are of smaller magnitude) to the domestic firm's operations.[1] This means that in addition to the differential costs of financing, we will also have to estimate these differential 'benefits' of POI as compared with the domestic alternative. These differential 'net benefit' effects can be divided into five broad categories.

First there may be differences in pure efficiency, so that the foreign firm can produce the same output with fewer inputs. This implies that the input-output coefficients will be different for POI and the domestic firm. This includes any differences in gestation lags before commencement of production. Secondly, there may be differences in the cost-benefits of 'training' labour and the associated externalities for the two types of firm. Thirdly, POI may enable the host country to 'keep up' with technical progress at lower social cost than the domestic alternative. Fourthly, there is a miscellaneous bunch of secondary 'linkage' effects which are claimed for one or the other type of investment. Finally, there are differential income-distribution effects which have been discussed in the literature on POI. We will discuss and take account of all these effects in our subsequent analysis.

The basic framework for the analysis can however be formalised very simply at this stage.

Suppose that the present value of the capital costs of financing the project domestically is PVC_d, and through POI is PVC_f, and the net benefits in any year n are given by B_{dn} and B_{fn} for domestic and foreign investment respectively, so that the present value of the net benefits for the two forms is:

$$PVB_d = \sum_{n=0}^{T_d} B_{dn} \left(1 + r_n\right)^{-n} \qquad (I.5)$$

$$PVB_f = \sum_{n=0}^{T_f} B_{fn} \left(1 + r_n\right)^{-n} \qquad (I.6)$$

where r_n is the relevant rate of discount for the economy,

1. See Streeten, 'New Approaches ...', op. cit.

and T_d and T_f are the lives of the respective domestic and foreign projects, we define:

$$B_{jn} = R_{jn} - C_{jn}$$

$$= X_{jn} \cdot P_{xn} + E_{jn} - \sum_i a_{ijn} \cdot P_{in} - \sum_k L_{kjn} \cdot W_{kn}$$

where $(j = d,f)$ (I.7)

where in period n, the R_n's and C_n's are the revenues and costs, X_n the output, P_{xn} the 'shadow' price of the output, E_n the net external effects, a_{in} is the input of the i'th intermediate good, whose 'shadow' price is P_{in}, L_{kn} is the input of the k'th type of labour, whose 'shadow' wage is W_{kn}. Then the net present value (NPV) of the two alternatives is:

$$NPV_d = PVB_d - PVC_d$$

$$NPV_f = PVB_f - PVC_f$$ (1.8)

The X, a_i, and L_k terms are technical coefficients, though it should be noted that they may differ for the two alternatives. In the next section we turn to the problem of estimating the P_x and P_i terms. Subsequent sections take up the problems of estimating the Ws, the E term, and the discount rates r_n $(n = 0 \ldots T)$. This is followed by a discusssion of the factors which lead to differences in PVC_d and PVC_f.

II.2   PRODUCED INPUTS AND OUTPUTS
The method we shall use to value produced inputs and outputs is that evolved by Little and Mirrlees (LM).[1]

It is widely recognised that in many developing countries, because of various market imperfections and non-optimal

---

1. I. M. D. Little and J. A. Mirrlees, *Manual of Industrial Project Analysis in Developing Countries: Vol. II — Social Cost Benefit Analysis* (OECD, Paris, 1969). Hereinafter referred to as the *Manual*. A revised edition has been published, entitled *Project Appraisal and Planning for Developing Countries* (Heinemann, 1974).

government controls, actual market prices often do not correctly measure the social costs and benefits of using and producing the relevant inputs and outputs of an investment project. The problem then is to derive 'shadow' prices which do provide the relative marginal social values of different goods and factors in the economy. Abstracting from the problem of the social valuation of labour inputs, we can usefully divide the produced commodities used or produced by the project into three categories: fully traded, non-traded and partially traded.

Fully traded commodities are those which are imported and exported and for which it can plausibly be assumed that an increase in domestic demand or supply as a result of the project will lead directly or indirectly to changes in foreign trade. This includes goods which are freely importable or exportable subject to given trade taxes or subsidies. The market prices of such goods will clearly be set by their border prices (CIF if importable; FOB if exportable) plus any given trade taxes. As the numeraire we are adopting is foreign exchange, the accounting (shadow) price of these goods will be just the CIF price *plus* internal transport costs if it is an importable, and the FOB price *less* internal transport costs if an exportable − that is their 'border' or 'frontier' prices. If for a particular good a country has monopoly or monopsony power in international trade, so that marginal and average revenue or costs are not the same, the relevant shadow price will be the marginal cost/revenue of importing/exporting the relevant good.

Non-traded goods are those which are not exported or imported at the margin, and for which therefore the market price will not be set by domestic demand and supply. An increase in domestic demand for such goods is assumed to be met on *Manual* procedures by an increase in supply. Hence the shadow price of such goods will be determined by the marginal social costs of producing such goods in terms of our numeraire − savings expressed in terms of foreign exchange. This is done by iteratively revaluing the costs of production of these goods at 'border' prices, that is, the costs of these goods are successively broken down into their component tradeable and primary factor costs, the former being valued as fully traded goods, and the latter on the lines discussed in Chapters II.3 and II.6 below.

Partially traded goods are an intermediate set of goods whose increased production by, or use on, the project might lead to changes not only in foreign trade (as for fully traded goods) and domestic production (as for non-traded goods) but also in domestic consumption of the good. The valuation of the two former sets of changes is as for fully traded and non-traded goods. This leaves the valuation of the proportion of the good's increase in supply or demand which affects domestic consumption. Consider the case of an increase in demand for a partially traded good, which is met in part by a reduction in its domestic consumption. This reduction will have been the result of a bidding up of the price of the good, and the consequent switch of part of consumer's expenditure away from the good to other goods and services. The social cost of acquiring the good for use on the project by this process will then just be the cost at accounting prices of providing the other goods and services to which consumers switch their expenditure. Assuming that for the economy as a whole this corresponds to the social cost of providing the average basket of commodities consumed, consumer expenditure data can be used to determine a consumption conversion factor, which converts say Rs. 100 of consumer expenditure into its accounting value in terms of foreign exchange. The accounting value of a change of Rs. X in domestic consumption can then be determined by simply multiplying Rs. X by the conversion factor. Moreover, if the breakdown of consumer expenditure by income/regional groups is available, specific consumption conversion factors for these groups can be calculated and used whenever changes in their consumption as a result of the project need to be valued at shadow prices.

Given these rules the shadow prices of most commodities can be determined. It is particularly useful to derive these shadow prices for the more important commodities in the economy. The ratios of these accounting prices to the market prices of these goods being denoted as accounting ratios. Thereafter, whenever the market values of particular commodities are to be converted into their social values, all that needs to be done is to multiply the market value by the appropriate accounting ratio.[1]

It should be noted that these accounting ratios and the accounting prices are not based on any necessary assumption of free trade.[2] Furthermore, in principle these LM rules are equivalent to those suggested for instance by UNIDO[3], which take aggregate consumption expressed in domestic currency as the numeraire. As we noted in the previous chapter, as long as the same relative prices are used to make the flows of foreign exchange and domestic currency items and of present and future consumption commensurable, it is purely a matter of convenience which of the two numeraires — future consumption (savings) expressed in foreign exchange, or present consumption expressed in domestic currency we take as our numeraire. However the LM methods which use the former numeraire are likely to be more convenient and more accurate in their application, as they imply the calculation of the *implicit* multiple exchange rates which are normally found in developing countries as a result of their highly differentiated tariff structures. The UNIDO procedures on the other hand use a single shadow exchange rate to convert foreign currency into domestic currency items, and this necessarily implies averaging across the existing multiple exchange rates, and, like any other process of averaging, the shadow exchange rate becomes extremely sensitive to the weighting system used. As a result widely divergent estimates of the shadow exchange rate can emerge (and have done so) from the same data for the same country. The Appendix to this Chapter substantiates these points, as well as providing a

---

1. A comprehensive set of such accounting ratios for Kenya is available in Scott, MacArthur and Newbery: *Project Appraisal in Practice* (Heinemann, forthcoming); and for the Philippines in D. Lal, *Men or Machines* (ILO, forthcoming). In addition also see the series on Cost-Benefit Analysis published by the OECD Development Centre. These are: No. 1 — D. Lal, *Wells and Welfare*; No. 2 — N. H. Stern, *An Appraisal of Small Holdings in Kenya*; No. 3 — I. M. D. Little and D. G. Tipping, *A Social Cost Benefit Analysis of the Kulai Oil Palm Estate*; No. 4 — F. Seton, *Shadow Wages in the Chilean Economy* (OECD, Paris, 1972).
2. See D. Lal, 'Adjustments for Trade Distortions in Project Analysis', *Journal of Development Studies* (Oct. 1974); and the Appendix to this Chapter.
3. UNIDO, *Guidelines for Project Evaluation*, by A. K. Sen, S. Marglin and P. Dasgupta (New York, 1972).

more rigorous justification for the *Manual's* valuation rules for commodities.

Two additional points may be noted. It may be the case that, for certain inputs, there may be unavoidable excess capacity for a long time in the domestic industries. Would it still be correct to use 'frontier' prices to evaluate the social cost of providing these inputs? The answer is yes, as long as it is remembered that the 'relevant frontier' price must be the marginal cost/revenue of importing/exporting the good. If there is excess capacity due to a shortage of domestic demand, then clearly the good is a potential exportable. It may however turn out that the marginal social cost (it should be noted that in the case of excess capacity, the marginal social cost is the short run marginal cost, valued at 'frontier' prices) of producing the good is greater than the marginal revenue which could be earned through exporting, taking into account export marketing problems, though less than the cost of importing the good. In that case, clearly the domestic social marginal cost of producing the good is its relevant shadow price. Our comparisons are still with the relevant frontier prices. In the above case the marginal cost of producing the input happens to lie between the marginal cost of imports and the marginal revenue of exports, and is hence the correct shadow price to use.

The second point concerns the widespread use of quota restrictions in developing countries. As long as trade restrictions are in the form of unchanging tariffs/subsidies, the *Manual* procedure as we have seen, will still be valid, as then the impact of a particular marginal project will still be on trade. If however the restrictions are in the form of a fixed import quota, then the 'frontier' prices will not provide the correct social measure of the costs and benefits of inputs and outputs. In this case the relevant goods will have to be treated as non- or partially-traded goods.

In short, therefore, the *Manual* framework of cost-benefit analysis, which we are basically adopting in these Guidelines, provides a method of investment appraisal for countries where a highly differentiated tariff structure results in complex and wide ranging divergences between the market and social relative values of goods and services. This is

particularly important when we are appraising foreign investment, for we should like to keep separate the effects which
can be ascribed to POI *per se*, and those which are the result
of general governmental policy, for instance the existence of
a highly differentiated and varying effective protective
structure. We have to be wary that the ill effects of the one
are not ascribed to the other. The *Manual* framework enables
us to do this and we shall therefore adopt it.

We turn next to the evaluation of labour costs, the W_i's of
Equation 1.7 of the previous chapter.

Appendix to Chapter II.2

The Rationale of LM Commodity Valuation Rules

The assumption and justification of the LM method are best
brought out in terms of the standard static two factor-two
commodity model of an open economy.[1] In this model
where both commodities are traded, given perfect international trading conditions, and assuming that any domestic
distortions can be corrected by appropriate tax/subsidy
measures, the optimal pattern of production and of trade will
be uniquely determined by the point of tangency of the
terms of trade line with the domestic production possibility
frontier. The relevant 'shadow' prices of the two commodities are then given by the international 'frontier' prices.
Furthermore, from Samuelson's theorem on the correspondence of factor and commodity prices it follows that relative
factor prices would be uniquely determined by the given

1. The following discussion is based on my article 'Adjustments for Trade
Distortions', op. cit. I had earlier discussed many of these issues in an unpublished
paper, 'Foreign Exchange Bottlenecks, Balance of Payments Investment Criteria
and the Optimum Pattern of Trade and Production', Oxford, Jan. 1967, mimeo.

'frontier' prices of the commodities. If now even a single money price of a domestic good or factor is given, all other money prices, and the foreign exchange rate which converts domestic money prices into foreign money prices, would be uniquely determined. Alternatively, if the foreign exchange rate were given, the domestic money prices would be uniquely determined. Moreover, in this model, a change in the foreign exchange rate would have no real effects on the economy, as it would affect only the absolute level of domestic money prices, without affecting the relative price structure which would remain the same as the unchanged 'frontier' price structure. The argument can be generalised to include traded intermediate goods and naturally carries over to the case of 'n' commodities which are all traded. Furthermore the model can be made dynamic given the intertemporal vectors of 'frontier' prices for the commodities, which will uniquely determine the intertemporal configuration of production and trade: the associated 'shadow' prices of the dated commodities and factors being determined by the terms of trade in each period. Note that in this model the optimal production point in each period is given independently of any specification of the pattern of consumer demand or any social objective function for the economy. The production decisions of the economy can be separated from the consumption decisions, and planners can achieve productive efficiency by merely using 'frontier' prices as their shadow prices, and this will maximise feasible social welfare.[1]

If we drop the assumption of perfect international trading conditions, production and consumption decisions can no longer be separated. As the terms of trade are variable, the efficient feasible commodity set will no longer be a straight line as in the constant terms of trade case. The efficient feasible commodity set will be given by the well-known

---

1. For a more rigorous analysis of a dynamic model of an open economy in which all goods are tradeable, see Hansen, *Long and Short-Term Planning in Underdeveloped Countries* (De Vries Lectures, North-Holland, Amsterdam, 1967), and Lal, 'Foreign Exchange Bottlenecks, Balance of Payments Investment Criteria, and the Optimum Pattern of Trade and Production', op. cit.

Baldwin envelope,[1] and the efficient production and consumption points will be jointly determined by the tangency of a community indifference curve with the Baldwin envelope. Moreover the 'shadow' prices in this situation will no longer be the 'frontier' prices corresponding to the average terms of trade, but will correspond to the *marginal* terms of trade at the optimum point, the difference between the 'frontier' and 'shadow' prices in this case being the familiar optimum tariff. Moreover, unless it can be assumed that the economy is already levying the optimum tariff on the relevant good, it will not be possible to derive the shadow price from the *observed* marginal rate of transformation of the good in international trade. It will therefore be necessary to estimate, or else guess, the marginal cost/revenue of the good after the levy of an optimum tariff, to obtain its shadow price. This complication may not however be of great importance in practice, as developing countries are likely to have a monopolistic position only in a few commodities.

Next introduce a single non-traded good into the model. The analysis immediately becomes more difficult. First, the optimal production of non-traded goods can no longer be determined independently of domestic preferences of consumers. The separation of production and consumption decisions which was possible as long as all goods were tradeable is no longer valid. Furthermore exchange rates will now have 'real' resource allocation effects in the economy, as they will determine the relative domestic money price of traded to non-traded commodities. This is best seen in terms of the following example, which also provides a way of justifying the use of a standard conversion factor, as in the *Manual* method of deriving the 'shadow' price of some non-traded goods.

Consider an economy which produces three goods, an importable (M), an exportable (X) and a non-traded good (N). These goods are produced by the two domestic factors of production capital (K) and labour (L). We observe the economy in a protection situation, with a tariff of t% on

---

1. R. E. Baldwin, 'Equilibrium in International Trade', *QJE*, 1948.

imports of M. Apart from this distortion, there are no other distortions in the economy, which is in external and internal balance, at an exchange rate e, with W, and R, the domestic money wage and rental rates of the two factors of production, K and L, and with eP_{xf}, $eP_{mf}(1 + t)$ and P_n, as the domestic money prices of the three goods X, M, and N, where P_{mf} and P_{xf} are the foreign currency prices of the two traded goods and A_{ij} is the input of the i'th factor in the production of the j'th good.

We now have the following production relationships:

$$A_{lm} W + A_{km} R = eP_{mf}(1 + t)$$

$$A_{lx} W + A_{kx} R = eP_{xf} \qquad\qquad (2.1)$$

$$A_{ln} W + A_{kn} R = P_n$$

At the existing domestic market prices, producers are indifferent as to whether a marginal increase in domestic resources is invested in X, M or N. However the tariff has introduced a distortion which will mean that investment decisions taken on the basis of market prices will not maximise feasible social welfare. The tariff as it were has introduced a wedge between the MSC of producing and the MSV of using a unit of foreign exchange. The MSC of producing foreign exchange will depend upon whether it is 'produced' by an expansion of exports and/or import substitute production. If the increase in foreign exchange is the result of a combination of both export expansion and import reduction, the MSC of 'producing' foreign exchange will be a suitably weighted average of the domestic resource costs of producing importables and exportables. The MSV of 'consuming' foreign exchange is given by the value of a unit of foreign exchange to consumers. Just as foreign exchange can be 'produced' by either expanding exports and/or reducing imports, it can be 'consumed' by either increasing imports and/or reducing exports and consuming exportables.

Now, consider the evaluation of the social costs and benefits of expanding production of the M(X) industry, with *domestic currency as the numeraire*. The social costs will be given by the left-hand side (LHS) of (2.1), for we are assuming the absence of any factor market distortions. The social benefits will be the $P_{mf}(P_{xf})$ units of *foreign currency*, whose MSV in *domestic* currency will be the social benefits from the unit expansion of M(X). If a unit increase in foreign exchange is 'consumed' by increasing imports of α, and reducing exports of β, in *foreign* currency ($\alpha + \beta = 1$), then the MSV of a unit of foreign exchange consumed (e') will be simply:

$$e' = \alpha e(1 + t) + \beta e = e[\alpha(1 + t) + \beta]$$

The shadow exchange rate (SER) will then be e', and its value will lie between $e(1 + t)$ when $\beta = 0$ and e when $\alpha = 0$. Thus in (2.1) the production of X will be socially more profitable than M.

Alternatively, we could have taken *foreign currency as the numeraire*, and worked out the social costs-benefits of the two traded goods industries (M, X) as follows. The social benefits (MSV's) of the two goods in *foreign* currency are their foreign currency prices P_{mf} and P_{xf}. To determine the social costs of production (MSC's) of the two goods, we have to revalue the inputs which enter into their production in foreign exchange. As in this model only primary factors enter as inputs, and with their physical quantities given, it is only the factor prices which need to be revalued in foreign exchange. Clearly the correct social value of the factors is their value marginal product (VMP) in an alternative use. Assume for the moment that there is no non-traded good industry (N). Then if the M(X) industry is being expanded, the relevant social cost of its factors will be the *foreign exchange VMP* of the factors in the X(M) industry, as its (M(X)) expansion, given our full employment assumptions must entail a withdrawal of factors from the X(M) industry. Furthermore, given our assumptions of the absence of factor market distortions, the factor prices in *domestic currency* must be equal to the *domestic currency VMP* of the two factors in the two industries. Hence the *foreign currency VMP's* of the two factors are obviously: W/e and R/e for factors *from* the X industry, and W/e(1 + t) and R/e(1 + t) for factors *from* the M industry, as the conversion of domestic currency VMP into foreign exchange VMP of factors from the X(M) industry is done at the effective exchange rate which applies to the X(M) good, namely $e(e(1 + t))$. The relative social profitability of the two goods using foreign currency as the numeraire is then:

$$A_{lm} W/e + A_{km} R/e > P_{mf}$$

$$A_{lx} W/e(1 + t) + A_{kx} R/e(1 + t) < P_{xf}$$

and once again X is socially more profitable than M.

The two methods would therefore give identical rankings of the two goods. Moreover if on the foreign currency as numeraire method too we had used a *single* conversion factor for converting values in domestic currency into foreign currency, equal to the SER of e', then the two methods would be identical except for the change in numeraire. However, as the above example shows even in this simple case the LM (foreign currency as numeraire) method would explicitly use the *multiple* conversion factors corresponding to the twin effective exchange rates (e and $e(1 + t)$) to convert domestic currency values into foreign currency, whereas the UNIDO (domestic currency as numeraire) method would average across these multiple exchange rates to derive the *single* conversion factor (the SER of e') to make the reverse conversions. The averaging process will naturally be sensitive to the weights α and β, and hence liable to error.

We next consider the relative social desirability of a marginal increase in the output of the non-traded good N, relative to the traded goods M or X. This will depend crucially upon what is expected to happen to the protective structure.

First, assume that the existing protective structure will remain unchanged. As 'ex hypothesi' a marginal investment project will not change the W's and R's in equation (2.1) above, the marginal social costs of production in *domestic currency* are given by the costs at market prices on the left-hand side of (2.1), and the only correction required is to the value of the outputs (the right-hand side of (2.1)) to reflect the marginal social values of the three goods, to obtain the correct relative social profitability of the three industries. In *domestic currency*, the MSV of M is $e'P_{mf}$, the MSV of X is $e'P_{xf}$ and the MSV of N is P_n. Thus the only adjustment necessary is the SER adjustment to the price of M and X, to provide the correct social ranking of the three industries — namely that the production of X, at 'shadow' prices is more profitable relative to both M and N.

Alternatively, using *foreign currency* as the numeraire, the MSV's of the two traded goods would be given by P_{mf} and P_{xf}. The 'shadow' prices of factors drawn from the two traded goods industries (X,M) will still be their respective foreign currency VMP's in the industry *from* which the factors are drawn. What of factors drawn from the non-traded good N to expand the output of a traded good X(M)? The first round effect will be to reduce output of N (as we are assuming full employment of factors in these simple models), which will tend to raise its domestic money price (as by definition all domestic demand for non-traded goods is met from domestic production). This will raise the money wage and rental rates in the N industry (as these are equal to the now higher VMP in domestic currency of the two factors in N production), which in turn will induce factors from the third industry (M(X)) to flow into N production (as the VMP's and hence factor prices in domestic currency in the M(X) industry are unchanged given the fixed border price of M(X)). This inflow of factors will reduce the wage-rental rates in N production, and hence the price of N in the second round towards their original values.[1] The net effect of expanding X(M) production will thus have been *indirectly* to reduce the output of M(X), with the factors required for expanding X(M) output coming *indirectly* from the M(X) industry. Hence the shadow prices of factors in this simple model, on LM lines, will still be their foreign exchange VMP in the relevant *traded* good industry M or X, even though the factors are drawn in the first instance from the non-traded good industry N; the shadow price of the non-traded good N being given on LM lines by the MSC of production in

---

1. But note that when resources are drawn from non-traded good production *both* consumption and output of the non-traded good could fall. It will then be necessary to value the change in consumption which is caused by using the consumption conversion factors described in Chapter II.2, above.

foreign exchange, the latter being dependent on the given input-output co-efficients of the two factors (in our model) and their foreign exchange VMP's in the traded goods industries from which they are drawn. Thus once again both the LM and SER methods would give the same ranking of the three industries, with the social profitability of M negative, of X positive, and of N equal to nought. However as before, whereas LM would use multiple conversion factors, the SER would again average across these, and hence be less accurate, and more difficult to compute.

Next assume that the protective structure will be removed in the future. Clearly, now the relevant shadow prices will be the prices of the goods and factors in the free trade situation.

To determine these prices, we consider what would happen to the prices of goods and factors in our model economy with removal of the tariff on M. The resulting changes are best considered in two distinct stages. In the first stage, we assume that all other domestic prices, the exchange rate, and domestic expenditure, remain unchanged. With a reduction in the price of M by t% (the tariff rate), the relative domestic prices of the three goods X, M and N will change. With a fall in the price of M relative to both X and N, there will be a shift in domestic consumption from X and N towards M, and in domestic productive resources from M to X and N. Now consider the markets for M, X and N. In the market for M there will be excess demand, whilst in the markets for X and N there will be excess supply. Unless the excess demand for M is matched by an equivalent excess supply of X (an exceptional circumstance) normally, there will tend to be a balance of payments deficit, given by the difference between the excess demand for M and excess supply of X. What is more, from Walras's law, this net excess demand for traded goods must be exactly equal to the *excess supply of the non-traded good N*. In the next stage, therefore, to restore equilibrium it will be necessary to cure the net excess demand for tradeables which is equivalent to curing the excess supply for the non-traded good N. This requires a fall in the relative price of the non-traded good N to the two traded goods. This change can be brought about by two alternative adjustment mechanisms (or a combination of both). The first is with *the exchange rate fixed, but with the domestic money price of* N flexible. (This is the 'classical' adjustment mechanism). The other is with the price of N fixed, but with the exchange rate flexible. Both adjustment mechanisms will lead to the same domestic relative price of the three goods in the free trade situation. Let these be e^*P_{xf}, e^*P_{mf}, and P_n, with exchange rate flexibility, and eP_{xf}, eP_{mf}, and P_n^* with the price of N flexible. As the relative price changes are identical on both adjustment mechanisms, they will lead to identical resource allocation effects, and factor price changes in the free trade as compared with the protection situation. Let these free trade factor prices be W^* and R^*. Then assuming that we know or can guess the price changes (in W, R and e or P_n), and assuming the same adjustment mechanism, then either of the two alternative methods of using domestic currency as the numeraire and a 'shadow' exchange rate, or foreign currency as the numeraire and the LM method will give the same ranking of the relative social profitability of investments in the three industries. But the shadow exchange rate will no longer be the UNIDO SER, but rather the free trade equilibrium exchange rate.[1]

We have thus shown that LM procedures do *not* need to assume free trade; that they are in principle equivalent to SER procedures, involving a mere change in numeraire; but in practice because they derive and use multiple conversion factors for converting domestic into foreign currency values, they are likely to be more accurate and also easier to apply than the SER procedures which average across these implicit multiple exchange rates.

II.3 LABOUR

In this section we discuss how the various types of labour which will be utilised by the investment project should be evaluated, together with any externalities that may arise as a result of the training imparted by the firm. We deal with all

---

1. See Lal, 'Adjustments . . .', op. cit.; and Bacha and Taylor, 'Foreign Exchange Shadow Prices: A Critical Review of Current Theories', *QJE*, May 1971.

classes of labour in one train of argument at first, and later differentiate different types of labour, for example by nationality (domestic or foreign), and take account of various other complications which may arise because of the typical wage structure which is claimed to be associated with most POI in developing countries.

First consider the simplest case, of a project which only employs unskilled labour, which is combined with various produced inputs, to yield the output of the firm. Assume that all managers or skilled persons are imported, so that their costs are direct foreign exchange costs, and can therefore be considered to be just like the produced inputs and outputs of the last section. We then only need to price the unskilled labour used on the project, the produced inputs and outputs being 'shadow' priced on the lines outlined above. Suppose that the labour to be used on the project comes from a low productivity agricultural sector, and that the output foregone in agriculture, by transferring the labour to the project valued at 'frontier' prices is m per man. Further assume that for various institutional reasons the wage that has to be paid to the worker on the project is c, which is greater than m. Also assume that all wages in the economy are consumed. Then the social cost of employing one worker (the SWR) on the project is given by:

$$SWR = m + (c - m) - (c - m)/s$$

where it is assumed that the overall level of savings in the economy is not optimal, so that one unit of current consumption generated is socially worth $(1/s)$ units of current savings. (This point is dealt with at greater length, together with the problem of determining s, in Chapter II.6.) In the above formulation, the first term on the RHS is the output foregone elsewhere in the economy by employing one more man on the project. In addition there will be the cost of the extra consumption $(c - m)$ to which the economy is committed (as $c > m$), and which has to be accounted for if current consumption is not as valuable as savings. Not the whole of this increase in consumption is however a social cost, as society does value s units of consumption as equal in social value to one unit of savings. Hence from the total

increase in consumption a proportion (1/s) must be sub-
tracted, to get the net social cost (in terms of the numeraire,
which is taken to be savings) of the increased consumption.
The above expression reduces to:

$$\text{SWR} = c - (c - m)/s \tag{3.1}$$

and is the *Manual* SWR.

The above formulation assumes that no social value should
be attached to the change in the net disutility of effort in the
economy which might follow the employment of one more
man on the project (which together with changes in output
elsewhere in the economy, and the change in aggregate
consumption caused by paying labourers a wage (c) greater
than the output figures elsewhere (m), gives the three
considerations relevant in shadow pricing labour).[1] If however disutilities of effort are taken into account, then the
SWR is given by:

$$\text{SWR} = c - (c - m)/s + \lambda(L - m)/s \tag{3.2}$$

where L is the supply price of labour to the project, the other
terms have the same meaning as before, and λ is the weight
society attaches to the changes in the private disutility of
effort. If $\lambda = 0$, that is private disutilities are not socially
valued, (3.2) reduces to the *Manual* SWR (3.1). If on the
other hand private disutilities of effort are socially valued at
par, $\lambda = 1$, and the SWR becomes:

$$\text{SWR} = L + (c - L)(1 - 1/s) \tag{3.3};$$

if the higher industrial wage (c) is therefore a competitive
wage, so that c -= L, then the SWR = c, the market wage.

One other complication needs to be introduced, namely
that as a result of increasing employment in the industrial
sector, in contrast to an implicit assumption in the above
analysis, more than one man may move from agriculture.
Suppose N people migrate to the towns with the creation of

---

1. The following discussion and derivations are based on my paper, 'Disutility of
Effort, Migration, and the Shadow Wage Rate', *Oxford Economic Papers*, March
1973. This paper also argues that in developing countries there may be a case for
not valuing the private disutilities of effort and hence assuming that $\lambda = 1$.

one more 'industrial' job; if the output foregone per worker is Y, and the supply price per worker is l, then m = NY and L = Nl, in equation (3.2).

We can formulate a simple and plausible rural-urban migration model, which would enable us to specify the values of N and l. Suppose that a rural migrant moves to the towns if the costs of migration are less than the expected benefits from migration, the costs being given by the income he foregoes in agriculture, say a (note that a is not necessarily equal to Y), plus actual migration costs, say g (which include both the real and 'psychic' costs of migration). He expects to obtain a job in the 'organised' urban sector at the institutional wage c, but if he cannot get this job, he can nevertheless find employment during his period of search in the 'unorganised' urban labour market at the competitive wage b. However by living in the town the migrant has to incur relatively higher costs of living of u, than in rural areas, to maintain the same standard of living as he enjoyed in the countryside. Finally, his chances of getting an 'organised' sector job, are given by the ratio of vacant jobs divided by the number of job seekers in any period, say P. Then, the costs of migration are given by (a + g + u) and the expected benefits by (Pc + (1 − P)b). Then at the margin the migrant will equate the costs of migration with the expected benefits, and hence in equilibrium:

$$a + g + u = Pc + (1 - P)b$$

which yields the 'equilibrium' value of $P = (a + g + u - b)/(c - b)$. If the number of 'organised' sector job vacancies is increased by one, this will alter the probability of finding a job from its equilibrium value P, and rural-urban migration will set in till $1/P$ migrants have moved and restored the probability of finding an urban sector job to P. Thus $N = 1/P$, and as m = NY, the total output foregone,

$$m = Y(c - b)/(a + g + u - b)$$

Also, given our assumptions the supply price of each migrant, $l = (a + g + u)$. Hence $L = Nl = (a + g + u)(c - b)/(a + g + u - b)$. Substituting these values of L and m in (3.2) above, yields the

$$SWR = c - 1/s\,[c - [Y + \lambda(a + g + u - Y)]$$
$$(c - b)/(a + g + u - b)] \quad (3.4)$$

If no social value is placed on the private disutilities of effort $(\lambda = 0)$, then the $SWR = c - 1/s[c - Y(c - b)/(a + g + u - b)]$, whilst if private disutilities are socially valued at par $(\lambda = 1)$, the

$$SWR = c - 1/s[c - (a + g + u)(c - b)/(a + g + u - b)]$$

Next relax the assumption that only domestic unskilled labour is employed on the project, for as Hirschman has rightly pointed out, 'very few countries would ever consciously wish to specialise in unskilled labour, while foreigners with a comparative advantage in entrepreneurship, management, skilled labour and capital take over these functions, replacing inferior "local talent"!'[1] More importantly, even though the project may initially employ raw unskilled labour, its use on the project will, through 'on the job' training, together with any more formal training the firm may impart, implant certain skills in it. The development of these skills is considered to be one of the most important aspects of development, and the transplanting of skills (or failure to do so) is considered to be one of the important external effects of foreign investment. To see how these aspects can be taken into account consider the following simplified example.[2]

We assume that initially the project employs foreign skilled personnel, whose shadow price is their wage (w) (assuming

1. A. O. Hirschman, 'How to Divest in Latin America and Why', *Essays in International Finance*, No. 76, Nov. 1969, Princeton.
2. The following analysis is based on the human capital approach which has been recently revived. See G. S. Becker, 'Investment in On the Job Training' in his *Human Capital* (Columbia, 1964); J. Mincer, 'On the Job Training: Costs Returns and Some Implications', *JPE*, 1962; J. Mincer, 'The Distribution of Labour Incomes', *Journal of Economic Literature*, 1970. The approach however goes back at least to Adam Smith, who wrote: 'When an expensive machine is erected, the extraordinary work to be performed by it before it is worn out, it must be expected, will replace the capital laid out upon it, with at least the ordinary profits. A man educated at the expense of much labour and time to any of these employments which require extraordinary dexterity and skill, may be compared

their consumption is entirely on imports and their savings are all repatriated), and unskilled labour which is paid a wage c, such that c = m = L, in our earlier equations, so that the SWR for unskilled labour is c. After say a year, as a result of training within and by the firm (the costs of training being assumed to be borne by the firm), the unskilled labour becomes skilled and replaces the foreign skilled workers, and is from then on paid a wage w, which is the wage previously paid to foreign skilled personnel, and which reflects the higher productivity due to the acquisition of skills (human capital), and which is equal to its alternative marginal product valued at 'frontier' prices in alternative employment within the country. The SWR for skilled and unskilled labour thus remains unchanged (except for the differences in the foreign exchange costs of consumption and savings by domestic and foreign skilled personnel, which are ignored at this stage). Suppose next, that the project comes to an end after T years, but that workers are immortal, and that the skills they have acquired do not depreciate and can furthermore be used with equal effectiveness in other domestic industries. In year T therefore, we will have to credit the project with the scrap value of its material assets plus the human capital which is now embodied in its domestic skilled workers. The value of this human capital, on our highly simplified assumptions, can be easily calculated. If the skills had not been imparted, the marginal product per worker would have continued to be c, the unskilled worker's wage. As a result of training, the marginal product has risen to w. That implies that from year T to infinity, the trained stock of workers can produce an incremental output compared with an equivalent unskilled stock of (w − c) per

---

to one of those expensive machines. The work which he learns to perform, it must be expected, over and above the usual wages of common labour, will replace to him the whole expense of his education, with at least the ordinary profits of an equally valuable capital. It must do this too in a reasonable time, regard being had to the very uncertain duration of human life, in the same manner as the more certain duration of the machine. The difference between the wages of skilled labour and those of common labour is founded upon this **principle'.** *The Wealth of Nations*, Book I, Chapter X, Part 1, p. 78, in the edition published by Routledge, London.

worker, per year. We cannot however take the whole of the
present value of this incremental stream of output as the
social value of the stock of skilled workers, for in any period
it will always be possible to train unskilled workers to the
same level of skill. Suppose that the real resource costs of
such training are k per period, and that it takes t' years to
train a worker. Then by having a skilled worker available
from the stock left by the project, the economy benefits by
first receiving the incremental output $(w - c)$, and secondly,
saving the resource costs k, in each period during the t' years
in which otherwise an unskilled worker would have to be
trained. The net present value of the social benefit of each
skilled worker left by the project, is therefore:

$$\sum_{n=0}^{t'} [(w - c) + k]/(1 + r)^n \text{ in year T}$$

The total stock of human capital which must therefore be
credited to the project in year T, will be

$$N . \sum_{n=0}^{t'} [(w - c) + k]/(1 + r)^n$$

where N is the number of skilled domestic workers on the
project at its demise in year T. The SWR during the project's
life however, in this example, will be c for unskilled and w
for skilled labour, that is, the same whether domestic or
foreign skilled labour is used. If only foreign skilled labour is
used till the end of the life of the project, then clearly, there
will be no stock of *human* capital to be credited to the
project.

We have so far implicitly assumed that workers, once they
are employed by a firm, stay with it till the bitter end.
Suppose however, that in year t, N_t domestic skilled workers
who have been trained in and at the expense of firm A, leave
to go and work in another firm B, in the country. As the N_t
who have moved to B, have been trained in firm A, so that
their productivity is higher by $(w - c)$ per worker over their
unskilled level, firm B, and the rest of the economy will have
the future benefits accruing from this training plus the
saving of the training costs during the period in which an

unskilled worker would otherwise have to be trained. The net present value of these benefits which must be credited to firm A in year t are therefore

$$N_t \cdot \sum_{n=0}^{t'} [(w - c) + k]/(1 + r)^n,$$

given our assumptions.

Next relax the unrealistic assumption we have hitherto made that workers are immortal. If the remaining effective working life of those skilled workers left on the project, and those leaving to join other firms is greater than t' — the period it takes to train an unskilled worker — our above formulae for the social value of the human capital to be credited to the firm which has borne the cost of their training remains unchanged. If however their remaining effective working life, say q years is less than t', then the term q, should be substituted for t' in the above formulae.

If we next relax the assumption that there is only one type of labour, the project should be credited with

$$\sum_i \sum_{n=0}^{t_i'} N_{Ti}[(w_i - c_i) + k_i]/(1 + r)^n$$

(for the skilled workers left at the demise of the project, in year T) and

$$\sum_i \sum_{n=0}^{t_i'} N_{ti}[(w_i - c_i) + k_i]/(1 + r)^n$$

(for those who migrate to other firms during the operation of the project, in year t).

Where the i subscripts refer to the particular class of labour, w_i is the competitive wage the particular class of labour received *before it left* the project (and in our present model *ex hypothesi*, what it will receive elsewhere, as it is its alternative marginal product) and c_i is the wage it received when it *entered* the project (which again *ex hypothesi*, was its alternative value marginal product when it was first employed by the firm); t'_i is the training time and k_i the real resource cost in each period of training labour from skill (wage) level c_i to w_i.

The general principles on which the external benefits from the acquisition of skills which may result from the investment's operations can be taken into account should now be clear. We have to try and estimate the net additions to the stock of human capital in the economy as a whole that the project makes possible at each point in time. As long as the capital produced by the firm is being utilised within it, then there is no need to take it into account any further, as its benefits and costs will already appear in the project's balance sheet. (Note that for our purposes it is irrelevant whether the costs of training are borne by the firm or by the workers themselves. In either case from the social point of view, given the assumptions we have made, these costs will have been taken into account in the other aspects of our calculations of the social profitability of the firm's operations.) However, as soon as the human capital created by the firm is no longer being utilised in the firm, but is available to be utilised elsewhere in the economy, and if the firm has borne the costs of providing this human capital, then the firm must be accredited with the NPV of the incremental output stream the net addition to the human capital stock makes possible during the period it would take to train a worker to an equivalent skill-level, plus the real resource costs of such training.

Obsolescence of skills or redundancy of specific skills in the absence of the project can again be taken into account. If skills depreciate or are specific to the project, the value-marginal product of the skilled labour will be less than the wage paid in the firm, and it is the former which should then be identified with the w terms in the formulas given above.

We next introduce a further complication, by relaxing the assumption we have made so far that wages of all classes of labour are determined in competitive markets, which reflect the alternative value marginal product of that particular class of labour. If this assumption is invalid, then the wage which the skilled labour is paid cannot be taken to be the shadow wage for that class of labour. But the general principles on which the divergence between m, the output foregone elsewhere by using a particular class of labour on the project, and c, the actual wage the labour is paid, should be taken into account, have already been stated. The SWR for any class of labour i, will be given by:

$$SWR_i = c_i - (c_i - m_i)/s_i \tag{3.5}$$

where the s_i are the weights (income distribution) to be attached to the social value of the increased income of the labour class i, above its social opportunity cost (value marginal productivity in an alternative use),[1] that is $(c_i - m_i)$. The determination of the s_i weights is taken up in Chapter II.6. It is important to remember that with the acquisition of skills, the c and m terms are likely to change for any particular *labourer*, but are less likely to change for any *class* of labour. If however they do change for classes of labour over time, these changes should be incorporated into a changing SWR for the particular class of labour over time.

Finally, the value of training to be ascribed to the project, in this more general case where labour markets are not competitive, will be given by

$$\sum_i \sum_{n=0}^{t_i'} N_{Ti} [(m_{Ti} - m_{\phi i}) + k_i] / (1 + r)^n$$

(in year T when the project ends)

$$\sum_i \sum_{n=0}^{t_i'} N_{ti} [(m_{ti} - m_{\phi i}) + k_i] / (1 + r)^n \tag{3.6}$$

(in year t, when the firm loses skilled labour whose training costs it has borne, to the rest of the economy).

where the m_T and m_t terms represent the value-marginal product of the particular class of labour in the rest of the economy when it leaves the project, and the m_ϕ terms represent the alternative value-marginal product of the relevant labour class when it entered the firm. For this

---

1. The discussion of unskilled labour was complicated by the impact of industrial employment on agricultural output. For skilled labour however these complications are not likely to exist, and hence it can be assumed that the m term will be equal to the value marginal product of that class of skilled worker in an alternative use. Equations 3.2 to 3.4 will therefore only apply to unskilled labour. See Lal, 'Disutility of Effort . . .', op. cit.

purpose some knowledge of turnover rates, wage rates in comparable relatively competitive markets for labour in the country and/or guesses of the orders of magnitude of the relevant m terms when they diverge from the c and w terms will be required.

It is claimed that POI has/does not have important external effects in terms of training labour. These mutually conflicting hypotheses are tested in a modest way in our cost/benefit studies in Parts III and IV. It is also claimed that POI distorts the income-distribution structure of the economy by paying its workers salaries above those for comparable classes of labour in the rest of the economy. As can be seen from Equation 3.5, in our estimation of the various SWRs, we shall be taking into account this divergence (distortion) and shall moreover be weighting the difference between c, and m, by income-distributional weights (the s_i terms), whose determination is taken up in Chapter II.6.

II.4 TECHNOLOGY

In the POI literature the most pervasive hypothesis about why POI exists and its most important characteristic feature relate to the advanced technological knowledge it owns.[1] The desire to acquire this advanced technology is given as one of the major reasons why POI may be allowed into developing countries (for example in India), whilst the existence of the special technological (including managerial) advantages of POI vis à vis actual or potential domestic competitors, is given as the reason why foreign firms may wish to invest in an alien socio-economic climate. The peculiar characteristics of particular technologies and the markets for their diffusion are in turn used to explain why the direct investment route is

1. Useful references are: C. Kindleberger, *American Business Abroad* (Yale, 1969); C. Kindleberger, ed., *The International Corporation* (MIT, 1970); R. Vernon, ed., *The Technology Factor in International Trade* (NBER, Columbia, 1970); Spencer and Woroniak, eds., *The Transfer of Technology to Developing Countries*, (Praeger, 1967); N. Rosenberg, ed., *The Economics of Technological Change* (Penguin, 1971); R. E. Cave, 'The Industrial Economics of Foreign Investment', *Economica*, Feb. 1971; whilst W. E. G. Salter, *Productivity and Technical Change* (Cambridge, 1966) still remains a very useful source for clarifying the various conceptual problems involved.

chosen by the parent foreign firm in preference to some other alternative, such as licensing arrangements with a local firm, or exports.

As we are concerned with appraising POI from the host country's viewpoint, it may seem unnecessary to dwell on the motives of foreign investors when making direct investments. As however, we are concerned with making comparisons of POI of different mixes, with each other, and with some (often hypothetical) alternative means of producing/obtaining the product, it is necessary to know the area of choice the host country has, in the sources from, and terms on which it can acquire the requisite technology. Given that the technology market is not a unified, perfectly competitive market for all products and processes, but is often likely to be monopolistic or oligopolistic, in order to know the alternatives available for acquiring the technology, it will be necessary to have at least some qualitative idea of the motives of different foreign investors in making direct investments in the host country, as this will in turn influence the terms on which the technology can be acquired.

It is unlikely that it will be possible to get anything more than qualitative evidence to form judgements about the reasons for particular direct investments. But it will be necessary to document these, together with any other information (quantitative if possible) on the alternative choices which might have been available to the host country to acquire the necessary technology. This information relates to the costs (direct and indirect) of acquiring the same or similar technology from alternative sources, if they exist. Some of the considerations involved will undoubtedly be game-theoretic in nature, and these will be dealt with in greater detail in Chapter II.8. Ideally, it is necessary to obtain data on the costs/benefits of the next best (or maybe even better) source for obtaining the requisite technology. This problem is part of the general one of searching out the best possible alternative, from a set of feasible investment projects, for producing a particular product.

This being said, we can very briefly state the various ways in which the technological factor can give rise to differential costs/benefits for different mixes of POI, and/or different sources of acquiring the necessary technology. These are:

(A) DIFFERENTIAL DIRECT COSTS OF ACQUIRING THE TECHNOLOGY

The foreign firm may be given equity in the local company in return for its technical know-how; it may be paid a fee, for instance, related to sales or output; or it may receive payment through a combination of a fee and local equity. The alternative costs of acquiring the technology could take any of the above forms.[1] These costs will however appear directly in the financial inflows and outflows of the firm's balance sheet, and will be taken into account in the same way as any other financial inflows and outflows (see Chapter II.7). There is no special problem involved in evaluating these costs. The problem is to delineate the relevant alternatives in each case, and to assign values to the 'expected' costs, which may often have to be hypothetical and based on the judgement of experts in the field.

(B) DIFFERENCES IN TECHNICAL EFFICIENCY

The different alternative forms of acquiring the technology may imply differences in technical (including managerial) efficiency of the firm. This will appear as a difference in the input-output coefficients of the various alternative technologies for producing the relevant good. Thus though the direct costs of acquiring a technology through route A may be less than those through route B, the technology acquired through A may be relatively inefficient (in the sense that it may require more inputs per unit of output than the alternative) compared with B. Here again if both the alternative sets of input-output coefficients are given, there is no further problem. The normal procedures of social evaluation will take into account the differential benefits of the two alternatives.

---

1. We will not consider the alternative of developing the technology indigenously, as this is not likely to be a relevant option for most developing countries. If however, in a particular case it is considered to be a relevant option, then the R & D costs of developing the technology should be evaluated in the same way as the rest of the social cost/benefit analysis, and included as part of the costs of the investment project.

It should be noted that the differences in efficiency need not be ascribed to purely technological factors, but more importantly may encompass differences in managerial efficiency. The latter is said to account for the advantages of POI in which the foreign firm has a majority equity holding. The differences in managerial efficiency may show up in a number of ways, for example, smaller working capital requirements, lower wastage rate for inputs and rejection rates for the output, lower rate of breakages, quicker reaction to mechanical and/or administrative faults and bottlenecks.[1] Though it may not be possible in practice to identify and quantify the precise reasons for differences in efficiency of the alternatives, some qualitative information may be available and should wherever possible be obtained. However, once again, if these differences in managerial efficiency exist, even though they cannot be pinpointed by source, they will nevertheless be taken into account in the normal way in the differences in the inputs and output of the alternative investments.

So far we have assumed that in fact we had certain and precise knowledge of the differences in input-output coefficients due to the differential technical efficiency of the various alternatives. In practice, it may not be possible to have this knowledge, and certainly for 'ex ante' appraisals it will be impossible to obtain for all cases. Here there is no escape from intelligent and informed guess work. From past experience in the industry in the host country (if it exists) or in other countries, some idea of the differential coefficients may be (and should be, wherever possible) obtained. As this is really an important area of uncertainty, probability weights should ideally be attached to the estimates on the lines suggested in Chapter II.8.

(C) DIFFERENCES IN GESTATION LAGS

This is really another aspect of (B) above. But as it is likely to be of great importance in determining the social rate of

---

1. For an illuminating qualitative discussion of the various characteristics associated with managers in different types of foreign investments see J. S. Fforde, *An International Trade in Managerial Skills* (Blackwell, Oxford, 1957).

return of the project, it has been put under a separate heading. The problem is again one of obtaining the information, and no special problems of evaluation arise.

(D) DIFFERENCES IN THE RATE OF TECHNICAL PROGRESS

One of the important advantages claimed for POI as opposed to licensing arrangements as a method of acquiring technology, is that it enables the domestic firm to keep abreast of technical progress. Different forms of acquiring technology will therefore have different effects in keeping domestic plants economically competitive, taking into account the development of new and better processes and products. The way in which these differential effects can be taken into account in cost/benefit studies is through the different lengths of economic life of the investment. In an industry with rapid technical progress, without access to new knowledge, the domestic plant will become uncompetitive sooner than one in an industry where technology is more stable, or where the domestic firm has access to the continuing R & D innovations of foreign firms.

The precise way in which these differential effects can be taken into account can be explained in terms of an example. Suppose there are two alternative investment projects A and B, for producing the same product. A is a fully-owned foreign subsidiary which has access to all the latest technological advances in the parent firm. B is a local firm which will buy the patented technology under a licensing agreement, but this agreement will not extend to future developments in technology. Further, assume that existing plants become technologically obsolescent T years from now. The foreign subsidiary's plant, on our assumptions, will never become technologically obsolescent, it being assumed that the costs of physical depreciation required to keep the plant physically intact from one year to the next also include any costs that may have to be incurred to incorporate the latest techniques in the existing plant. The costs of this continuing access to the latest technology will appear in the repatriation of dividends and in any direct technical fees that may be paid to the parent company. For the domestic company, on the other hand, on our assumption, the plant will become technologically obsolescent T years from now. The benefits to be ascribed to its operations will therefore cease on that date. Hence, if B_t is the social value of the net output of the plant in any year, and z_t the physical depreciation to keep the physical capital intact, and q_t the depreciation to be set aside each year to keep up with technical progress, the present values of the net benefits (NB) of the two plants foreign (f) and domestic (d) are given by:

$$NB_f = \sum_{t=0}^{\infty} (B_t - z_t) - \sum_{t=T}^{\infty} q_t$$

and

$$NB_d = \sum_{t=0}^{T} (B_t - z_t)$$

In these expressions it has been assumed that there is no difference in the B_t and z_t terms for the two alternatives, till year T, and furthermore that no q_t outlays are required to keep up with technical progress for the two options till then. These assumptions can be relaxed in a number of ways. First, there may be q_t payments required for both alternatives, till year T, to keep the plants competitive, and moreover they may differ for the two alternatives. Secondly, even with the q_t payments, the domestic plant may become progressively more (technologically and hence economically) uncompetitive, before year T, so that the B_t for this alternative may be lower progressively, as compared with the foreign subsidiary alternative. Finally, the assumption that the domestic firm cannot have access to new technology after year T can be relaxed. This access is, however, likely to be more expensive than for the foreign subsidiary. This will appear as higher q_t payments than in the foreign alternative, plus of course the actual capital costs, in the form of licensing fees, etc., which will have to be paid to acquire the technology. The general formulae will therefore become:

$$NB_f = \sum_{t=0}^{\infty} (B_{ft} - z_{ft} - q_{ft})$$

$$(4.1)$$

$$NB_d = \sum_{t=0}^{\infty} (B_{dt} - z_{dt} - q_{dt} - 1_{dt})$$

where the f and d subscripts refer to the two foreign and domestic alternatives, and the l term is on account of licensing fees etc., which the domestic firm has to pay to acquire the requisite technology. This last term does not appear in the formula for the foreign subsidiary's operations, as it is assumed that the relevant costs appear in the form of dividend repatriations in the capital account. If, however, there is some fee which still has to be paid for acquiring new techniques from the parent company, then this should be included in the NB_f formula too, as it is in the NB_d formulation.

Equation 4.1 provides the terms which have to be estimated for the different alternatives. Past experience may be of some help, but often it will be necessary to obtain the judgements of competent experts about the 'expected' values of these terms. It should be noted that the accountant's depreciation and other capital allowances are worthless for this purpose and should be ignored. The depreciation which is relevant is that due to normal wear and tear, which is necessary for keeping existing physical capital equipment intact (the z terms) and the depreciation which is caused by technological obsolescence, and which is required to embody the relevant new technology to keep the plant technologically up to date (the q terms).

(E) DIFFERENCES IN QUALITY OF PRODUCTS

One of the important effects of production behind protective structures is likely to be a reduction in the quality of the goods being produced. Thus producers may recoup the implicit subsidy given them by protection, by reducing the quality of the output (which implies incurring lower costs) rather than by raising its price over the free trade level. The implicit assumption in our analysis that the locally produced output is homogenous with imports of the same good may be invalid. If the good is an importable, the CIF price may not represent the real social value of the domestic import substitute if it is of lower quality. Clearly in this case we need an estimate of the import cost of an equivalent lower quality importable. (This problem does not arise with a product which is actually exported.) When no such importable exists it will be necessary to guess the price, or else make deductions from the CIF price of close substitutes of the domestic import substitute.

The same considerations apply to future changes in the quality of the product. One form of technical progress may be in improvements in the quality of the product, and if the outputs produced by POI and the domestic alternative differ in this respect the differences must be taken into account, by suitably adjusting the social value attached to the output produced by the domestic firm. The principle on which the adjustment has to be made must be the same as in the previous paragraph, namely the CIF value for an import substitute of an importable of equivalent quality or of a close substitute. The costs involved will again be taken into account in the same manner as for technical progress in the production of the good as outlined in (D) above.

One practical problem which may confront a number of countries purchasing technology through the agency of international firms may be noted. This is the least cost form of payment for this technology from the host country's viewpoint. The main choice is between payments in lump-sum in the early years of the project, or annual royalties over a longer period during the operation of the firm. If the firm is a profit maximiser, with a rate of discount, π_f, and the annual royalty payments it would require over T years are F per annum, then it would equivalently be satisfied with a lump sum payment in lieu of annual royalties, of

$$\sum_{n=1}^{T} F/(1 + \pi_f)^n.$$

What would be the relative *social* costs of paying the annual royalties, or the lump sum in year 1? The net present value of the social costs of paying the royalties, given that the host country's rate of discount is r, will be

$$\sum_{n=1}^{T} F/(1 + r)^n.$$

The social costs of paying the lump sum in year 1 are its

nominal costs, viz,

$$\sum_{n=1}^{T} F/(1 + \pi_f)^n,$$

and clearly it will be desirable to pay a lump sum, or royalties as:

$$\sum_{n=1}^{T} F/(1 + \pi_f)^n \lessgtr \sum_{n=1}^{T} F/(1 + r)^n \qquad \text{i.e. } \pi_f \lessgtr r;$$

that is, if the host country's rate of discount is lower than the foreign firm's, which is likely, then it will be better to pay a lump sum rather than annual royalties from the host country's viewpoint. The converse case would hold if $r > \pi_f$.

II.5 EXTERNALITIES

Are there any special costs and benefits of projects which will not be taken into account through the procedures hitherto suggested for valuing the inputs and outputs of the project? One such externality, which is normally not part of the firm's private profitability calculation has already been taken into account, namely the training of skilled labour which may be provided and paid for by the firm. Some other forms of externalities which are often adduced to investment projects, will also be taken into account. These include divergences between private and social profitability because of differences between the private and social rates of time preference (Chapter II.6) which result in private producers discounting future benefits from projects to a shorter time horizon (or equivalently at a higher discount rate) than is socially desirable; failure to anticipate lowering of future costs through the operation of 'learning by doing' within the firm.[1]

Certain other externalities are misconceived from our viewpoint. This applies particularly to the type of externalities adduced by Hirschman.[2] Hirschman's backward and forward linkages are really concerned with the overall

1. The *Manual*, Chapter XVI, contains a good discussion of the externalities normally claimed for industrial projects, and shows how these are often included in the procedures of evaluation it provides.
2. A. O. Hirschman, *The Strategy of Economic Development* (Yale, 1958).

inducement to invest in the economy, and not with the optimum allocation of given resources, which is our concern. The inducement to invest aspects would only be relevant if aggregate investment in the economy were not limited by the availability of savings. However, one of the common features of most developing countries is the relative scarcity of savings relative to investment opportunities and the divergence between social and private preferences for present versus future consumption. These are the considerations which will be taken into account in Chapter II.6, when we discuss the sub-optimality of savings and the desire of governments to use project choice as a means of shifting the existing savings constraint.

The cases where so called 'linkage' effects may be relevant are confined to the cases of non-traded goods (and traded goods for which foreign trade is not perfect) in which there are indivisibilities in production.[1] But these cases are the same as those under the heading 'non-traded goods production with economies of scale'. In such cases we have to estimate the relevant 'producers' and 'consumers' surpluses to obtain the social values to be used in the evaluation. No new measures are required. For tradeables for which foreign trade elasticities are infinite, even in the presence of indivisibilities the CIF/FOB prices will still give the correct marginal social costs/revenues of using/producing the input/output.

One other source of externalities, it is claimed, is due to differential 'multiplier' effects of the project resulting from the different pattern of expenditure generated by the project. For these multiplier effects to be ascribed to the project, and hence to be included in its social benefits, it is necessary that the inadequate effective demand in the absence of the project which gives rise to them should not be curable by more direct instruments of public policy. That is, these effects must in a sense be 'tied' to the project.[2] Moreover for our purposes in

1. Note that the 'linkage' argument in its resource-allocation aspects is really part of the problem of optimal investment for non-tradeables in whose production there are indivisibilities.

2. Note that the full shadow wage formula takes account of any multiplier effects of paying labour a wage above its shadow wage. For a formal demonstration of this see M. Fg. Scott, 'Shadow Wages for "Surplus" Labour in Mauritius' (mimeo), Nuffield College, Oxford, 1972.

comparing the different mixes of POI and domestic investments, it is the differential 'multiplier' effects of these
alternatives which are relevant. If these effects can be
carefully identified, and quantified, their evaluation for the
purposes of our social cost/benefit analysis is straightforward.
We need to ascertain the net increases in these secondary
output/incomes, and their valuation is the same as for the
primary output/incomes from the project.

Finally, there are the various externalities which are
claimed to accrue from the agglomeration of projects. These
may occur if a number of investment projects are complementary.[1] In such cases the correct procedure is to evaluate
the interdependent projects together, the principles of
evaluation remaining unchanged. Secondly, there may be
externalities from agglomeration as the closeness of supplying
industries may reduce the uncertainties associated with
obtaining supplies from a greater distance, as also the costs of
transportation. But both these aspects will be adequately
considered, if the principles for evaluating produced inputs
and outputs are correctly applied. The first factor should
show up as a reduction in working capital requirements
and/or a shortening in the time lag in obtaining supplies of
relevant inputs; the second will be taken into account by the
adjustments we have to make to 'border' prices for internal
transport costs.

In conclusion therefore, it must be emphasised that it is
important to check and see that, first, a presumed externality
actually exists, and secondly, that it has not already been
taken into account in the rest of the social cost/benefit
analysis. Wherever genuine externalities can be identified and
measured, they should be included in the cost/benefit
studies. But what must be avoided is a recourse to
Hirschman's 'hiding hand' to justify any and every investment.[2]

1. See Streeten, 'Economic Models and their usefulness for Planning'. Appendix 3,
in Myrdal, *Asian Drama* (Pantheon, 1968).
2. A. O. Hirschman: *Development Projects Observed* (Brookings, 1967).

II.6 INCOME DISTRIBUTION[1]

In our discussion so far we have only concentrated on the economic efficiency aspects of project choice. This would be sufficient if the government could deal with the equity aspects by independent tax-subsidy measures. It has been argued however that the government's fiscal powers to redistribute incomes intra-temporally and inter-temporally are likely to be limited in developing countries, and hence equity considerations cannot be separated from those of efficiency in project choice. We have to take account of the income-distributional impact of the project's benefits, in the ensuing second-best world.

There will be two dimensions of income distribution which will be relevant in assessing the impact of the investment project on social welfare. These concern, first, the impact on inter-temporal income distribution via the savings-consumption distribution of the net benefits of the project, and secondly, on the intra-temporal distribution of income via income accruals from the project to different income classes amongst contemporaries. In large countries where there may be large inter-regional disparities of income, which again are sought to be alleviated through project choice, there will be a third dimension of income distribution, the inter-regional, which will need to be taken into account. We shall ignore the last aspect for most of this chapter, only stating the formulae which can be used if this aspect is important, and if the same considerations which are relevant to the other two dimensions apply.

We begin by considering the weighting of income accruals to different income classes amongst contemporaries. Assuming that we can employ a constant elasticity social utility function for valuing changes in income (consumption), we can derive these weights as follows.

Let the social valuation function for valuing changes in income assuming diminishing marginal utility from increasing incomes (which for simplicity we assume are all consumed)

---

1. This chapter is based on my paper, 'On Estimating Income-Distribution Weights for Project Analysis', IBRD Economic Staff Working Paper No. 130, March 1972, revised June 1973.

both for individuals and for society as a whole, be:

$$U'(C) = k/C^e \tag{6.1}$$

where $U'(C)$ is social marginal utility, C is income (consumption) and e is a constant parameter ($-e$ is the elasticity of marginal utility defined as $[U''(C)/U'(C)]C)$, and k is a *constant of scale* which converts the private 'utils' accruing to particular income groups into *social* utils.

We next make use of a property of certain 'positive' measures of the size distribution of income (like the Gini coefficient), that with a given distribution of income, an equiproportionate rise in all incomes, raises the mean income but leaves the value of the distributional measure unchanged. We *define* our social utils in terms of this 'distribution-neutrality' property, by making the change in total private income socially valuable at par, if it is distributional neutral. That is if there is an equiproportionate rise in all incomes of $\theta\%$, this will result in a rise in social utils (N) of[1]

$$N = n\bar{C}\theta \tag{6.2}$$

where n is the number of incomes, and $\bar{C}$ is the arithmetic mean income in the country. But, equivalently, this change in social utils (N) should also be derivable from our general social valuation function (6.1). That is, N is also given by

$$N = \int_0^\infty f(C) \int_C^{(1+\theta)C} (k/Y^e)\, dY \,.\, dC.$$

$$= \frac{k}{(e-1)} \cdot \frac{(1+\theta)^{(e-1)} - 1}{(1+\theta)^{(e-1)}} \cdot \frac{n}{C^*_{(e-1)}} \quad \text{for } (e>1) \tag{6.3}$$

where $f(C)$ is the frequency of those obtaining income C, and where

$$\frac{1}{C^*_{(e-1)}} = \frac{1}{n} \int_0^\infty \frac{f(C)}{C^{(e-1)}}\, dC$$

---

1. I owe these derivations (6.2 to 6.7) to Francis Seton, who developed them in his *The Shadow Wage Rate in Chile* (OECD, Paris, 1972), in the context of a different argument to estimate the Little-Mirrlees 's' factor. They have been derived in the form given in this chapter in my paper, op. cit.

that is, C^*_{e-1} is the harmonic mean of degree $(e-1)$ of the national income distribution, and n is the number of incomes.

When e = 1, equation 6.3 becomes

$$N = k \log (1 + \theta)n \tag{6.3a}$$

From (6.2) and (6.3) it follows that

$$k = \theta \frac{(e-1)(1+\theta)^{(e-1)}}{(1+\theta)^{(e-1)} - 1} \cdot \bar{C} C^*_{(e-1)} \quad \text{(for } e > 1) \tag{6.4}$$

and

$$k = \frac{\theta}{\log(1+\theta)} \bar{C} \quad \text{(when e = 1)} \tag{6.4a}$$

If we are now considering marginal changes in income (consumption) in the limit $\theta \to 0$, the equations (6.4) and (6.4a) become

$$k = \bar{C} C^*_{(e-1)} \quad \text{(when e} > 1) \tag{6.5}$$

$$k = \bar{C} \quad \text{(when e = 1)} \tag{6.5a}$$

And hence substituting (6.5) in (6.1) our generalised utility function becomes

$$U'(C) = \bar{C} C^*_{(e-1)} /C^e \quad \text{(when e} > 1) \tag{6.6}$$

and

$$U'(C) = \bar{C}/C \quad \text{(when e = 1)} \tag{6.6a}$$

We can now socially value any income accrual to any particular income class in the country. Suppose that the income of group y rises to a level Cy from a level pCy. Given our valuation function (6.6) the value of this increase in terms of N units is

$$\Delta N = \int_{pCy}^{Cy} \frac{\bar{C} \cdot C^*_{(e-1)}}{Cy^e} \, dCy \quad \text{when e} > 1$$

and

$$\Delta N = \int_{pCy}^{Cy} \frac{\bar{C}}{Cy} \, dCy \quad \text{when } e = 1$$

$$\Delta N = \frac{\bar{C} \cdot C^*_{(e-1)}}{(e-1)Cy^{(e-1)}} \cdot \frac{1 - p^{(e-1)}}{p^{(e-1)}} \quad \text{(when } e > 1) \qquad (6.7)$$

and

$$\Delta N = \bar{C} \log(1/p) \quad \text{(when } e = 1) \qquad (6.8)$$

Equation 6.7-8 is our basic formula for valuing income accruals to any particular income class. To use it we need to know $\bar{C}$, C^*, which are characteristics of the country's income distribution, and the value of e, which is a value parameter, namely the elasticity of social marginal utility of income (consumption).

By an extension of the same argument we can also take account of inter-regional disparities of income in our project evaluation criteria. The relevant formulae are:[1]

(a) when $e > 1$

$$\Delta N = \frac{n_z \cdot \bar{C}_R C^*_{R(e-1)}}{(e-1)} \left[\frac{(\bar{C}_z + \Delta \bar{R}_z)^{(e-1)} - \bar{C}_z^{(e-1)}}{\bar{C}_z^{(e-1)}(\bar{C}_z + \Delta \bar{R}_z)^{(e-1)}} \right] \qquad (6.9)$$

where

$$\Delta \bar{R}_z = \frac{\bar{C}_z C^*_{z(e-1)}}{(e-1)Cy^{(e-1)}} \left[\frac{1 - p^{(e-1)}}{p^{(e-1)}} \right] \frac{1}{n_z}$$

the z subscripts refer to the region z in which the income increase $(1 - p)Cy$ accrues to income group y, n_z are the number of incomes in the region, $\bar{C}_z$ and $C^*_{z(e-1)}$ are the arithmetic mean income and the harmonic mean of degree $(e-1)$ of incomes in the *region*, and $\bar{C}_R$ is the arithmetic mean. $C^*_{R(e-1)}$ is the harmonic mean of degree $(e-1)$ of

1. For these derivations see my paper, 'On Estimating Income Distribution Weights for Project Analysis', op. cit.

the inter-regional incomes given by

$$\frac{1}{C^*_{R(e-1)}} = \frac{1}{\theta} \int_0^\infty \frac{f(\overline{C}_z)d\overline{C}_z}{\overline{C}_z^{(e-1)}}$$

where $\theta = \sum_z n_z$, and $f(\overline{C}_z)' = n_z$.
(B) when $e = 1$.

$$\Delta N = n_z \overline{C}_R \log \left[\frac{\log(1/p)}{n_z} + 1 \right] \qquad (6.9a)$$

Having obtained a measure of the income (consumption) generated by the project in terms of national homogenous units N, we next need to take into account the intertemporal income distribution in terms of the social valuation of present versus future consumption. If we take current savings (which will determine future consumption) as our numeraire (this is the Little-Mirrlees numeraire), we essentially have to convert the N units of present consumption into their savings equivalent. Given the non-optimality of savings, which is assumed to be a common feature of most developing countries, there will be a premium on savings vis à vis consumption, say of 's', so that the final social value (W) of an increase in consumption (income) to group y, will be given by

$$W = \frac{1}{s} \Delta N \qquad (6.10)$$

Our final problem then is to determine 's'. Its value will depend upon the opportunities open to society to convert one unit of present consumption into future consumption, and the weight society places on one unit of future consumption in terms of present consumption. The former factor represents society's opportunities, the latter its impatience in deciding the optimal inter-temporal consumption profile, given the constraints of existing resources and present and future technology. In an optimal savings situation 'impatience' must be balanced against 'opportunity' till, at the margin, the social return from one unit of current savings (net present value of the consumption stream made possible by one unit of current savings) is equal to the social value of one unit of current consumption. If however, as is normally assumed, the developing country is in a non-optimal savings situation, and project choice is the only instrument available to the government for altering the aggregate consumption savings balance in the economy towards the optimal one, then the social return r (the *Manual* ARI) will not be equal to the rate of indifferent substitution between present and future consumption, i (the *Manual* CRI). The divergence between r and i will determine the premium on current savings, 's'. This divergence is likely to change over time, and assuming first that it is turned into an equality at some date T, and secondly, that the divergence diminishes linearly from the present date to T, we can use a formula derived in the Little-Mirrlees *Manual* to determine the current value of s, that is s_1, as follows:

$$s_1 = [1 + \tfrac{1}{2}(r_1 - i_1)]^T \tag{6.11}$$

This necessitates estimating i_1, and r_1.

The consumption rate of interest, or social discount rate, i_t, in any period t, is defined as

$$i_t = [U'_t/U'_{t+1}] - 1 \tag{6.12}$$

where U' is the marginal utility of consumption in the relevant period.

Once again using our social valuation function (6.2), we can derive the value of i_t as

$$\begin{aligned}
i_t &= [k\, C_t^{-e}/k\, C_{t+1}^{-e}] - 1 \\
&= [C_{t+1}/C_t]^e - 1
\end{aligned} \tag{6.13}$$

Defining the growth rate of per capita consumption between periods t and t + 1 as G_t, we have $(1 + G_t) = (C_{t+1}/C_t)$ and hence

$$i_t = (1 + G_t)^e - 1 \tag{6.14}$$

Thence substituting in (6.11) we find that

$$s_1 = [1 + \tfrac{1}{2}[r_1 - (1 + G_t)^e + 1]]^T \tag{6.15}$$

r is the social rate of return, which is also the discount rate to be used for discounting the stream of benefits and costs to obtain the net present value of the project. Alternatively it provides the cut off internal rate of return above which the project is socially profitable. r is thus the own rate of return to investment on the marginal investment project in the economy. For ways of making estimates of r, the *Manual* may be consulted for a number of helpful suggestions. To estimate i, it will be necessary to have some estimate of the expected future growth rate of consumption (G_t). This may be provided by projections made in perspective plans, or else the past rate of growth of consumption may provide some indication of what the future rate is likely to be. The time (T) when consumption and savings are likely to be equal is needed in order to estimate s. This again will require some sort of optimal, perspective planning type exercise.

Finally, in both equation (6.15) which determined the inter-temporal distributional weights, and in equations (6.7) and (6.8) which determine our intra-temporal weights, we require an estimate of e, the elasticity of marginal utility. Different values of e reflect different degrees of concern for inequalities of income in all our dimensions. Once however a value is assigned to this parameter, then all the other parameters needed to estimate the distributional weights in equations 6.15 and 6.8, which jointly determine 6.10, can be derived from 'objective' features of the economy, which are the parameters of the existing income distribution, the social rate of return to investment in the economy, and the expected rate of growth per capita consumption.

There is a method developed by Frisch-Fisher, recently revived by Fellner,[1] which can be used to make empirical estimates of e, and this method was used to make estimates for India.[2] This may however give a spurious air of 'objectivity' to what is an important social value judgement, about the degree of concern for equality. It may therefore be better to derive the relevant distributional weights for different values of e (say ranging from 1 to 2), and let the

1. See W. Fellner, 'Operational Utility: The Theoretical Background and a Measurement' in Fellner et al., *Ten Economic Studies in the Tradition of Irving Fisher* (John Wiley and Sons, 1967).
2. See my *Wells and Welfare* (OECD Development Center, Paris, 1972).

policy-makers pick the set of weights, and hence implicitly the value of e, which best conforms to their judgement of the social values of income increments to different income classes in the country.

By applying formula (6.10) we will get W_i the social value of a given increase in the income/consumption of a particular income group. These weights must be applied to the excess of the existing wage rate (c_i) over its social opportunity cost (m_i) in the SWR formulae given in Chapter II.3.

Furthermore if project benefits accrue to different income groups, then the part which is consumed by each income group, will again have to be converted into its social value (W_i) by applying formula (6.10).

II.7 FINANCING

POI characteristically entails a net increase in the investible resources of the host country, whereas the use of domestic capital on the same project will be at the cost of investment and/or consumption elsewhere in the economy. But whereas the return to domestic investment remains within the host country, whose social welfare is our concern, part of the return from POI accrues to foreigners in the form of dividends, and retained earnings, which does not increase the social welfare of the recipient country, but on the other hand imposes a cost in terms of the real domestic resource cost of transferring these foreign earnings abroad. All these aspects need to be taken into account in our cost-benefit analyses.

As we have to make discounted cash flow calculations, we need to date the various capital inflows and outflows associated with the project. Then the Net Social Benefit from the operation of POI in any year n is given by:

$$NSB_n = P_{xfn} \cdot X_n - \sum_i a_{in} \cdot P_{ifn} - \sum_j h_{jn} \cdot W_{sjn}$$
$$+ E_n + K_n - \delta_n - v_n \quad (7.1)$$

where: in any period n

P_f — is the border price of the output (x) and the inputs (i)

P_d — is the domestic price of the output (x) and the inputs (i)

X — is the output

a_i — the input of the i'th good, which includes costs of plant and machinery

h_j — the input of the j'th type of labour

W_s — the shadow wage of the relevant type of labour (when income distribution effects are neglected, that is, it is equal to m_i in Equation 3.5)

W — the actual wage of the relevant type of labour

E — represents the net external effects of the project

K — the capital inflow, inclusive of retained earnings

δ — are the dividends and capital repatriated in foreign exchange

v — is the foreign exchange value of the retained earnings of the foreign investment.

It is a matter of definition that

$$\delta_n + v_n = P_{xdn} \cdot X_n - \sum_i a_{in} \cdot P_{idn} - \sum_j h_{jn} \cdot W_{jn} - \rho_n - \tau_n$$

$$(7.2)$$

as this expression gives the actual return to the foreign investor in year n. All the terms have the same meaning as given above (but note that the relevant prices are actual as compared with the shadow prices in (7.1)) except for two additional terms:

ρ — is the return (profit) to domestic capitalists (if the POI is a joint venture. If the POI is 100% foreign-owned, this term is = 0)

τ — is the sum of all the direct taxes levied on the foreigner.

Substituting (7.2) in (7.1) we get

$$NSB_n = (P_{xfn} - P_{xdn})X_n + \sum_i a_{in} \cdot (P_{idn} - P_{ifn})$$

$$+ \sum_j h_{jn} \cdot (W_{jn} - W_{sjn}) + E_n + K_n + \rho_n + \tau_n \qquad (7.3)$$

This expression is the one normally associated with the social benefits from POI, as presented, for example, by

MacDougall.[1] The last four terms are self-explanatory, and provide the direct benefits to the country from POI, namely, through the taxes levied on POI (τ), the return to any domestic capital that may be associated with POI (ρ), the net inflow of capital (K), and the net external effects of the POI (E). The next term (working backwards), in the W_s is also traditionally associated with the benefits to the host country from POI, that is the excess of actual wages paid over the shadow wage (exclusive of distributional considerations). The first two terms on the RHS may be a little unfamiliar. The first represents the social cost/benefit from producing the POI product as an import substitute/export good under a protective structure. If the good is an import substitute, the P_{xd} is the domestic price of an importable inclusive of the tariff. When an import substitute is produced, tariff revenue equal to the difference in price of imports P_{xf} and the tariff-inclusive price P_{xd}, is lost, and this is a net social loss to the country.[2] If there had been no protection of the good before POI, P_{xd} and P_{xf} would be the same, and the first term would be zero. The second term represents the net social benefit/cost from the effects of the protective structure on the price of intermediate inputs used in the POI project. If the POI is forced to buy an import substitute intermediate input at the domestic price P_{id} which is above the import price P_{if}, the difference between the two prices represents the implicit (actual) tariff, or 'monopoly' profits which accrue to domestic producers of the import substituting intermediate good, and are equivalent to a tax which the host country imposes on the POI. If however, the POI is allowed to import its intermediate inputs at border prices, then $P_{id} = P_{if}$, and once again, the second term will be zero.

As (7.3) is implied in (7.1), we are assured that the latter formula incorporates all the elements which have been traditionally identified with the social costs and benefits of

1. G. D. A. MacDougall, 'The Benefits and Costs of Private Investment from Abroad: A Theoretical Approach', *The Economic Record*, 1960.
2. If the good produced under POI is exported, then for these exports to be privately profitable, either $P_{xf} > P_{xd}$, or else the government will have to give an export subsidy of $P_{xd} - P_{xf}$, if $P_{xd} > P_{xf}$. The latter case leads to social costs, the former to benefits, as is correctly shown by the formulation in (7.3).

POI to the host country, as given by the former formulation. The social rates of return we shall estimate will therefore be derived from (7.1). If the time stream of cost-benefit is properly behaved,[1] we can derive the internal rate of return (IRR), which will be the social rate of return to the project, and the solution of

$$\sum_{n=0}^{T} \frac{NSB_n}{(1 + IRR)^n} = 0 \qquad (7.4)$$

where T is the terminal date of the project. This social rate of return can then be compared with the ARI (the r determined in Chapter II.6), for the economy, and the project is socially profitable only if its social rate of return is equal to or greater than the ARI.[2]

Having obtained the IRR of the project from (7.1) we might however, be interested to make estimates of the various factors which contribute to it. This can be done by using the same information which is needed to estimate (7.1), to estimate the various components on the RHS of (7.3), and by calculating the percentage contribution of the various components in the social rate of return to the project.

The same formulation (7.1) will also give the correct answer to the NSB, and hence the social rate of return (from 7.4) for the wholly domestic-owned alternative to POI. In this case, the last three terms in $(7.1) - K, \delta, v -$ will be zero. Also for various reasons outlined in the previous chapters, the X, a_i, h_j, E, terms may have different values for the two alternatives.

It would be advisable to carry out sensitivity tests to see which components of the NSB of the foreign and domestic alternative crucially affect the social rates of return of the two alternatives.

---

1. See Feldstein and Flemming, 'The Problem of time-Stream Evaluation: Present Value versus Internal Rate of Return Rules', *Bulletin of Oxford Institute of Statistics*, Feb. 1964, for the conditions when the IRR gives the correct decision rule in project analysis.
2. When calculating the social rate of return from (7.1), it should be remembered that the W_s term should now *include* the distributional effects discussed in Chapter II.6. We had *excluded* them in the formulation in the text to enable comparisons between equations (7.1) and (7.3) to be made.

We may also consider the case of takeovers by foreign firms of domestic firms. If the takeover is financed by a net inflow of capital, then no amendment to the above procedures and formulae for taking into account foreign financing is required. If however the takeover is financed from the retained earnings of a foreign enterprise currently operating in the host country, then the project should *not* be credited with an initial inflow of capital in the K term in expression (7.1) above. For as is evident from this expression, the retained earnings of the foreign firm taking over the domestic enterprise, will already have been included as part of host country benefits in the earlier operations of the foreign firm. To include them again as a benefit in its operations in the taken-over firm, would be double-counting. Moreover, in both cases, the payments made to the owners of the taken-over firm may not necessarily be saved and invested, but a part may be consumed. This part will not be as socially valuable as savings, on distributional grounds discussed in Chapter II.6, and hence only the portion which is socially as valuable as savings should be counted as a net capital inflow in the first case, and in the second the portion which is not socially valuable should be added to the costs of the project.

Finally, we may consider some possible objections to the procedures for taking into account financing, suggested in this chapter. First, it may be argued that we have not taken into account the transfer problem associated with the inflows and outflows of capital and interest which are claimed to be an important cost of POI. This objection is misplaced. In our evaluation procedures we have been estimating the border prices (or shadow price equivalent) of all inputs and outputs; changes in these shadow prices (particularly those for non-traded goods, and labour) will already have taken into account any terms of trade type changes which may pose a transfer problem. Furthermore we will be taking into account capital inflows and outflows in the years they occur, and hence adding/subtracting them from the net social benefits of the project in the year that they cease or impose a transfer burden on the host country. No further consideration therefore needs to be given to the transfer problem. Secondly, it may be objected that we have not taken into account the balance of payments effect of the POI investment. This objection is again mistaken. Our procedures represent net social benefits in terms of savings expressed in foreign exchange, after taking into account the social value of any additional consumption that may be generated by paying labour a wage above its social opportunity cost. If the full potential balance of payments effect needs to be estimated, this will be given by our procedures *with the restriction* that the accounting wage is set equal to the market wage.[1] The actual balance of payments effect of course depends upon the short-run domestic expenditure and exchange rate policies of the host country.[2] It is a short-run phenomenon, and should clearly not be confused with the long-run investment decisions of the economy with which we are concerned. Finally, it may be noted that we have not included any opportunity cost of domestic capital in our calculations in (7.1). This is as it should be, for the social opportunity cost of domestic capital is given by the ARI, and we shall be comparing the IRR given by (7.1) and (7.4) with the ARI (determined in Chapter II.6), as the criterion for accepting or rejecting a particular investment project.

II.8 UNCERTAINTY

So far our analysis has been conducted on the assumption that all the relevant inputs, outputs and prices could be assigned values with certainty. In practice, however, considerable uncertainty will surround the likely values these variables will take, especially when making projections for a long time into the future. In such cases we will adopt the 'expected value' criterion, for dealing with uncertainty.[3]

On this approach, once the various possible outcomes of the relevant variables are known, and probabilities assigned to

1. See I. M. D. Little, 'On Measuring the Value of Private Direct Overseas Investment', IEA 1970 Conference on 'The Gap Between the Rich and the Poor Nations' (Macmillan, 1972).
2. See W. M. Corden, 'The Balance of Payments Effects of Foreign Investment: Some Theory', mimeo, OECD/UNCTAD 1970, for a clear and neat demonstration of this point.
3. See *Manual*, op. cit., Chapter XV, and K. J. Arrow, *Aspects of the Theory of Risk-Bearing* (Yrjo Johansson Lectures, Helsinki, 1965).

each outcome, the expected value is obtained by multiplying each possible outcome by its probability of occurrence and then summing over all possible outcomes. Thus for example, if a particular price is likely to take values p_i, where $i = 1 \ldots n$, and the probability of the price p_i actually ruling is ϵ_i, then the expected value of the price p, is $\sum_i \epsilon_i . p_i$ $(i = 1 \ldots n)$.

No allowance is made in this expected utility approach to uncertainty for the attitudes towards risk of the individuals who may have to bear the uncertainty. For as we are concerned with evaluating investment projects from a social viewpoint, given the possibilities open to society for spreading and pooling risks, social welfare is maximised, in an expected utility framework, with social investment decisions taken in a risk-neutral manner. The basic argument is that as fluctuations in the project inputs and outputs are likely to be small compared with those in national income, when the result of these fluctuations is spread over the whole population it will involve only very small changes in per capita income.[1] If however, risks cannot be spread, but have to be borne by particular individuals, and the resulting fluctuations are large in relation to the incomes of these individuals, and/or if the value of the output of the project is correlated with national income, then the risk-neutral procedure advocated by the 'expected value' approach will be invalid. In these cases we shall have to identify the groups which are likely to bear the burden of the fluctuations, and the likely increases/decreases in their incomes will have to be weighted by the relevant income distribution weight for their group (see Chapter II.6) to obtain the social wefare value of the likely change in incomes.

It should be noted that the most important area of uncertainty in making ex-ante appraisals will concern the expected differences in the values of the various variables for the foreign and domestic alternatives. Here it may be advisable to carry out a sensitivity test to find out which of the various variables are crucial in deciding the relative social

1. See K. J. Arrow and R. C. Lind, 'Uncertainty and the Evaluation of Public Investment Decisions', *AER*, June, 1970.

profitability of the two alternatives, and then to seek out as much detailed information as possible, concerning the likely values of these crucial variables for the two alternatives. But in the last resort, good judgement and intelligent guesswork would remain indispensable.

II.9 BARGAINING

In concluding these Guidelines, we may briefly state the various stages involved in evaluating a POI project, and then go on to consider the most distinctive feature of appraising POI projects, namely the problem of bargaining with the foreign investor.

The first stage in appraising the project will be to delineate various alternatives to the project under consideration (Chapters II.1 and II.8). Next it will be necessary to obtain, or estimate the input, output, and market price data, for the various alternatives (Chapter II.4). At the third stage the external effects from the project should be delineated (Chapters II.3 and II.5). The final stage consists of shadow pricing the various inputs and outputs (Chapters II.2 and II.3), taking into account the different income distribution effects (Chapter II.6) and inflows and outflows of capital (Chapter II.7). The basic formulae are given in Chapter II.7.

Finally we need to say something about the 'bargaining' aspects of POI. A great deal of the heat generated by debates on the costs/benefits of POI is due to an essential feature of certain forms of POI, namely that the relationship between the foreign investors and the government of the host country is in the nature of a non-zero sum game.[1] As Kindleberger puts it: 'Most instances of direct investment in less developed countries are akin to bilateral monopoly, where the reserve prices of the two parties are far apart, and there is no determinate solution such as the competitive price'.[2] In such cases it will be insufficient to look at just one foreign

---

1. See C. Kindleberger, *American Business Abroad* (Yale, 1969), and A. K. Sen, 'Cost-Benefit Analysis of Private Foreign Investment and the OECD-UNCTAD Meeting in Paris', mimeo, 1971.
2. Kindleberger, op. cit., p. 149.

investment project, for there may be a whole range of projects which imply different shares of the potential net benefits between the host country and the foreign investor. What the host country must undertake is an analysis of the minimum share of the POI's social profitability which will justify the project from the host country's point of view. This minimum is given by the rate of social profits accruing to the host country being at least equal to the ARI, as shown in Chapter II.7. To determine the social profit rate to the host country, the rules suggested in these Guidelines will need to be applied. The other limit of the possible range of social profitability to the host country is given by the minimum rate of profit that is acceptable to the foreign investor. In practice this will not be known to the host country, and must be a matter of judgement. In the ensuing negotiations, the host country should naturally try and get the best terms it can, above the minimum social profitability given by the ARI, and in doing so, it must naturally explore other alternative sources of POI, and evaluate them on the lines suggested in these Guidelines, and try and choose the best alternative that is available.

In this context it may be important to bear in mind that, for most POI in developing countries, as emphasised in Part 1, the degree of effective protection offered is an important determinant of the share of the potential social benefits from POI between the foreign investor and the host country. In the small sample of case studies presented in Parts III and IV we found that this was the single most important variable explaining the relative social profitability of different POI projects to the host country. As can be seen from expressions (7.2) and (7.3) of Chapter II.7, the social profitability to the host country varies inversely with the degree of effective protection offered, whilst the private profitability varies directly. Thus a useful calculation when appraising POI would be to calculate the degree of effective protection which would reduce the net present value of the social benefits accruing to the host country to zero, at the ARI, and the degree of effective protection which would make the private profitability to the foreign investor zero, at the expected foreign investor's rate of profit (which as we have seen in Part I is likely to be about 15%). The former would give the maximum degree of effective protection compatible with the POI project being socially profitable to the host country, whilst the latter would give the expected minimum effective protection which would yield the minimum acceptable private profit to the foreign investor. The area of bargaining will then lie between these two limiting degrees of effective protection, and the host country should obviously try to approach the lower limit in the bargaining process.

At this point it is important to mention one particular feature of certain types of foreign investment, which forms part of the vertically integrated operations of an international firm, namely the problem of 'transfer' pricing. So far in these Guidelines it has been implicitly assumed that goods and services are exchanged at 'arm's length' prices. If however the transactions take place as between different parts of the same international firm, the prices charged will not necessarily be these 'arm's length' prices. The actual 'transfer' prices being determined most often, if the international firm is a global profit-maximiser, by its minimisation of declared profits in high-tax areas, and correspondingly maximisation of declared profits in low-tax areas. In such cases especially if it is difficult or impossible to arrive at 'arm's length' prices on any objective basis, it may be advisable for the host country to negotiate directly on the total tax to be paid by the foreign investor, based on physical output levels, rather than on the conventional value of sales or profits. Joint ventures would also seem to be particularly useful in preventing some of the abuses of transfer-pricing in which global profit-maximising vertically integrated international companies might otherwise be tempted to indulge.

This having been said, the rest must remain a matter of playing a rather difficult bargaining game, but it must be emphasised that in this game the government of the host country must be armed with the knowledge of the true social profitability to it of the various alternatives, and for that the social evaluation of the costs/benefits remains essential, and it is to this task that these Guidelines are dedicated.

PART THREE

Aspects of Foreign Investment in India

This Part presents the results of the cost-benefit studies carried out in India, using the Guidelines of Part II. The first three chapters set these studies in perspective, by delineating the special features of foreign investment in India. They are followed by two chapters which deal with the case studies proper.

This part is based on a report prepared by Paul Hare. The data for the case studies was collected by him in a field trip during the summer of 1971, and supplemented by information I collected in field trips to India during 1971. The numerical results derived, and their presentation, have also been Paul Hare's responsibility.

III.1 POLICY-FRAMEWORK

(i) GOVERNMENT AIMS AND POLICIES

After Independence in 1947, the main principle behind India's economic policy was the desire to promote industrialisation, preferably under Indian rather than foreign ownership, management and operation of the industrial concerns. This basic goal is set out clearly in the government's Resolution on Industrial Policy, announced in April 1948.[1]

> The government of India agree with the view of the Industries Conference that, while it should be recognised that participation of foreign capital and enterprise, particularly as regards industrial technique and knowledge, will be of value to the rapid industrialisation of the country, it is necessary that the conditions under which they may participate should be carefully regulated in the national interest. Suitable legislation will be introduced for this purpose. Such legislation will provide for the scrutiny and approval by the Central Government of every individual case of participation of foreign capital and management in industry. It will provide that, as a rule, the major interest in ownership and effective control, should always be in Indian hands; but power will be taken to deal with

1. Quoted in *Foreign Technology and Investment* (NCAER, Delhi, 1971), p. 53,

exceptional cases in a manner calculated to serve the national interest. In all cases, however, the training of suitable Indian personnel for the purpose of eventually replacing foreign experts will be insisted upon.

In practice, exceptions to this principle of Indian owner-ship were allowed, partly to obtain needed foreign exchange, and partly to obtain up-to-date technology for the new industries. In the late 1950s, increasing stress was laid on the need for import substitution in a situation where foreign exchange was needed for capital imports to sustain further growth, and export prospects were regarded as unpromising. By the mid-1950s, the government was becoming more concerned about Indian economic growth, and was more determined to play an active role in its promotion. Thus in 1956, the Industrial Policy Resolution then issued established the basis for greater government initiative by dividing industries into three basic categories. In the first, schedule A industries, further development was to be the exclusive concern of the State; in the second, schedule B industries, the State would increasingly take the initiative in development, while in the remaining category of schedule C industries, private enterprise would continue to play the leading role. One consequence of the government's more active role was its encouragement of foreign collaboration agreements; the rate of approval of agreements rose from an annual average of about 50 in the period 1948—1958, to over 300 after 1958.[1] As a result of these collaborations, many new industries such as plastics and petro-chemicals were established in India in the late 1950s and early 1960s, as well as a great diversity of small consumer-goods industries, the latter mainly serving the middle-class urban market.

Later in the 1960s, however, government policy towards collaboration agreements became somewhat stricter, as a result of studies of foreign investment in India which were critical about some of its effects.[2] The new government policy put greater emphasis on keeping royalties below a

1. *Foreign Collaboration in Indian Industry*, Survey Report by the Reserve Bank of India (Bombay, 1968), pp. 3—4.
2. See for example M. Kidron's *Foreign Investment in India* (Oxford, 1965).

ceiling of 5% of net sales, and on limiting foreign equity participation to a minority of the total capital of any new firm established. The sanctioning of agreements which failed to meet these conditions depended on the goods concerned being particularly essential for India or on their having good export prospects. In some cases, the level of the foreign technology was such that agreements were allowed.[1] Thus in general, the implementation of the government's basic principles regarding foreign collaborations has been extremely pragmatic, adjusting to what were regarded as the main needs of the time, though it is not clear that the measures adopted were economically very satisfactory. But, essentially, the government's approach to foreign collaborations has become more selective, as the early concentration on achieving a fast rate of economic growth has given way to more diverse objectives.

(ii) ADMINISTRATIVE PROCEDURES
In line with their intentions expressed in the Resolution on Industrial Policy of 1948, the government established an administrative procedure for controlling both foreign collaborations and general industrial development in the national interest. The legal basis for this was laid down in the Industrial (Development and Registration) Act of 1951 and the Registration and Licensing of Industrial Undertakings Rules of 1952; Acts which required that any new industrial unit or any substantial expansion of existing units, with or without foreign collaboration, must obtain a licence from the government if they belonged to any of the industries included in schedules attached to the Acts. The procedure for obtaining such a licence was and remains a complex and time-consuming process for the firms concerned.

An application for a licence had first to be submitted to the Ministry of Industrial Development and Company Affairs, which would then forward copies of the application to the relevant technical authorities. In consultation with the appropriate Administrative Ministry, they would then collect information on existing licensed capacity in the industry

1. NCAER, op. cit., p. 59.

concerned, also its present production levels, foreign exchange requirements of the project, and other factors considered to be relevant to each particular case. The Licensing Committee, a statutory body set up under the 1951 Act, would then have to make a recommendation to the government on the desirability of issuing a licence.

For projects involving foreign collaboration, the procedures were rather more complex. Firstly, a letter of intent concerning the proposed terms of the collaboration had to accompany the initial application for a licence. Import proposals would be submitted to the Directorate General of Technical Development, and then the appropriate administrative Ministry would put the case before the Capital Goods Committee. This body would accept or reject the application in principle, the licence itself only being issued after the financial terms of the collaboration had been finally negotiated with the collaborator and accepted by the government. An additional licence would also be issued to permit the imports required by the project. Proposals with a foreign equity participation in excess of 50% had to be approved by the Foreign Investment Committee, while decisions about projects costing less than Rs 5 crores could be expedited by the Committee of Secretaries to Guide Negotiations. The financial terms of collaboration agreements had to be endorsed by the Reserve Bank of India, which also had to approve actual payments made abroad under such agreements.[1]

In the 1960s, the government became increasingly concerned about the long delays to which applications to enter into collaboration agreements were subject before decisions were taken on them. In 1964 an attempt was therefore made to streamline the procedures for some key industries. As a result of studies begun then, the Foreign Investments Board was established in 1968, with the aim of reducing the time taken to process applications concerning foreign collaborations to about three months, and to make known to intending collaborators the procedures and facilities available for foreign investment. This new Board was given the

1. Reserve Bank Survey, op. cit., pp. 4–6.

responsibility for handling all foreign collaboration applications except those in which the project would involve more than Rs 2 crores of equity capital, or where the foreign participation would exceed 40% of the total capital issued. In order to publicise the opportunities available for foreign investment, the government also grouped industries into two lists, namely those industries in which no further foreign collaboration would be allowed, and those in which it would still be permitted; in the latter group, standardised royalty rates were indicated, too.[1]

Unfortunately, government efforts to eliminate delays in the disposal of applications have not been very successful, as yet. In the period before the Foreign Investment Board was established, surveys suggest that the average time taken for the government to approve proposals from a sample of 23 firms was one year and nine months; delays were almost certainly longer for projects which were not approved. This contrasts markedly with the target figure of three months laid down in the government Press Note of July 1968 announcing the formation of the Foreign Investment Board. What evidence there is concerning the period since 1968 suggests that the new Board has made very little difference in the average time for decisions to be reached on applications relating to foreign collaborations. Consequently, firms continue to complain of their difficulties in keeping foreign collaborators interested, while they await the necessary government approval of their projects.[2]

(iii) THE LONG-TERM LENDING INSTITUTIONS
Since Independence, a number of financial institutions have been established in India to promote the country's economic development. Typically, these specialise in the provision of long-term credit, of which there was formerly a shortage. This is usually provided at low interest rates, often in situations where other banking institutions would have been unwilling to extend credit. These institutions have also served

1. The policy of the Foreign Investments Board and the lists of industries mentioned are set out in 'Foreign Investment and Collaboration' guidelines published by the Indian Investment Centre, Delhi.
2. NCAER, op. cit., p. 55.

to coordinate credit available from different sources. In projects involving some foreign participation, three of these agencies have been especially important: these are the Industrial Finance Corporation of India (IFCI), the Industrial Credit and Investment Corporation of India (ICICI), and the Industrial Development Bank of India (IDBI).

The Industrial Finance Corporation of India (IFCI)[1]

Established in 1948 to provide medium- and long-run credits to industrial concerns, the IFCI is authorised to guarantee for periods of up to 25 years loans floated in the market by industrial firms, and also to underwrite the issue of stocks, shares, bonds, and debentures of these firms. From its initial coverage of manufacturing, mining, electricity, power and shipping the Corporation has subsequently extended its activities to include non-manufacturing industry and public limited companies. Loans are given in domestic and foreign currencies. Although other institutions have later been established, the Industrial Finance Corporation continues to play an important role in the provision of credit to industry. One of the firms reported in Chapter III.5 obtained a loan from the IFCI.

The Industrial Credit and Investment Corporation of India (ICICI)

This institution was set up in 1955 with support from the Indian government as well as from international organisations like the World Bank and the Commonwealth Development Finance Company. Its loanable funds arise from Rs 25 crores of authorised capital, supplemented by loans from the Government of India amounting to Rs 32.5 crores up to 1968, from the World Bank amounting to about 165 million dollars in foreign currencies, and loans of about Rs 10.5 crores, of which an equivalent of 137.38 million dollars was available in foreign currencies.

The stated purpose of ICICI is to assist limited liability companies within the private sector to establish, expand or modernise themselves. This it achieves by providing finance

---

1. Govt. of India, *Pocketbook of Economic Information 1970*, p. 11.

as long- or medium-term loans, sometimes in foreign currency for the import of capital equipment, as well as sponsoring or underwriting new issues of shares and securities. The Corporation also guarantees loans from other private investment sources and generally serves to coordinate alternative means of finance, apart from giving managerial, technical and administrative advice where appropriate. The importance of ICICI in facilitating foreign collaboration is shown by the fact that of the total of 486 enterprises assisted up to 1968, more than half had some sort of collaboration agreement with a foreign company. Moreover, of the Corporation's total net sanctions up to 1968 of Rs 230.51 crores, Rs 131.88 crores were given in the form of foreign currency loans to 328 companies.

Although the Corporation is stringent in its requirements for information on each project which it considers supporting, it does not always insist on a minimum rate of return on capital. The minimum requirement employed is that the firm should have the ability to pay back ICICI's loan eventually, which in most cases would amount to an implicit rate of return criterion being employed. However, in a few cases where a project may not be immediately profitable, if it is regarded as important for the national economy and is likely to be profitable in subsequent years, ICICI has been ready to support it. An example of this is their support for a paper mill in Assam being established in an area of high unemployment.[1]

The Industrial Development Bank of India (IDBI)

The Industrial Development Bank of India was established in 1964 as an additional lending institution with the additional aim of providing better coordination of the activities of the other institutions. As a subsidiary of the Reserve Bank, the IDBI has wider functions and larger resources than those of the already existing long-term lending institutions, and it also holds some shares in the others, especially the IFCI. Loans are provided both to private and public sector industrial

---

1. Information obtained from ICICI's booklet, 'A source of capital for private industry', and also from interviews, Bombay 1971.

concerns at a lower rate of interest if the projects being supported would increase exports. For expansion and diversification of enterprises, finance is provided for some public sector concerns and the Bank also offers loans on 'soft' terms to small and medium projects in backward areas. In addition to acting as a source of finance, the IDBI is also important as a development agency for planning and promoting new industries. It also undertakes marketing and investment research, techno-economic surveys, and gives technical and administrative assistance to firms.

Until 1971 the method of project appraisal used by the IDBI was similar to that now used by the ICICI, although perhaps somewhat more formal and stringent. However, from early 1971, the Bank adopted a new method of project appraisal which involves evaluating each project's net present worth using a discount rate of 15% and Indian prices. An additional check is made on the cost of saving one dollar through import substitution or earning it through exports. The Bank appears to be critical of the Little-Mirrlees method of investment appraisal because of its complexity, particularly of the difficulties in finding 'correct' world prices to use for any particular study, and in working out the multipliers for non-traded goods. However, their own method was defended by the claim that it would reject any project which the Little-Mirrlees method would reject.[1]

III.2 POLICY EFFECTS

Although wishing to benefit from imports of foreign technology and capital, the Indian Government has been concerned to keep to a minimum the costs to India of the resulting collaboration agreements with foreign firms. One aspect of this has been the government's recent attempt in 1968 to keep down royalties paid abroad, by publishing schedules of standard rates. While some reduction seems to have been achieved, the success has been partially offset by a tendency for foreign firms to take what they would have previously

1. Information from *Pocketbook of Economic Information 1970*, pp. 12–13, and from interviews in Bombay, 1971.

wanted as royalties in the form of a lump sum payable for technical information, in some cases the lump sum payments completely substituting for royalties. This was the situation in one of the case studies reported later.

Also, the NCAER, in its recent survey of foreign investment in India, found that several firms complained that the lower royalty payments insisted upon by the government had reduced the quality of the technology offered by the foreign partner.[1] In order to reduce Indian dependence on foreign know-how, the government has tried to limit the period of royalty payments to five years since 1968, but it is not clear yet whether this has had any significant effects. Government experience in trying to limit royalty payments does, however, suggest that little can be achieved without a simultaneous effort to develop Indian know-how to replace foreign techniques. In fact this conclusion seems to be accepted by the government, which is now trying to encourage indigenous R&D, after a long period of neglect.

Stipulations on exports and imports have been another feature of government policy towards collaborations, particularly since 1962. Initially, export stipulations were in the form of requirements that exports should cover the foreign exchange costs of a project, though more recently clauses have been inserted in agreements insisting that a certain proportion of the output be exported. Thus for one firm which we began to investigate, it had been stipulated that 50% of the output should be exported from the second year of production in its new plant. The firm in question[2] expected to make a loss on this, which suggests that the government may be trying to apply such requirements too strictly. In practice, firms have tended to be rather backward in fulfilling these export requirements, partly because their high costs made them unable to compete on the world market, and partly because of the profitability of the protected domestic market. Consequently, the requirements have not been very effective. On the other hand, stipulations on imports, taking the form of phased reductions of the import

1. NCAER, op. cit., p. 56.
2. A chemicals firm based in Bombay.

content of new products, have generally been much more effective, since the government has been able to use its import licensing powers.[1]

One important objective which has motivated fiscal policy in India has been the discouragement of foreign majority control of Indian companies. For this purpose, dividends paid abroad by Indian companies with foreign majority control are taxed at higher rates than those with Indian majority control. The difference between these two rates has risen progressively to the present level of about 30%. Further objectives of government policy have been to encourage import substitution and to protect Indian industries once they are established through an extensive system of import duties and restrictions. This has provided foreign investors with considerable scope for high profits in the protected domestic market, which probably explains the government's strong desire to control the firms which are allowed to operate there and repatriate their profits. Since the devaluation of the rupee in 1966, the government has laid more emphasis on encouraging exports than on restricting imports though the basic policy of import restriction remains. However, one of the case studies reported in Chapter III.5 has suffered considerable competition from imports.[2]

To see how foreign investors are actually affected by Indian fiscal policy, it is instructive to look briefly at the current pattern of corporate taxation. Four main taxes are important for foreign investors. Firstly there is the usual corporate income tax, levied at a rate of 55% on Indian companies with a substantial public interest, defined as those companies where 40% or more of the shares are held by the general public or by the government, rather than by other firms. For companies without such a public interest, the rate of tax is 65%, while for branches of foreign companies it is 70%. However, in the case of priority industries, the profits are reduced by 8% before the tax is calculated.

A second important tax is that on dividends remitted abroad. This is deductible at source and amounts to 24.5%,

---

1. Discussed in NCAER, op. cit., p. 59.
2. Polyolefins Industries Ltd.

except for priority industries where it is 14%. Thirdly there is a surtax on corporate profits when these exceed 10% of capital employed; the surtax amounts to 25% of the firm's net income at present. Finally, there is a tax on payments of royalties and technical fees which is levied on the difference between the fees and the costs incurred by the firm in earning them; the rate of tax is 50% on agreements made since 1961, and 70% on agreements made earlier.

Reducing these basic tax rates are a number of concessions which are important for foreign investors. For newly established firms a tax holiday of five years is provided, during which time no tax is paid on profits up to 6% of capital employed, and there is no income tax on the dividends paid out of these profits. Where profits are actually less than 6% of capital in these five years, the deficiency may be carried forward for up to three more years and offset against profits earned then. There is also a development rebate of 20% on new plant and equipment; this means that 20% of the cost of plant and equipment is allowable against income tax in the first year that a plant operates. The rebate is, however, subject to the condition that 75% of it should not be distributed for at least eight years. The rate of the rebate is increased to 35% in the case of priority industries. Finally, one may mention a concession to foreign personnel working in India; the income of technicians is exempt from income tax for three years, while that of managers is exempt for six months.[1]

An important adjunct to fiscal policy for achieving the objective of Indian control of enterprises has been government regulation of capital issues. Thus whenever a new company is established, its capital structure must be approved by the Controller of Capital Issues; also if a company wishes to expand or capitalise its reserves, it too must get approval from the Controller. These requirements give the government a powerful instrument of control which has been used to considerable effect; very few exceptions to

1. Details of the current tax position are taken from NCAER, op. cit., pp. 66—7. Also see Ajit Mazumdar, 'Overseas Investment and Indian Taxation' in P. Ady, ed., op. cit.

the rule of majority Indian control have been allowed recently, and these few have mainly been in branches where India needed the foreign technology. Thus in 1964, there were three initial issues approved in which the firm had foreign majority ownership, from 1965 to 1967 only two annually, and in 1968 only one. In all cases since 1965, the foreign investment involved was less than Rs 10 million, with an average total issue of Rs 7.4 million; this compares with the average total issue of Rs 19 million, for issues involving some foreign collaboration. This reflects the government policy of keeping down the size of foreign-controlled firms, to leave room for Indian-controlled firms where these can be established. The result of this policy appears to have been the encouragement of joint ventures in which foreign participation has been in the range 40% to 50% of the capital employed.

In addition to controlling new firms, the Controller of Capital Issues has also been concerned to put pressure on existing Indian firms to make them increase their Indian shareholding. Similar pressure has also been applied by the licensing authorities, 100% foreign-owned subsidiaries being required to allow a minority Indian shareholding, and companies already having minority Indian participation being required to extend it to a majority Indian shareholding. The latter group have often been reluctant to comply with these impositions, preferring instead to set up other affiliates or license out their know-how. Nevertheless, the Indian government does seem to have been successful in extending Indian control of enterprises which operate in India.[1]

III.3 FOREIGN COLLABORATIONS

PAST TRENDS

Since Independence, the annual number of foreign collaboration agreements in India has progressively risen. Up to 1958, the rate of increase was fairly steady, then in 1959 the total was almost double that of the previous year, and rose rapidly

1. Material taken from NCAER, op. cit., Chapter 7.

from then until 1963. Since 1964, the number of agreements approved annually has fallen somewhat. Overall, there were 2792 proposals agreed between 1946 and 1967. This total can be broken down as shown in the following summary table:

Table 1 Collaboration Agreements in India, 1946–67[1]

Form of Collaboration Agreement	1946–50	1951–58	1959–67	Total
Licences	4	230	831	1,065
Other production know-how	—	163	844	1,007
Plant construction	—	32	222	254
Major imports of technology	4	425	1,897	2,326
Pre-investment services	—	5	74	79
Problem solving services	—	15	77	92
Indian personnel abroad	—	1	2	3
Foreign personnel to India	—	1	9	10
Drawings and specifications	—	14	117	131
Patents	—	79	56	135
Others	—	2	14	16
All Proposals	4	542	2,246	2,792

From the table it can be seen that by far the greater majority of foreign collaboration agreements were concerned with the transfer of production know-how, and in just over 50% of cases through licensing agreements. Other factors such as the training of Indian personnel were much less important. The industrial pattern of collaborations is also of interest, and this is shown in the table below; the entries in the table only show the pattern of agreements in the main industries where collaborations have been important, and consequently, the columns do not add to the totals at the bottom.

1. Summary of table 39, NCAER, op. cit., pp. 124–5.

Table 2 The Industrial Pattern of Collaborations[1]

Industry	1946—50	1951—58	1959—67	Total
Textiles		49	57	106
Chemicals		42	225	267
Pharmaceuticals		46	102	148
Iron and steel		18	120	138
Metal goods		34	138	172
Machinery	1	122	681	804
Electricals	1	59	314	374
Automobiles	1	19	90	110
All manufacturing	4	508	2,175	2,687
All proposals	4	542	2,246	2,792

It is clear from this that there was a dramatic increase in the number of agreements in practically all industries during the second period. The greatest rise is evident in the categories of machinery, electricals and chemicals, which probably reflects their basic importance for the Indian goal of self-sufficiency. In industries such as textiles, there was already considerable Indian production, so not such a large rise in number of agreements took place there. Given that an important goal of Indian government policy is to reduce the dependence of Indian firms on foreigners, the duration of collaboration agreements is quite significant. This duration for the agreements where information was available, is shown in Table 3. Before drawing any conclusions from the table it should be pointed out that in the period 1951—58 the number of unspecified agreements is nearly one third of the total, although the ratio falls in later years. This may affect slightly the inferences drawn from the table.

If we assume that the duration of the unspecified agreements would be similar to that of the ones given in the table (actually one might expect it to be longer on average), then the table shows two things. Firstly, about one-third of all agreements were intended to endure for at least ten years, with few significantly longer than ten years; secondly, there

1. Summary of table 44, ibid, pp. 148—9.

Table 3 The Duration of Agreements[1]

Duration of agreement	1946–50	1951–58	1959–67	Total
Short term		57	307	364
1–4 years		22	75	97
5 years		65	496	561
6–9 years		21	87	108
10 years		134	799	933
Over 10 years	4	46	32	82
Unspecified		197	450	647
Total	4	542	2,246	2,792

seems to be a trend towards a higher proportion of shorter-term agreements, with more bunching of agreements on durations of ten, five and less than one year. Thus the Indian government has had only limited success in its aim of reducing the period for which agreements were made with foreign firms.

Finally, in order to give some idea of the magnitude involved we give some figures for the net inflow of investment into India, with breakdown by the major countries involved. This is shown in Tables 4 and 5 below, where it can be seen that in spite of some fluctuations from year to year, a substantial net inflow of funds has taken place each year. In recent years, the U.S.A. has consistently invested more than Britain, although the value of Britain's total investments in India is still higher than that of any country, standing at 48% of the total. Japan's investment in India has been rising rapidly from the early 1960s, and Japan now ranks fourth behind West Germany in terms of its total outstanding investment in India.

SOME EFFECTS OF COLLABORATION AGREEMENTS
After initial enthusiasm for foreign collaboration agreements in the late 1950s and early 1960s, the Indian government has subsequently tended to be rather more cautious in approving agreements. Their aim has been to try to reduce some of the

1. Summary of table 52, ibid, p. 139.

undesirable effects of foreign investment, and we can therefore usefully look briefly at some of these effects to get some idea of likely trends in government policy.

Table 4 Inflows of Investment[1]

Net inflow of investment (Rs million)	W. Ger.	U.K.	U.S.A.	Others	Total
1961	n.a.	138	229	82	449
1964—65	68	298	525	153	1,044
1965—66	75	105	326	232	738
1966—67	233	362	621	391	1,607

Table 5 Total Outstanding Investments[2]

Outstanding investments to date (Rs million)	W. Ger.	U.K.	U.S.A.	Japan	Internat. Insts.	Others	Total
1955	24	3,659	396	2	27	340	4,448
1962	120	4,822	1,062	33	719	576	7,332
1965	309	5,390	2,148	373	683	1,047	9,950
1967	815	6,554	3,758	692	1,066	1,939	14,824

It has been argued that one important effect of foreign collaborations has been to encourage wasteful use of scarce investment resources. Thus during the late 1950s especially, the government's enthusiasm for foreign collaboration agreements seems to have resulted in their accepting a large number of proposals in industries which the government itself regarded as low priority. For example, of the 250 agreements approved in 1964, 42 were for radios and components, 15 for refrigerators, 14 for yeast and Ovaltine, 12 for garments, 8 for pens, 8 for needles and 7 for printing,

1. *Pocketbook of Economic Information 1970*, table 8.2, p. 82.
2. *Pocketbook of Economic Information 1970*, table 8.1, p. 82.

making a total of 106, that is just under half of the agreements made.[1] Hence instead of restricting luxury consumption, and hence imports, by taxation, the government has effectively encouraged domestic production to cater for it; as a result, a balance of payments cost due to remittances of royalties and dividends is substituted for that due to the initial imports, while the new production contributes very little to raising the general standard of life of the people.

A related problem is voiced in complaints of waste through multiple collaborations; this is the situation which arises when more than one firm imports the same technology. Here we have evidence only for a few small industrial groupings, though what we have does lend support to complaints about this problem. Thus from 1950 to 1964, a total of 33 agreements was approved in castings, 22 each in cables, radios, and transistors, and 18 in ball bearings.[2] Two reasons for this wasteful import of technology appear to be inadequate coordination of information on agreements, and the xenophilia of Indian firms. Nothing has yet been done to implement proposals for the establishment of a central agency to coordinate imports of technology; moreover it is hard to see such an agency being effective in a market economy in which firms are normally so secretive about detailed technical information. But the second reason, the xenophilia of Indian firms, is probably more important, since many firms admit that the acquisition of a foreign trade mark is an important motive for establishing a collaboration with a foreign firm. Such a trade mark is considered a valuable weapon for a firm competing on the Indian market, which is probably correct given the prevailing low opinion of Indian goods among the Indian middle classes. Recently the government has tried to fight this by attempting to restrict the use of foreign trade marks in the Indian market, though this has been offset by increased liberality where such trade marks would be used on exported goods.

1. Figures quoted in Chapter 7 of 'A Study of Foreign Private Investment in India since 1950', by K. K. Subrahmaniam, Bombay University, 1967.
2. Ibid.

Apart from waste caused by the actual imports of technology, it has also been suggested that the development of Indian technology has been inhibited. In the early 1960s, government concern over the rise in imports of technology led to an attempt to develop indigenous technology by setting up research laboratories; but firms have been slow to take up processes developed there. Firms complain that such processes tend to be obsolete, and that the laboratories are unable to offer help with detailed production and development problems which would be encountered in using any particular process for the first time. Probably these complaints have some force, though it seems likely that if it were more difficult to import technology, indigenous methods would be developed at a faster rate. By the late 1960s the government itself seemed to have accepted this conclusion, and began to apply a policy of import substitution to technology as well as goods. For this purpose, the recently established Council for Scientific and Industrial Research (CSIR) is represented on the committee approving foreign collaboration proposals; then if a technique is considered to be available in India a firm is unlikely to be allowed to import it. Unfortunately, this can only work if Indian firms are willing to sell their technical information to potential competitors, and this is not at all clear as yet.

Not only does foreign collaboration tend to inhibit the use of Indian techniques of production already developed, but it also seems to have an adverse effect on Indian R&D. Partly with encouragement from the foreign partners, Indian firms with collaboration agreements tend to rely on the foreign firm not only for the initial technology, but for results of subsequent research which could improve the process. Such dependence reaches its most extreme form in the case of subsidiaries of foreign firms in India. Evidence of this effect is provided by a study of R&D in the Indian chemical industry which found that the average rate of expenditure on R&D amounted to no more than 1% of sales, which compares unfavourably with international levels between 5 and 15% of sales. Moreover, within India, the foreign-controlled firms were much less R&D conscious than the rest. There seemed to be little relation between R&D outlays and size of firm, according to this study.[1]

However, before condemning foreign technology too harshly, it should be noted that in many industries it has served to stimulate Indian techniques, especially when opportunities are seen for adapting it to Indian conditions.[2] Unfortunately, we lack evidence on this point. On the other hand, such benefits would be unavailable to many firms whose collaboration agreements include restrictive clauses to the effect that product designs may not be changed, or new products may not be developed within a specified period. Dissemination of information to other firms is often forbidden, too. A study of restrictive clauses in collaboration agreements showed that nearly one third of such agreements contained restrictions of the types just mentioned.[3] Government policy is now tending to oppose such restrictions, so they are probably becoming less common in contracts; however, in some cases informal arrangements between the collaborators could maintain the restrictions in practice.

Turning now to the effects of foreign collaborations on the inflows and outflows of foreign exchange, it is important in principle to distinguish two components of the effects. There is first the direct effect of the inflows of capital and outflows of dividends, royalties and various technical fees, and secondly the indirect effect through the impact of capital flows on imports and exports when the new plant is operating. Table 6 below shows the capital account effects for the period 1948—61; more recent information seems not to be readily available, either for the capital account or for the current account effects.

We suspect that the situation has not radically changed since these figures were reported. These figures should not, however, be taken to be the balance of payments effects of

1. 'Market Structure and R&D Activity — A Case Study of the Chemical Industry', by K. K. Subrahmaniam, *Economic and Political Weekly*, Bombay, August 1971.
2. NCAER, op. cit., p. 47.
3. See footnote 1, p. 111.

Table 6 *Net Foreign Exchange Inflows: 1948—1961*[1]

		Rs crores
Foreign exchange losses (1948—61)		
Repatriation of capital		141.1
Profits paid abroad		381.0
Royalties, fees, etc.		196.3
	Total:	718.4
Foreign exchange gains (1948—61)		
Gross investment in cash		60.2
Gross investment in kind		186.9
	Total:	247.1
	Debit:	471.3

POI, for the reasons outlined in Part I, Chapter I.3. As the time stream of these inflows and outflows is not available, it is not possible to calculate the internal rate of return (IRR) of the flows. If such an IRR could have been calculated, then it would have been possible to compare it with the ARI for India, to see whether, on the limiting assumption that the only difference between the domestic alternative and POI was financing, the POI was socially beneficial.

III.4 CASE STUDIES I: NATIONAL PARAMETERS
All our case studies in India are of chemical plants. Some of the general problems posed by using the Guidelines of Part II in India are discussed in the first section below, whilst the two succeeding sections derive certain common (or 'national') parameters used in all the case studies, namely the shadow wage rate, the accounting rate of interest, and the conversion factors for non-traded goods.

(i) GENERAL PROBLEMS IN USING THE GUIDELINES
A fundamental assumption of the original *Manual* method on which the 'Guidelines' of Part II are based is that government

1. M. Kidron, 'Indo-Foreign Financial Collaboration in the Private Sector', paper prepared for the Seminar on Foreign Collaboration of the Centre of Advanced Studies in Economics, 1965.

policy is 'sensible', in the sense that if a particular good is cheaper in terms of accounting prices to import than to produce domestically (i.e. in India), than the government will encourage such imports and will not impose prohibitive duties. However, such a view of government policy overlooks aims other than inter-temporal efficiency, and for India these are important. For example, the Indian government has encouraged the development of many new factories in industries not previously existing in the country, which at world prices are probably inefficient, and which only survive because of comprehensive import controls and duties.

This aspect of government policy is quite important for the projects analysed below. For in several of these cases, the government did indeed restrict competing imports, and seems reluctant to reverse this policy purely on efficiency grounds. In principle, the *Manual* would suggest treating the relevant goods as non-tradeables, and computing the marginal social cost of increasing their production as for other non-tradeables. So in the case studies below, the calculation is done in two ways — one in which we assume 'sensible' government policy, and another in which we do not make this assumption.

Even when using world prices, however, there is the further problem that these are often not well defined for many goods. For example, the IDBI considered using the *Manual* method and found that 'world' prices varied considerably depending on the country of origin of the product concerned. Nor is it satisfactory just to take the lowest price (for imports) or the highest (for exports), since it is unlikely that Indian firms will always find the best market. Also some of the price variation is probably accounted for by quality variation, or variation in delivery times. The procedure followed in most of the case studies below was to use average world prices computed from Indian foreign trade statistics, which at least reflects the average past performance of Indian firms.[1] There is some chance that data could be spurious because they combine both large and small orders in the same

1. In some cases the firms themselves supplied information about the relevant 'border' price.

entry in the statistics. However, this should not cause too much distortion in our case studies, since we are mainly concerned with chemicals which are normally transported in bulk.

Another difficulty concerns the conversion factors for non-traded goods. Lack of time for the present study forced the use of various figures prepared for an OECD report on cost-benefit analysis in India,[1] as well as some data prepared by M. Scott et al., breaking down the Indian prices of non-tradeable goods into tradeable, labour and residual components.[2] Since the latter data were based on a rather aggregated input-output table prepared by the Indian Planning Commission for 1966, and the former figures referred to the periods immediately before and after the 1966 devaluation, there may be some doubt about their reliability for the case studies below. But more recent information which would permit updating of the conversion factors is not easily available.

At this point it is convenient to summarise symbolically the formulae used in the case studies, to avoid repetition later. This is a simple transformation of equation (7.1) of Chapter II.7 in Part II. Let $N(r)$ be the project's net present value when the discount rate is r; $N_A(r)$ is the same project evaluated in accounting prices, where we should recall that this may be computed in two ways depending on whether certain tradeables are treated as non-tradeables. Then the following equations hold by definition:

$$N(r) = S(r) - C(r) - M(r) - L(r) - I(r) - F(r),$$

and

$$N_A(r) = S_A(r) - C_A(r) - M_A(r) - L_A(r) - I_A(r) - F_A(r),$$

where $S(r)$, $S_A(r)$ are the present values of sales revenue at Indian and accounting prices respectively;

1. See Appendix II of the OECD's Industrialisation and Trade Project, entitled 'Guide to the Methods used in Cost Benefit Studies of Industrial Projects in India', OECD Development Centre, 1970.
2. The method used is described in 'Note on the Estimation of Accounting Prices for some Non-tradeable and Tradeable Goods and Services in Kenya', M. Scott, 1970, mimeo.

$C(r)$, $C_A(r)$ are present values of costs other than labour and materials;

$M(r)$, $M_A(r)$ are present values of material costs;

$L(r)$, $L_A(r)$ are present values of labour costs net of any imputed benefit from training;

$I(r)$, $I_A(r)$ are present values of capital costs;

and

$F(r)$, $F_A(r)$ are present values of net cash flow abroad associated with the project.

The internal rate of return of the project is the solution of the equations $N(r) = 0$ at Indian prices, or $N_A(r) = 0$ at accounting prices; that is, it is the rate of discounting at which the present value is zero. If the solution of $N_A(r) = 0$ exceeds the accounting rate of interest, then the project should be accepted. In the present study no fresh attempt has been made to estimate the ARI. The estimate derived in my *Wells and Welfare,* may however be used which, with one slight modification to the value of one of the parameters initially assumed (discussed below), yields an ARI of approximately 6%. Consequently, we shall consider a project to be acceptable if its internal rate of return exceeds 6 per cent.

It is also interesting, as was suggested in Chapter II.7, to analyse the difference between $N_A(r)$ and $N(r)$. Now, since our numeraire is free foreign exchange, it is clear that $F(r)$ and $F_A(r)$ are equal; thus by combining the above formulae, the following equation is easily derived:

$$N_A(r) = (S_A(r) - S(r)) + ((C(r) + M(r)) - (C_A(r) + M_A(r))$$

$$+ (L(r) - L_A(r)) + (I(r) - I_A(r)) + N(r).$$

The term $N(r)$ is the discounted sum of the return to domestic capitalists, retained profits, and taxes on the foreign returns from the project. If we call this the market return, then the above equation expresses the social return from the project as the market return plus a series of terms which measure the social cost or benefit of the various distortions in the domestic economy, as Chapter II.7 explained. It will be observed that our equation contains no separate term for externalities; reasons for this omission are given in the conclusions following the reports of the case studies.

(ii) THE SHADOW WAGE

In the evaluation of each project, the shadow wage is used in two ways. These are:

(a) evaluation of the project's direct labour costs;
(b) computation of the multipliers for evaluating non-tradeable goods produced or used by the project.

Both of these evaluations will vary with the method used to compute the shadow wage, and although direct labour costs are quite small for most chemical projects, the labour component in non-tradeables makes the total significant enough to affect the overall evaluation of the project. It may reasonably be argued that it is not appropriate to use the same shadow wage for both (a) and (b) above, because it is not obvious that an adjustment to be made to allow for income distribution should be the same in all branches. In spite of this, lack of information forces us to use the same shadow wage throughout, so that the presented calculations should be seen as illustrative rather than theoretically exact.

Now, in working out the shadow wage, we first need to evaluate consumption of workers at accounting prices, since their entire savings is assumed to accrue to government, and is counted as a benefit. The Indian *Pocket Book of Labour Statistics* for 1971, table 9, 4(d) shows that 176,000 out of 214,000 chemical workers were covered by the Employees' Provident Funds Scheme with contributions amounting to 8% of pay, as of March 31st 1970. In addition, an NCAER survey of Urban Income and Saving (1962)[1] gives average net household saving of 13.9% after various adjustments, and including contractual saving. On the basis of this, we assume for present purposes the following rates of saving:

Unskilled workers	10%
Skilled workers	15%
Managerial staff	20%

To convert consumption at Indian prices to its value in accounting prices, we use deflators contained in an OECD Guide on project appraisal in India (already referred to); this provides different deflators for the consumption of managerial staff before and after the devaluation of 1966, and we

1. NCAER, *Survey of Urban Income and Saving* (Delhi, 1962).

assume that the same deflators can be used for the consumption of other categories of workers. Thus in order to arrive at consumption in accounting prices, the following multipliers should be applied to the wage costs in project reports:

	Before deval.	*After deval.*
Unskilled workers	0.900	1.200
Skilled workers	0.850	1.133
Managerial staff	0.800	1.067

As outlined in Part II, Chapter II.3, the increase in employment caused by some project implies a certain commitment to extra consumption, not all of which is to be counted as a benefit from the project; the reason for this is that we are supposed to be in a situation where savings in the economy are sub-optimal in the government's view, and where project choice is the only policy tool available to raise the savings rate over a period. This may be because it is not considered politically feasible to raise taxation substantially. The result is that an extra unit of saving is valued more highly than an additional unit of consumption. Thus we take as the shadow wage the quantity $c - (c - m)/s$, where $(c - m)$ is the increased commitment to consumption from employing an additional worker, and c is the worker's consumption evaluated in accounting prices. 's' is a factor to be worked out below, which expresses the value of a marginal unit of savings in terms of consumption.

'm' is the value in accounting prices of the consumption of an additional worker if he had not been employed on the project which concerns us. This is taken to be the value of the agricultural marginal product, since we assume that the net effect of employing an extra industrial worker will be the migration of one more person from the countryside. It is hard to estimate the reasonableness of this assumption, but it will be seen later that the calculated shadow wage is fairly insensitive to it. Assuming that real agricultural incomes and consumption have not increased in the last decade on average, m can be estimated as Rs 600 for 1970/71 and Rs 565 for 1968/69.[1]

1. This is based on an estimate of Rs400 for 1963/64, made by A. Chakravarti in 1970, and price indexes taken from *Economic Survey 1970–71*, Delhi 1971.

We next calculate the factor 's'. Now, project choice is an instrument for adjusting savings towards optimality; and as a consequence of the present non-optimality, the social rate of return on investments, r, will be greater than i, the rate of indifferent substitution between present and future consumption. Assuming that by suitable project choice and other policies, the difference $r - i$ can be reduced to zero in T years, and falls linearly over time, then according to the *Manual*, the savings premium is given by the formula:

$S_O = (1 + .5(r_O - i_O))^T$, where the o-suffix denotes current values.[1] To estimate r_O and i_O it is necessary to postulate some form of social utility function, which following Chapter II.6 above we take in the constant elasticity form as a function of aggregate consumption:

$U'(C) = kC^{-e}$, where the factor k depends on the actual income distribution and will be evaluated below, and the parameter e expresses our preferences about income distribution; thus large values of e indicate greater egalitarianism. In the calculations below we use the two values $e = 1$ and $e = 2$; the former means that if consumption is doubled its marginal utility is halved, while the latter means that if consumption is doubled, its marginal utility is to be divided by four. Following Fisher-Frisch-Fellner, an empirical estimate I made[2] of e for India was about 2. In the same study I also argued that $e = 1$ to 2 was a reasonable range for e in the case of India.

With this kind of utility function, i is given by the relation $i_t = (C_{t+1}/C_t)^e - 1$, so that we need some estimates of the rate of growth of consumption. Over the period 1950/51 up to 1964/65, the average growth rate of per capita consumption was .7% per year. Thus if we use this as an estimate of future growth, we get:

$e = 1$ $i_O = 0.007$
$e = 2$ $i_O = 0.014$

---

1. This is explained in the Little—Mirrlees *Manual*, op. cit., Appendix to Chapter XIII.
2. Lal, *Wells and Welfare* (OECD, Paris, 1972).

Chakravarti[1] has estimated that given past trends it would take 40 years for India to raise its savings level to about 18–20% of national income. When this savings rate is achieved, it may be assumed that savings will be as valuable as consumption, that is $T = 40$ years. Using estimates of the social return to investment derived in my previous study,[2] we obtain the relationship

$$s_0 = (1 + .5(.0378 + .0822/s_0 - i_0))^{40}$$

where .0378 is the part of the return to investment which is saved and .0822 the part which accrues as consumption and hence has to be deflated by s_0, to convert it into savings, which is our numeraire.

Solving the above equation by a method of successive approximation gives the desired values of s_0, and simultaneously of r_0, in the two alternative assumptions of the value of e.[3]

$e = 1$; $s_0 = 4.05$ falling to unity $r_0 = 5.8\%$ which is

                   after 40 years and   approxi-

$e = 2$; $s_0 = 3.76$ $r_0 = 5.96\%$ mately 6%

Finally, we need to estimate the factor k, the effect of income distribution on the evaluation of a consumption increase, and then combine all the above calculations into an estimate of the shadow wage. Income distribution is important because we do not consider as equivalent the same gain to a rich as to a poor man. Following the derivations in Chapter II.6, allowance for these effects amounts to finding an appropriate value for the factor k of the utility function introduced above. This factor turns out to be $\bar{C}C^*_{(e-1)}$, where $\bar{C}$ is the mean consumption and $C^*_{(e-1)}$ is the harmonic mean of degree $e - 1$ of the income distribution. Unfortunately Indian data on income distribution is rather sparse, with no details of regional distribution, and only

1. A. Chakravarti, 'The Social Profitability of Training Unskilled Workers in the Public Sector in India', *Oxford Economic Papers*, March 1972.
2. Lal, op. cit.
3. These estimates are slightly different from those I obtained in *Wells and Welfare*, as there I had arbitrarily taken T = 100 years.

national data for 1955/56[1] Consequently, we have to assume that the basic distribution has not changed since then, and use data from the recent study, *Poverty in India*[2] to adjust for the changes in average consumption levels. The result is as follows:

$$e = 1 \quad k = 488.4$$
$$e = 2 \quad k = 1.605 \times 10^5, \text{ for the year } 1968/69.$$

Using our earlier estimates of s_0, the shadow wage can now be expressed in the following form:[3]

$$e = 1. \quad w_a = c - \frac{488.4}{4.05} \cdot \log(c/m) = c - 120.6 \log(c/m)$$

$$e = 2. \quad w_a = c - \frac{160500}{3.76}(1/m - 1/c)$$

$$= c - 42680(1/m - 1/c)$$

Inserting into these formulae some concrete estimates of income levels for workers in the chemical industry,[4] it is at last possible to express the shadow wage as a fraction of the wage costs as these appeared in project reports. As can be seen below, it turns out that in all cases, the ratio w_a/c is quite close to one when income distribution is allowed for, meaning that for the industrial workers with whom we are concerned, income is so high compared to the average income that the social value of their gain from the project is very small compared to their final consumption. The table is worked out for the year 1968/69, but the ratios are assumed to be valid over a longer period.

1. Report of the Committee on Distribution of Income and Levels of Living, Part I, Delhi, 1964.
2. V. M. Dandekar and N. Rath, *Poverty in India*, Ford Foundation, 1970.
3. These formulae follow from the arguments of Chapter II.6; they are based on the general relation

$$w^e = c - \frac{k^{(e)}}{s_0^{(e)}} \int_m^c x^{-e} \, dx.$$

4. The data used for these calculations came from Herdillia Chemicals Ltd.

Wa/C		Income dist. ignored	/	allowed for
	Managers	0.76		0.98
$e = 1$	Clerical & skilled	0.78		0.95
	Unskilled	0.78		0.94
	Managers	0.74		1
$e = 2$	Clerical & skilled	0.76		0.99
	Unskilled	0.77		0.99

From the table it is clear that the variation of e from 1 to 2 makes little difference to the results, and for this reason, all subsequent calculations will be based on the value e = 1. Also, strictly speaking, the above calculation is not correct for managerial staff, since the short supply of these workers means that 'm' for this group is equal to 'c'. In this case we simply need to calculate the value of the consumed part of wages as already explained. The next table gives the final figures used for the accounting wage, for the case e = 1, w_a being expressed as a fraction of the wage w_p which appears in the project reports.

W_a/W_p	Before devaluation		After devaluation	
	Income dist. ignored	Income dist. allowed for	Income dist. ignored	Income dist. allowed for
Managerial staff	0.80	0.80	1.05	1.05
Skilled workers	0.70	0.80	0.95	1.10
Unskilled workers	0.70	0.85	0.95	1.10

This table completes the determination of the shadow wage to be used in the project reports given below.

(iii) MULTIPLIERS FOR NON-TRADED GOODS
In order to evaluate the accounting values for these goods we use data provided by M. Scott which breaks down the marginal cost of these goods into tradeable, labour and residual components.[1] By applying the above factors for the shadow price of labour, we get the following factors which convert data in project reports to accounting values, as shown in Table 7. The pre-devaluation figures are probably rather spurious, since devaluation was accompanied by changes in

1. Data for India were supplied by M. Scott; see also M. Scott, op. cit. and OECD 'Guide . . .' op. cit.

import duties on many goods. This is confirmed by the figures in brackets which are worked out in the OECD *Guide* on investment appraisal in India; they agree with our calculations for the post-devaluation period, but differ substantially for the earlier period. As far as possible we shall avoid using multipliers for the earlier period, and in any case will prefer the OECD calculations where they differ from ours. Since activities of the firms reported on below mainly concern the post-devaluation period, this difficulty will hardly affect our results.

It should be noted that after applying shadow wage multipliers and the multipliers for non-traded goods to data in project reports, the results must still be converted to foreign exchange, which is taken as numeraire; this means

Table 7 Multipliers for Non-traded Goods

v_a/v_p	Before devaluation		After devaluation	
	Income dist. ignored	Income dist. allowed for	Income dist. ignored	Income dist. allowed for
Construction	0.79	0.84	0.88	0.94
Road transport	0.68	0.71	0.74	0.77
Rail transport	0.86	0.89	0.92	0.96
Communications	0.76	0.85	0.93	1.03
Admin. O/H	0.75	0.79	0.82	0.86
Business services	0.70	0.80	0.93	1.07
Banking & insurance	0.75	0.83	0.93	1.04
Misc. services	0.73	0.84	0.94	1.07
Electricity	0.81	0.84	0.87	0.90
Misc. indus. mat.	0.91 (0.67)	0.91	0.91 (0.91)	0.91
Dom. machin. & equip.	0.78 (0.50)	0.78	0.78 (0.78)	0.78
Iron and steel	1 (0.83)	1	1 (1)	1
Cement	1	1	1	1
Glass & glassware	1	1	1	1
Other forest prod.	1	1	1	1
Petroleum prods.	0.29	0.29	0.29	0.29
Coal & coke	1	1	1	1
Uniforms	1	1	1	1
Average multiplier: (Standard Conversion Factor)	0.73	0.85*	0.89	0.92

*This value is probably too high; in the calculations below we use the value 0.76. In addition, instead of the figures in this column given for Miscellaneous industrial materials, Domestic machinery and equipment, and Iron and steel, we use the corresponding OECD figures from the previous column.

that cash flows before 1966 are to be divided by 4.76, and those after 1966 by 7.5, these being the rates of exchange in rupees per dollar in the two periods.

III.5 CASE STUDIES II: EVALUATION

As stated, industrialisation has been one of the paramount objectives of the Indian government since Independence. A series of three five-year plans (1951–56, 1955/56–60/61, 1960/61–65/66), and an initially abortive fourth five-year plan, now completed, have achieved a rate of growth of industrial production of just over 6.5% per year over the period 1951–68.[1] This growth rate is about double that of overall national income, and has brought the share of industry in national income from 17% to the still rather low 20%. Concurrently, the structural changes taking place within the industrial sector have been quite dramatic. Thus in prices of 1960/61, the share of machinery in industrial value added rose from 8% to 22% from 1951–68, while the share of consumer goods fell from 67.9% to 34% over the same period.[2] In terms of growth rates, therefore, the leading sectors in India's post-Independence industrialisation have been intermediate and investment goods sectors, as is confirmed by the Economic Survey of India for 1970/71, where the following figures are quoted:[3]

Table 8 Growth Rates of Major Industries

	1960–65 average p.a. growth	1967	1968	1969	1970 Jan–Oct, over same in 1969
Machinery (except electrical)	43.2	2.8	9.1	6.9	4.9
Railway equip.	31.8	−21.5	−8.5	−10.6	−19.4
Metal products	21.1	−7.8	−5.6	13.1	3.9
Elec. machinery	20.9	8.1	14.0	16.2	11.8
Elec. generation	18.2	11.0	15.6	12.9	11.3
Rubber products	11.9	7.0	17.9	6.6	−2.9
Petroleum refinery products	11.7	19.6	11.1	8.0	6.2
Chemicals	10.8	2.3	14.6	10.2	8.2
General Index	10.8	−0.8	6.4	7.1	4.7

1. R. Datt and K. Sundharam, *Indian Economy* (Delhi, 1971), p. 513.
2. Ibid., pp. 513–14.
3. *Economic Survey of India 1970–71* (Delhi, 1971), pp. 13–14.

The previous table contains a selection of the fastest growing branches of Indian industry in the 1960s, as compared to the overall industrial average, which is the General Index in the table. The reader can observe that the chemicals sector, from which the four case studies to be reported on below were drawn, grew at about the average rate in the early nineteen-sixties, and at about double the average rate in the late sixties. The chemical industry is making an important and increasing contribution to India's industrialisation, involving the introduction of many new production processes into India.

Currently, about 5% of India's factory labour force is employed in the chemical industry, that is about a quarter of a million workers out of a total factory labour force approaching five million. The industry contributes about seven and a half per cent of industrial production in India.[1] Regionally, the industry is extremely concentrated with one third of it being in the Calcutta region, and a further third being in the Bombay area and Gujarat State. The remainder of the industry is quite thinly dispersed over the country, some of the larger plants outside Bombay and Calcutta being in Madras, Visakhapatnam, and Uttar Pradesh.

The recent increase in the rate of introduction of new technology into the chemical industry is reflected quite clearly in Table 2 of Chapter III.3 above, which shows foreign collaboration agreements in an industrial breakdown. The annual average of such agreements was more than five times as high in the 1960s as in the 1950s, a change equalled only by the machinery and the electrical sectors. Thus the chemicals sector is not only fast growing, but also technically progressive, especially in recent years; it was largely for these reasons that it was decided to present case studies from this sector.

The procedure for each of the case studies is as follows. Firstly, the project itself is described, which includes its main

---

1. See the *Pocket Book of Labour Statistics* (Delhi, 1971), table 2.4(a), p. 13; see also the *Pocket Book of Economic Information* (Delhi, 1970), table 6.3, p. 59.

processes and products, the collaborators and details of the collaboration agreements, and relevant government policy. Then we attempt to work out the project's rate of return using the methods described above, in terms of both market prices and accounting prices. For each case, when collecting data with which to carry out the necessary calculations, attempts were made to discover evidence of significant externalities associated with the projects, for example arising from the training of labour. It turned out, however, and not surprisingly, given the high capital intensity of typical chemical projects, that although some labour training always occurred, this normally involved only a small number of the plant's most senior staff. Consequently, no attempt has been made to estimate separately what could only have been a quantitatively insignificant component of the social benefit from each project.

·Now, at market prices, many of the collaborations look profitable for the Indian firm concerned, though not always; but as the results below show, the situation is not so simple when the shadow price calculations are done for the projects. The firms reported on were all producing a product previously unknown to India's domestic production, which had earlier been imported. Usually, either concurrently with or soon after the start up of the projects, the Indian government was prevailed upon to restrict imports of the goods now being produced, to enable the new firms to sell all their output profitably. Thus when evaluating the projects, we have to decide whether this restrictive government policy will be continued or not, since this will affect the shadow prices which will be attached to the final products. As a consequence of this difficulty, the results are presented for four cases, as follows:

M   evaluation at market prices, but ignoring taxes which are merely a transfer between the firm and the government;

A_1 evaluation according to the 'classical' Little-Mirrlees method;

A_2 evaluation as for A_1, except that the shadow wage includes the effect of income distribution;

A_3 evaluation as for A_1, except that the restrictive government policy is assumed to continue.

For each case study, there are four tables, on which can be found data[1] on capital costs and working capital, operating costs and current revenue, foreign exchange flows associated with the project, and a graph of the net present value as a function of the rate of return, r, with one line for each of the above cases M, A_1, A_2, and A_3. From these graphs, it is usually possible to work out the project's internal rate of return for the four cases, as we shall show in the discussion below. The tables are in the Statistical Appendix to Part III, whilst the graphs follow each case study.

Case Study 1: Herdillia Chemicals Ltd.

This firm was incorporated in Bombay in 1963 for the manufacture of heavy organic chemicals, and was formed as a result of collaboration between B.P. Chemicals (U.K.) Ltd. (formerly Distillers Chemicals and Plastics Ltd.), Hercules, Inc. of U.S.A., and the Indian company of E.I.D. — Parry Ltd., to develop a project approved by the Indian government in 1961. According to the terms of the collaboration, an initial Rs. 440 lakhs of equity capital was issued, of which Rs. 110.99 lakhs was held by B.P., Rs. 69.30 lakhs by Hercules Inc., Rs. 13.33 by the C.D.F.C. London, and the same amount by the Finance and Development Corporation of the National & Grindlays Bank Ltd., U.K.; the remainder was held in India by E.I.D. — Parry and the Indian public. In addition, technical know-how fees of Rs. 51 lakhs, and engineering fees of Rs. 7 lakhs were paid to the foreign collaborators. The project was also supported by a number of long-term loans from Indian and foreign lending institutions.

Herdillia's project involved the construction of plants to produce phenol, acetone, diacetone, phthalic anhydride, and dioctyl phthalate. These are all important intermediates used

1. Most of the project data was obtained from published sources, especially from company annual reports and accounts, company prospectuses, and publications of the Bombay stock exchange. In addition, some information was obtained from executives of the companies reported, during interviews held in Bombay in August and September 1971.

in the manufacture of plastics, dyes, pharmaceuticals, and so on. The plant capacities are small by international standards, and are listed below in metric tons per year.

Phenol	10,160
Acetone	6,096
Diacetone	2,032
Phthalic anhydride	6,096
Dioctyl phthalate	3,048

Some waste hydrocarbon is produced as a not very valuable by-product. Hydrogen, benzene, and propylene, three of the main raw materials needed, are obtained locally from other plants in the same chemical complex; these are converted, via the usual cumene intermediate and an oxidation process, into acetone and phenol. Some of the acetone is then used to make diacetone alcohol. In the phthalic anhydride plant, locally available naphthalene, or more recently, imported o-xylene, is combined with air to form phthalic anhydride. Part of the latter reacts with 2-EH (2-ethyl hexanol), which is mostly domestically produced now, in the presence of a catalyst, to form dioctyl phthalate. It is therefore clear that the net outputs of acetone and phthalic anhydride must be much less than the gross capacities given above: when all plants operate at full capacity, the maximum net annual outputs of these two chemicals are around 4000 and 3000 tons respectively. The economic life of the plant is expected to be around 15 years.

Construction of the plant began in October 1965, at a site prepared by the Maharashtra Development Corporation about 30 miles from Bombay, which also contains a number of other new chemical plants, including that of Case Study 2. In 1968, the plants began regular production under rather unfavourable conditions of erratic raw material supplies, and power failures; sales were also limited by competing imports. However, since then, the supply position has vastly improved, and the Indian government has imposed restrictions on imports of chemicals which would compete with Herdillia. It now seems likely that from 1971, until the end of the project's life, all plants will operate at full capacity. Since the company's position in the domestic market is strong, particularly in connection with phenol and phthalic anhydride, where it is at present (1972) still the only domestic producer, the output will be sold in India without difficulty. Only acetone has been exported, and that only in small amounts, as a result of a 10% export incentive, but this is expected to cease as the export incentive is reduced and domestic demand rises.

The detailed calculations for this project, the results of which are tabulated in the Statistical Appendix, and exhibited graphically by Figure III.1, show that it is extremely unprofitable, even at market prices. Only in case A_3, where the government restrictions on imports of competing products are maintained, is it profitable socially, with an internal rate of return of just under 19%.[1] It is possible that the apparent unprofitability of the project in general arises from an over-estimate of the capital costs, since much of the existing plant and buildings could accommodate much higher throughputs than current levels; thus the marginal cost of expansion is probably quite low. Lack of time prevented the collection of enough data to allow for this factor.

Ignoring this possible source of error, it is instructive to examine the present values of the project for cases M (market prices) and A_3 (government restrictions maintained), using the approach outlined above on page 117, and in Chapter II.7. This will enable us to understand what factors contributed to A_3's profitability; the comparison is effected with a rate of discount, r, equal to 10%. In the notation on page 116, it is easily calculated from the tables that:

$N_A(10) = 5.09$; this is the sum of the following quantities
$N(10) = -5.12$; $(S_A(10) - S(10)) = -6.67$; and
$(C(10) + M(10) - C_A(10) - M_A(10)) = 9.09$; and
$(L(10) - L_A(10)) = .06$; $(I(10) - I_A(10)) = 7.73$

This shows that case A_3 is socially profitable largely because the project's social costs, both current and capital,

---

1. This should not be taken to imply that any project can be made 'socially' profitable by means of deliberate government policy, since the word socially should imply that the government has reasons for maintaining e.g. a tariff apart from its effects on the project under consideration.

are much less than the market costs, while the cost distortion in the product market is smaller, since for case A_3 the product is not considered to be tradeable; that is, it is treated as a non-tradeable good. The distortion in the labour market appears to be negligible, a result which will also arise with the other projects, not surprisingly in view of the shadow wage calculations given earlier.

From the graph, we can see that for cases A_1 and A_2, which correspond to the classical Little-Mirrlees approach with or without some allowance for income distribution, the present values of the project are higher at an interest rate of 20% than at 10%. This 'perverse' result seems to be explicable by the fact that I and F are both large relative to the value-added terms as compared to the other projects. If, in order to make some allowance for the possible error in investment costs noted above, we replace investment costs, I, by the lower amount of .61, then the resulting graph of present value against the discount rate has 'normal' slope.

Case Study 2: Polyolefins Industries Ltd.

In 1964, the Bombay firm of National Organic Chemicals Ltd. (NOCIL), and the West German firm of F. Hoechst A. G., collaborated in the formation of Polyolefins Industries Ltd., in which they each hold one third of the issued equity, the remaining third being held by the Indian public. Polyolefins Industries Ltd. (PIL) was set up for the manufacture of high density polyethylene (HDPE), and polyethylene products, and Ziegler catalysts, technical information being supplied by Hoechst, and raw materials by NOCIL. In payment for the technical information, and licences for the use of patents, PIL pays a royalty of 1.5% of the net value of sales to Hoechst for ten years from the first year of production, and a further royalty over the same period of around 3% of the net values of sales (depending on the volume of sales), which is transmitted to the Max Planck Institut für Kohlenforschung (West Germany). The company has contracted with the West German engineering firm of Friedrich Uhde GmbH an agreement that it should undertake all arrangements concerned with design, construction and start-up of PIL's plant. This involved PIL in a fixed cost of

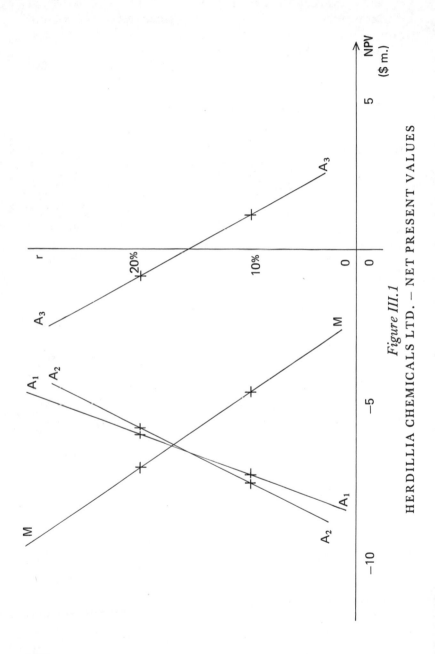

Figure III.1

HERDILLIA CHEMICALS LTD. — NET PRESENT VALUES

DM. 3,770,000, plus the cost of equipment etc. Arrangements were made to obtain foreign exchange loans from West German institutions, and rupee loans from Indian long-term lending institutions.

The project, as approved by the Indian government at the end of 1964, envisaged construction of plants to produce the following amounts of chemicals annually (in metric tonnes).

HDPE	20,000
Processed polyethylene products	5,600
Ziegler catalysts	320

The actual capacity to produce HDPE appears to be somewhat more than the designed capacity, being around 22,000 tonnes per annum. As noted above, ethylene, the main raw material used, is supplied by the new plant of NOCIL, which occupies a site very close to PIL's, in the same industrial area. The ethylene is polymerised in the presence of Ziegler catalysts, to form HDPE; some of the latter is then moulded to make various goods like buckets, bowls, and other containers. Since demand for such products is rising very quickly in India, and since PIL was India's first producer of HDPE, the firm need only maintain reasonable prices to be sure of a ready market. The firm expects present plant to be operating at full capacity from 1971, until the estimated end of the project's life in 1982; moreover, in 1969 it applied to the government for a licence to expand capacity, but a reply had not been received by mid-1971.

By 1965, construction was well under way, on a site adjacent to Herdillia's (Case Study 1); but completion was slightly delayed, and production did not begin until 1968. In spite of some initial difficulties with raw material supplies, sales increased rapidly, from 2900 tonnes in 1968, to 13,000 tonnes in 1970 in the domestic market, while exports in 1970 amounted to 4,700 tonnes of HDPE. The latter were encouraged by Indian government export incentives, but will probably fall as the result of the reduced incentive, and the growth in home demand, especially if the Indian government delays further its approval of PIL's expansion.

From the tables in the Statistical Appendix labelled Polyolefins Industries Ltd 1-3, and the graphs (Figs. III.2 and

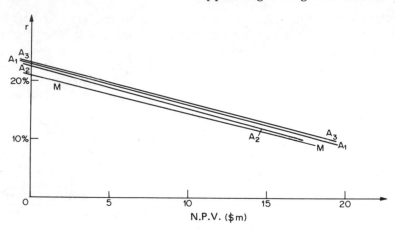

Figure III.2
POLYOLEFINS LTD. – NET PRESENT VALUES

III.3) above and on the next page, it is clear that this is an extremely successful collaboration, with an internal rate of return in excess of 20%, whatever the basis of the calculation (M,A_1,A_2,A_3). The graphs of present value against the discount rate are close together, but this should not lead one to assume that PIL's project is unaffected by trade distortions of any kind. For example, we can compare cases M and A_1, using the method on page 117, and a discount rate of 20%. Straightforward calculation from the table yields:

$N_A(20) = 3.48$; this is the sum of the following:
$N(20) = .99$; $(S_A(20) - S(20)) = -4.69$;
$(C(20) + M(20) - C_A(20) - M_A(20)) = 2.74$;
$(L(20) - L_A(20)) = 0.05$; and $(I(20) - I_A(20)) = 4.39$.

The present value in accounting prices is therefore reached by adding to the value in market prices the difference between two quite large distortions, namely that arising in the product market (4.69), and that arising in markets for current and capital inputs (2.74 and 4.39).

It is also interesting to look at the effects on present values of changes in the relation between the accounting price (i.e. border price) and the domestic market price of PIL's

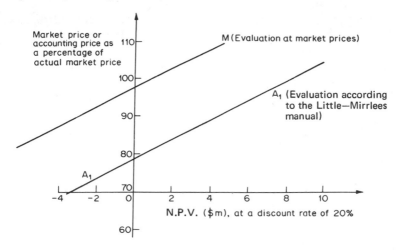

Figure III.3

POLYOLEFINS INDUSTRIES LTD. – PRICE VARIATIONS

products. There are two considerations here. Firstly, since we are concerned with a private firm, the market price must allow the firm to earn a certain normal level of commercial profit; this means that the project would no longer be viable if the market price fell by more than a certain amount below the present market price. Secondly, in the evaluation in accounting prices, the project is only socially profitable if the accounting price of the output is above a certain level. This means that if the market price were too high relative to the accounting price, the project would not be socially beneficial since it would be better to import the product. These two points establish a region within which the market price must lie, in order for the project to be both socially and privately profitable. Actual choice of price in this region just affects the distribution of benefits between the firm and the government, and may therefore be the subject of bargaining between the two agents. Results of such a calculation for Polyolefins Industries Ltd are shown on the graph in Fig. III.3, which gives the relation between present value and product price using a discount rate of 20%; prices on the graph are expressed as percentages of the currently ruling market price. The line MM shows that the firm will earn a 20% rate of profit at market prices, provided that the market price of the product does not fall below 97.5% of the current price; on the other hand, the line $A_1 A_1$ shows that it is socially profitable to allow the firm to operate provided that the accounting price does not fall below 79% of the current market price. If the world price were lower than this, it would be optimal to import high density polyethylene into India, instead of letting PIL produce it. A similar analysis of the effects of price variations is given in slightly more detail for one of the Kenya case studies reported in Part IV.

Case Study 3: Synthetics and Chemicals Ltd.

This is the only one of our case studies where the factory is not in the Bombay area; although the offices are in Bombay, the factory is in Uttar Pradesh, to the north of Delhi. Synthetics and Chemicals Ltd was formed as a joint venture between the Firestone Tire and Rubber Company, U.S.A., and the Indian firm of Kilachand Devachand and Company (P) Ltd., each of whom held about a quarter of the total paid up capital, the remainder being taken up by the Indian public. The aim was to manufacture synthetic rubber, for which Firestone provided know-how and technical assistance at the construction phase, and will provide further know-how for ten years after start-up. For these services the following fees either have been, or are to be, paid: firstly a fee for design work etc. of 750,000 dollars, and an initial disclosure fee of 300,000 dollars, followed by amounts of 285,000 dollars per annum for 10 years, as know-how fees. The Firestone Corporation, various United States banks, and the Indian government, provided the necessary foreign exchange loans; rupee loans were provided by AID, and the Export-Import Bank of Washington, from PL480 counterpart funds.

The project was planned to produce 30,000 tonnes of synthetic rubber annually, using a process which utilised alcohol available as a by-product of sugar production in Uttar Pradesh. The Indian government imposed this technical condition on the project, although it is probably not the cheapest process available. This explains the location, which is near the main centres of sugar production in North India.

Benzene is available as a by-product of steel production, and other raw materials are only needed in small quantities, some of which are imported. Using the benzene, some alcohol is converted to styrene, while another plant converts alcohol to butadiene. A third unit combines styrene and butadiene to form synthetic rubber. In most years, a small excess of styrene over requirements has been produced, but this was easily sold.

Commercial production began in 1963, after a two-year construction period. The performance of the plant was poor, partly due to high costs — benzene was dearer than expected, and rubber imports were considerable, competing strongly with Synthetics and Chemicals' output. At the end of 1965 the plant was suffering from poor labour relations, when it was damaged by a large explosion; repairs cost about rupees 1 crore. In 1967 production was low because of an alcohol shortage, arising as a result of a drought, which severely affected the sugar yields. However, in spite of these difficulties, sales gradually rose, and by 1970 full capacity operation was finally attained. This is likely to be maintained over the project's remaining expected life, that is up to 1981. Thus, although the project began rather badly, its future looks much better, especially as Synthetics and Chemicals is still India's only manufacturer of synthetic rubber, in a market now growing rapidly.

From the graph for Synthetics and Chemicals, Fig. III.4,

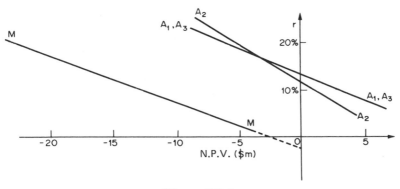

Figure III.4
SYNTHETICS AND CHEMICALS LTD. —
NET PRESENT VALUES

the reader can see that although the project is unprofitable at market prices (case M), it is profitable in terms of any of the accounting prices used, with an internal rate of return between 11% and 13%, depending on the case; this is in excess of the ARI of 6% determined in Chapter III.4. The unprofitability at market prices is undoubtedly explicable mainly by the slow build up of sales to full capacity, and the extra expenses incurred after the explosion at the plant in 1965. It is also interesting to compare the present value of the project in case M with that in case A_1, say; to do this, we use a discount rate of 10%, which gives:

$N_A(10) = 2.80$; as the sum of:
$N(10) = -12.98$; $(S_A(10) - S(10)) = -13.84$;
$(C(10) + M(10) - C_A(10) - M_A(10)) = 7.53$;
$(L(10) - L_A(10)) = .75$; and $(I(10) - I_A(10)) = 21.34$.

The main factor in the explanation of $N_A(10)$ appears, therefore, to be the distortions in investment costs; this should not be too surprising if one recalls that most of the project's investment costs were incurred before India's 1966 devaluation. At that period trade barriers were much higher than they are now, and it has been estimated that plant and machinery in India cost about double the world price (see Table 7 on page 124).

Case Study 4: Albright, Morarji and Pandit Ltd.

This firm was formed in Bombay in 1965, as a collaboration between the British firm of Albright and Wilson Ltd., London, who hold 46% of the equity, and the Indian firm of Dharamsi Morarji Chemical Company Ltd., with 27% of the equity; the remaining share capital is held by the Indian public. The object of the firm is to manufacture phosphoric acid and phosphates, as permitted by a licence granted by the Indian government in late 1965. For technical know-how, about one quarter of the shares issued to Albright and Wilson were credited as fully paid-up, the others being paid for in cash; in addition, Albright and Wilson were paid on a cost-plus basis for technical services related to construction and start-up of the plant. The Dharamsi Morarji Chemical Company Ltd. was also paid for various initial services, and each year since start-up, it is paid rupees 60,000, plus 1% of the sales value of the company's products (excluding inter-company transfers). Finally, rupee loans were provided by Indian banks and long-term lending institutions, while a foreign currency loan was provided by Albright and Wilson Ltd.

The industrial licence specified that the project may produce 20,000 tonnes per annum of phosphoric acid, provided that 12,000 tonnes of this are sold back to Dharamsi Morarji Chemical Company, for manufacturing triple superphosphate fertilizer. In fact, the constructed plant had a phosphoric acid capacity of around 20,000 tonnes per annum, as specified, and a sodium tripolyphosphate capacity of 12,500 tonnes per annum; as a result, only a little over 4,500 tonnes per annum of the phosphoric acid are sold to make fertilizer. The firm claims that it is happy to go on producing phosphoric acid somewhat above its own needs, as this has enabled it to achieve an economic size. The sodium tripolyphosphate produced is mainly used to make household detergents, which replaces some imports, and also releases some vegetable oil previously used to make soap, for consumption or export. The project has a monopoly of production of this product in India, but it is likely that at least one other project will be sanctioned by the Indian government in the near future.

The main raw materials needed by this firm are rock phosphate, sulphuric acid, soda ash, fuel oil, and a few other chemicals in small quantities. About 90% of the rock phosphate is currently imported, but all other materials are indigenously available, sulphuric acid being obtained from one of the parent companies, Dharamsi Morarji Chemical Company Ltd. In the production of sodium tripoly-phosphate, first sulphuric acid and rock phosphate are combined, using the Wet process, to obtain phosphoric acid; most of this is then converted to sodium tripolyphosphate, by combination with soda ash and fuel oil.

The plant was erected during 1965-1968, and commercial production began early in 1968, later than expected because of some delays in delivering equipment. In the accounting year 1967/1968, sales were lower than expected, because of high costs and competing exports, but sales improved rapidly thereafter, as a result of a government ban on imports of sodium tripolyphosphate. By 1970/71, the plant was almost at full capacity operation; it was expected to operate at full capacity for the remainder of its useful life, namely up to 1981/82.

Turning now to the economics of the project, the graph for Albright, Morarji and Pandit, Fig. III.5, shows that for case M (evaluation at market prices), and case A_3 (assuming continued government restriction), the project is highly profitable, with an internal rate of return in excess of 25%. On the other hand, evaluation of the project at world prices with a 'free trade' assumption about government policy (cases A_1 and A_2) suggests that the project's internal rate of return barely exceeds zero. In order to explain this result, we compare the present value of cases M and A_1 using a discount rate of 10%. From the tables for the project, we get:

$N_A (10) = -1.28$; as the sum of:
$N(10) = 11.43$; $(S_A (10) - S(10)) = -18.03$;
$(C(10) + M(10) - C_A (10) - M_A (10)) = 4.26$;
$(L(10) - L_A (10)) = 0$; and $(I(10) - I_A (10)) = 1.06$.

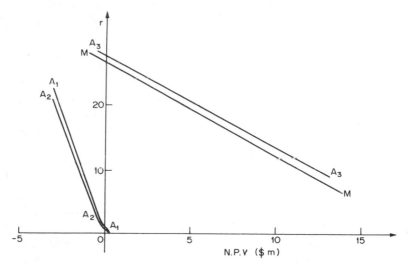

Figure III.5
ALBRIGHT, MORARJI AND PANDIT LTD. —
NET PRESENT VALUES

It seems from these numerical results that the most significant distortion for this project is that in the product market, which produces a difference of 18.03 million dollars between the net present worth at market prices, and that at world prices. Such a distortion, and the relative smallness of other distortions, would also explain the similarity in results obtained from cases M and A_3 with this project.

III.6 TECHNOLOGY

One of the problems facing decision-makers in appraising POI has not been dealt with so far. This is the question of determining whether the particular POI alternative adopted was the best available. In the case of India, especially in the chemical sector, this is basically a question of choosing the least cost source of technology. No direct information was obtainable on the relevant choices available as regards the actual projects presented in the case studies, in this chapter. However, from interviews with officials in the Indian Ministry of Petroleum and Chemicals, some qualitative information was obtained on this choice of technology issue for the NOCIL petrochemical complex, which as can be seen from Case Study No. 2, provides the basic raw materials for one of the projects. This information is presented in this section.

The NOCIL complex's main plant is an olefins plant which consists basically of a naphtha cracker. The main sources of technology for this plant are two international firms — Stone-Webster and Lummus. Other possible firms are Lurgi, Lindz and Foster-Wheeler, though they were not considered as good as the first two. The plant was actually set up in collaboration with Stone-Webster, who charged between $1-1.5 million for a turn-key project. Recently, Lummus have set up a similar plant in the public sector, for which they have only provided the basic engineering drawings, called the Black Book, and for which they charged $400,000. The rest of the engineering in the public sector plant had been done by Indian engineers. However, it seems that in 1961, when NOCIL was set up, Indian engineers would not have been able to set up a plant just by purchasing the Black

Book. Thus the price charged by Stone-Webster for the turn-key arrangement was probably not uncompetitive, and moreover, there was no alternative to obtaining the whole technology package from abroad at that time. It may, however, be noted that the Stone-Webster turn-key plant turned out to be faulty, because of the inadequate design of the furnace, and as a result the plant has not operated at rated capacity. Its output has been 20% below capacity, which has meant that the rest of the complex's output, which is dependent on the naphtha cracker has also been affected. Revamping of the furnace will, it is estimated, cost about Rs. 300 crores. The faulty furnace was however, something which could not have been predicted.

The technical collaboration for the remaining products produced by NOCIL is with Shell. Payments for this are in part based on royalties at about 2½% of sales value, and operating service charges at 1% of sales value. For some products these rates of payment were considered to be too high, but for some they were relatively cheaper. For one product we were informed that the particular process could be earning a royalty of 6-7% of sales value. On balance, it seemed that NOCIL's payments of royalties of 2½% on sales value were economical.

There is, however, the general problem connected with payments for technology transfers, viz. whether it would not be better to pay for the technology in a lump sum, rather than on the basis of royalties on sales value. Particularly in countries with high rates of protection, domestic product prices are artificially raised, and hence royalty payments based on sales value can be relatively more onerous than lump sum payments. The alternative of fixing royalties on the basis of sales value at international prices has been mooted but not implemented, partly because of the difficulty of identifying a genuine international price for petrochemical products. Thus it seems that in a protection situation it may be better to make lump sum payments. This case is further strengthened by the considerations we noted in Chapter II.4, namely the divergences in the rates of discount of the foreign investor and the host country. As long as the latter is less than the former, as is likely, lump sum payments will be cheaper from the host country's point of view than royalty payments. Domestic entrepreneurs, however, do not, it appears, like to pay lump sums for technology transfers as this increases the amount of capital that they have to raise domestically.

The great advantage of POI for NOCIL has been the role of the foreign investor in extending the demand for the final product. Thus, in the first year of full operation, the demand for one of the main products was only 4,000 tonnes when the rated capacity of the plant was 20,000 tonnes. In this year NOCIL made a loss of about Rs. 30 million. The next year the foreign collaborator, largely as a result of its marketing skills and experience pushed up sales to 8,000 tonnes and in the third year to 20,000 tonnes, Here, to some extent, the royalties based on sales gave an incentive to foreign investors to use and transfer their marketing skills to increase sales; something which the domestic collaborator did not have the know-how to do on its own.

III.7 CONCLUSIONS

The conclusions which can be derived from the case studies of this chapter can be briefly summarised.

First, the methods of appraisal presented in Part II are operational.

Second, the main determinant of the social profitability of the POI projects studied has been the degree of effective protection offered. This appears to be the most important area, quantitatively, where the host country should bargain, at least in the manufacturing sector.

Third, externalities seem quite unimportant, at least in the capital-intensive chemical industry. There was little training of labour, and no externality which we could identify which would have made any significant difference to the rate of return of the projects evaluated.

Fourth, given the capital-intensive nature of the projects examined, the income distributional factor made an insignificant difference to the social rates of return of the projects.

Fifth, the financial flows abroad associated with the projects seem to have only small effects on the evaluation of the projects examined.

Sixth, there is some evidence to suggest that the marketing skills POI brings may be important in achieving the full potential social benefits of the project.

Seventh, at least in high technology industries like chemicals, there is not likely to be any other alternative to POI, and the main problem is to consider alternative means of paying for the technology, as well as ensuring that the least costly and most efficient source of technology has been chosen. On the first issue there seems to be a case for preferring lump sum payments to royalty payments, and in any case the relative social costs of these two sorts of payments need to be evaluated with care when allowing particular foreign collaborations. On the second issue it appears from the admittedly meagre evidence we were able to obtain that at least in the chemicals sector India has been fairly successful in obtaining the requisite technology from the least costly and most efficient source.

Finally, though we did not conduct any sensitivity analyses of variations in the relevant parameters for a hypothetical domestic alternative, as such an alternative was clearly not feasible for the projects we studied, this may be important in appraising other POI projects.

Herdillia Chemicals Ltd. — Table 1
CAPITAL COSTS AND WORKING CAPITAL[a,b]

	1965				1966				1967				1968				1969–82			
	M	A_1	A_2	A_3	M	A_1	A_2	A_3	M	A_1	A_2	A_3	M	A_1	A_2	A_3	M	A_1	A_2	A_3
Imported Plant & Mach.	51.42[c]	25.70	25.70	25.70	205.80	131.71	131.71	131.71		160.52	160.52	160.52	17.10	13.34	13.34	13.34				
Indigenous Plant & Mach.	54.31	27.16	27.16	27.16	217.40	139.14	139.14	139.14		169.57	169.57	169.57	18.10	14.12	14.12	14.12				
Buildings	19.74	15.59	16.58	15.59	79	66.36	70.31	66.36		69.52	74.26	69.52	6.60	5.87	6.20	5.81				
Land	20.50	13.74	13.74	13.74	—								—							
Total Capital	145.97	82.19	83.18	82.19	502.20	337.21	341.16	337.21	502.20	399.61	404.35	399.61	41.80	33.29	33.66	33.29				
Stock in Trade													72.60	66.07	66.07	66.07	75	68.25	68.25	68.25
Stores & Spares													41.60	37.86	37.86	37.86	43	39.13	39.13	39.13
Debtors — Cred. & Cash													35.50	35.50	35.50	35.50	36.50	36.50	36.50	36.50
Total Working Capital													149.70	139.43	139.43	139.43	154.50	143.88	143.88	143.88
Annual Economic depr.[d]													102.40	71.28	71.48	71.28	102.40	71.28	71.48	71.28
Total (Rs) (excl. some W/C, incl. in NPVs below)	145.97	82.19	83.18	82.19	502.20	337.21	341.26	337.21	502.20	399.61	404.35	399.61	293.90	244	244.60	244	102.40	71.28	71.48	71.28
Total ($)	3.07	1.73	1.75	1.73	8.19	5.50	5.57	5.50	6.70	5.33	5.39	5.33	3.92	3.25	3.26	3.25	1.37	0.95	0.954	0.95

NPV:

$I(r)$	M	A_1	A_2	A_3 (NPV)	A_3 (NPV)
10%	26.22	18.49	18.49	18.01	18.49
20%	20.41	14.57	14.57	13.87	14.57

Herdillia Chemicals Ltd. — Table 2
ANNUAL REVENUE AND OUTLAYS

	1968				1969				1970				1971–82[g]			
	M	A_1	A_2	A_3	M	A_1	A_2	A_3	M	A_1	A_2	A_3	M	A_1	A_2	A_3
Sales[a]	296.10	199.30	199.30	263.50	546.80	368	368	486.7	736.60	495.70	495.70	655.60	827.30	556.80	556.80	736.30
Other Income	4	3.60	3.70	3.60	4.50	4.10	155	4	5.05	4.50	4.60	4.50	5	4.60	4.60	4.40
Materials purchased[b]	260.80	186.20	186.20	186.20	217.10	45.70	45.70	155	324.20	231.50	231.50	231.50	342.60	244.60	244.60	244.60
Utilities	36.91	32.10	33.20	32.10	50.74	44.10	45.70	44.10	59.15	51.50	53.20	51.50	70.64	61.50	63.60	61.50
Transport	1.74	1.44	1.50	1.44	1.89	1.57	1.63	1.57	2.32	1.93	2	1.93	2.77	2.30	2.38	2.30
Repairs[c]	5.09	4.48	4.78	4.48	9.29	8.18	8.73	8.18	8.46	7.44	7.95	7.44	8.88	7.81	8.35	7.81
Stores[d]	11.68	10.63	10.63	10.63	16.14	14.69	14.69	14.69	24.24	22.06	22.06	22.06	28.95	26.34	26.34	26.34
Overheads	19.23	15.77	16.54	15.77	22.22	18.22	19.11	18.22	22.41	18.38	19.27	18.38	22.31	18.29	19.19	18.29
Insurance etc.	13.65	12.69	14.20	12.69	16.71	15.54	17.38	15.54	19.61	18.24	20.39	18.24	22.63	21.05	23.54	21.05
Other outlays on labour[e]	2.57	2.11	2.21	2.11	3.77	3.09	3.24	3.09	4.99	4.09	4.29	4.09	6.50	5.33	5.59	5.33
Value Added	−51.57	−62.52	−66.26	1.68	213.44	111.61	106.60	230.30	276.27	145.06	139.64	304.96	327.02	173.98	167.81	353.48
Management[f]	6	6.30	6.30	6.30	6.40	6.72	6.72	6.72	8.29	8.70	8.70	8.70	9.81	10.30	10.30	10.30
Skilled Workers	6.17	5.86	6.79	5.86	6.52	6.19	7.17	6.19	2.87	2.73	3.16	2.73	1.39	1.32	1.53	1.32
Unskilled labour	18.11	17.20	19.92	17.20	21.34	20.27	23.47	20.27	21.39	20.32	23.53	20.32	21.40	20.33	23.54	20.33
Operating surplus Rs	−81.85	−91.86	−99.27	−26.68	179.18	78.43	69.24	197.12	243.72	113.31	104.25	273.21	294.42	142.03	132.44	321.53
$	−1.09	−1.22	−1.32	−0.356	2.39	1.05	0.923	2.63	3.25	1.51	1.39	3.64	3.93	1.89	1.77	4.29
$S(r)-C(r)-M(r)-L(r)$	10%								20%							

	M	A_1	A_2	A_3,(NPV)
	19.46	8.74	7.77	18.15
	8.84	3.78	3.40	10.18

Herdillia Chemicals Ltd. — Table 3
FOREIGN FINANCIAL FLOWS[a]

	1965	1966	1967	1968	1969	1970	1971	1972	1973	1974	1975	1976	1977	1978	1979	1980	1981	1982
Tech. know-how fees			48.26															
Engineering fees					6.77	2.66												
Equity	−295.50	−218																
Dividends paid abroad[b]		−90		29.55	29.55	29.55	13.08	26.16	26.16	26.16	26.16	26.16	26.16	26.16	26.16	26.16	26.16	26.16
Loans from abroad (and repayments)							29.55	35.18	40.80	40.80	40.80	40.80	40.80	11.25	11.25	5.62		
Interest on loans		16.85	24.05	23.72	22.09	20.46	18.83	17.20	14.90	12.36	9.84	7.30	4.16	2.02	1.12	0.22		
Total outflow of funds (Rs)	−295.50	−291.15	72.31	53.27	58.41	52.67	61.46	78.54	81.86	79.32	76.80	74.26	71.12	39.43	38.53	32.00	26.16	26.16
Total outflow of funds ($)	−3.94	−3.382	+0.964	+0.710	+0.779	+0.702	+0.819	+1.047	+1.091	+1.058	+1.024	+0.990	+0.948	+0.526	+0.514	+0.426	+0.349	+0.319
F (10)	−1.636																	
F (15)	−2.997																	
F (20)	−3.854																	

147

NOTES ON TABLES

Herdillia Chemicals Ltd.

Table 1 (a) The construction period was from October 1965 to January 1968, and outlays are assumed to have been made at a constant rate over the period, with the exception of that on land. Miscellaneous outlays amounting to Rs 169.17 lakhs have been added to those on buildings and indigenous plant and machinery in the same ratio as the original figures.

The economic life of the plants is assumed to be 15 years and the constructed capacities are:

Phenol	10,160 metric tonnes p.a.
Acetone	6,096 metric tonnes p.a.
Diacetone	3,032 metric tonnes p.a.
Phthalic anhyd.	6,096 metric tonnes p.a.
Dioctyl phth.	3,048 metric tonnes p.a.

(b) The breakdown of working capital for 1969—82 is derived from the company's 1970 annual report; the figures for 1968 assume the same proportional breakdown of the total.

(c) In all these tables, figures in Rupees are in units of 1 lakh, which is 100,000 Rupees; figures in dollars are in units of 1 million.

(d) Depreciation is based on 10% of the project's plant and equipment cost plus 2% of the cost of buildings, as was recommended in the OECD guide to project appraisal in India.

Table 2 (a) Inclusive of a small excise on waste hydrocarbons, and exclusive of export incentives for acetone.

(b) This includes both chemical raw materials, and packing materials, the latter treated as miscellaneous industrial materials. In total, packing materials amount to:

1968	1969	1970	1971—82
14.3	27.7	36.18	43.21

(c) Including repairs to both plant and buildings.

(d) These are treated as miscellaneous industrial materials.

(e) Including welfare expenditures, insurance, etc.

(f) Estimated as 3% of value added as recommended in the OECD guide.

(g) Estimated by assuming full capacity operation and constant input coefficients.

Table 3 (a) The current exchange rate of Rs 7.5 = 1 dollar should be used throughout, to obtain the last row of the table.

(b) Net of Indian taxes.

Polyolefins Industries Ltd. – Table 1
CAPITAL COSTS AND WORKING CAPITAL[a]

	1965				1966				1967				1969/70				1971–82			
	M	A_1	A_2	A_3	M	A_1	A_2	A_3	M	A_1	A_2	A_3	M	A_1	A_2	A_3	M	A_1	A_2	A_3
Imported plant & Mach.	15.40	7.70	7.70	7.70	305.30	195.39	195.39	195.39	125.50	97.89	97.89	97.89	89.09	81.07	81.07	81.07	108.24	98.50	98.50	98.50
Indigenous plant & Mach.	2.97	1.48	1.48	1.48	141.67	90.67	90.67	90.67	110.15	85.92	85.92	85.92	23.44	21.33	21.33	21.33	28.48	25.92	25.92	25.92
Buildings	2.27	1.79	1.91	1.91	55.24	46.40	49.16	46.40	29.15	25.65	27.40	25.65	90.40	90.40	90.40	90.40	109.80	109.80	109.80	109.80
Land	6.48	4.34	4.34	4.34	2.42	1.91	1.91	1.91	8.49	7.73	7.73	7.73	202.93	192.80	192.80	192.80	246.52	234.22	234.22	234.22
Miscellaneous	8.31	6.56	6.98	6.56	27.26	22.63	24.26	22.63	71.22	62.67	66.95	62.67	71.80	49.38	49.47	49.38	71.80	49.47	49.47	49.38
Tech. & other fees to collaborators[b]	19.91	19.91	19.91	19.91	46.77	46.77	46.77	46.77	91.44	91.44	91.44	91.44								
Total Capital	55.34	41.78	42.32	41.78	578.66	403.77	408.16	403.77	435.95	371.30	377.33	371.30								
Stock in trade									27.37	24.91	24.91	24.91								
Stores & Spares									0	0	0	0								
Debtors – Cred. & Cash									104.09	104.09	104.09	104.09								
Total Working Capital[c]									131.46	129	129	129								
Annual economic depr.[d] (1968–82)									35.90	24.69	24.74	24.69								
Total (Rs) (excl. some W/C, incl. in NPVs below)	55.34	41.78	42.32	41.78	578.66	403.77	408.16	403.77	603.31	524.99	531.07	524.99	71.8	49.38	49.47	49.38	71.8	49.38	49.47	49.38
Total ($)	1.16	0.875	0.889	0.878	9.44	6.59	6.66	6.59	8.04	6.99	7.08	6.99	0.957	0.658	0.66	0.658	0.957	0.658	0.66	0.658

I(r) 10% M A_1 A_2 A_3(NPV): 22.75 17.03 17.24 17.08

A₃(NPV): 17.08

I(r) 20%

I(r) M A_1 A_2 A_3(NPV): 18.23 13.84 13.84 13.98

Polyolefins Industries Ltd. – Table 2

ANNUAL REVENUE AND OUTLAYS

	1967[d]				1968				1969				1970				1971–82[e]			
	M	A_1	A_2	A_3	M	A_1	A_2	A_3	M	A_1	A_2	A_3	M	A_1	A_2	A_3	M	A_1	A_2	A_3
Sales[a]	51.60	44.50	44.50	45.90	246.40	212.40	212.40	219.30	703.30	606.20	606.20	625.90	944.90	814.40	814.40	841	1148.40	1020.80	1020.80	1022.10
Other income	1.90	1.69	1.75	1.69	3	3.56	3.68	3.56	85.80	76.36	78.94	76.36	17.30	15.40	15.92	15.40	20	17.80	18.40	17.80
Materials purchased[b]	47.40	40.70	40.70	40.70	164.90	141.60	141.60	141.60	269	231.10	231.10	231.10	290	249.10	249.10	249.10	352.50	302.80	302.80	302.80
Product purchased[b]	56	48.29	48.29	48.29	0	0	0	0	1.30	1.12	1.12	0.70	0.70	0.60	0.60	0.60	0	0	0	0
Utilities	0	0	0	0	45.70	39.76	39.76	39.76	54.40	47.33	48.96	47.33	57.10	49.68	51.39	49.68	69.40	60.38	62.46	60.38
Maintenance/repairs	0	0	0	0	10.10	8.89	8.89	8.89	20.20	17.78	18.99	17.78	31.20	27.46	29.34	27.46	35.00	30.80	32.90	30.80
Insurance	0.20	0.19	0.21	0.19	9.40	9.78	9.49	8.74	16.20	15.07	16.85	15.07	15.40	14.32	16.02	14.32	18.70	17.39	19.45	17.39
Land rent	0.60	0.55	0.55	0.55	2.40	2.18	2.18	2.18	2.80	2.55	2.55	2.55	2.90	2.64	2.64	2.64	2.73	2.73	2.73	2.73
Admin O/H.	4.20	3.44	3.61	3.44	28.90	24.85	23.70	23.70	38.80	31.82	33.37	31.82	48.10	39.44	41.54	39.44	50	41	43	41
Value added	−54.90	−46.98	−47.11	−45.58	−11.20	−8.91	−12.95	−2.01	386.40	335.79	332.10	355.49	516.80	446.56	439.69	473.16	639.80	583.50	575.86	584.80
Management[c]	3	3.15	3.15	3.15	3	3.15	3.15	3.15	10.30	10.82	10.82	12.40	12.40	13.02	13.02	13.02	15.90	16.70	16.70	16.70
Other wages	0.20	0.19	0.22	0.19	27.20	25.84	29.92	25.84	31.30	29.74	34.43	29.74	39.80	37.81	43.78	37.81	39.10	37.14	43.01	37.14
Operating surplus (Rs)	−58.10	−50.32	−50.48	−48.92	−41.20	−37.90	−46.02	−31	344.80	295.23	286.85	314.93	464.60	395.73	382.89	444.33	584.80	529.66	516.15	530.96
Operating surplus ($)	−0.775	−0.671	−0.673	−0.652	−0.549	−0.505	−0.614	−0.413	4.60	3.94	3.82	4.20	6.19	5.28	5.11	5.92	7.80	7.06	6.88	7.08
$S(r)-C(r)-M(r)-L(r)$	10% 38.93	34.91	33.87	35.65 [A_3(NPV)]					20% 17.77	15.87	15.35	16.35 [A_3(NPV)]								

Polyolefins Industries Ltd. — Table 3

FOREIGN FINANCIAL FLOWS

	1966	67	68	69	70	71	72	73	74	75	76	77	78	79	80	81	82
Royalties[a]	10.08		3.93	11.52	10.52	16.94	16.94	16.94	16.94	16.94	16.94	16.94					
Loans (incl. repayments)	1.20	0.60	-319.40	32	32	32	32	32	32	32	32	32	32				
Interest on loans				17.94	16.10	14.26	12.42	10.58	8.74	6.90	5.06	3.22	1.38				
Equity	-120																
Dividends paid abroad[b]						7.20	14.40	14.40	14.40	14.40	14.40	14.40	14.40	14.40	14.40	14.40	14.40
Net outflow (Rs)	-108.72	0.60	-315.47	51.46	58.62	70.40	75.76	73.92	72.08	70.24	68.40	66.56	47.78	14.40	14.40	14.40	14.40
Net outflow[c] ($)	-1.45	0.01	-4.21	0.819	0.782	0.939	1.01	0.986	0.961	0.936	0.912	0.887	0.637	0.188	0.188	0.188	0.188
F(r) 10%	-.199		20%	-1.45													

NOTES ON TABLES

Polyolefins Industries Ltd.

Table 1 (a) The data in this table are mainly derived from company balance sheets. Figures for 1965 include small amounts spent at the end of 1964, while those for 1967 include small amounts spent in 1968. Expenditure in the first three rows has been estimated on the basis of a constant rate of outlay over the construction period, and a total outlay on imported equipment of Rs 294 lakhs, estimated from the prospectus.

(b) This item includes engineering fees, technical and project staff salaries, and other expenses paid to the collaborators.

(c) The breakdown of working capital is derived from the company's annual reports; the figures for 1971—82 are adjusted to a full capacity basis, using the 1969/70 figures.

(d) Economic depreciation is taken to be 10% of the cost of plant and equipment plus 2% of the cost of the buildings; the plant's economic-life was originally expected to be 15 years but may now be less.

Table 2 (a) Includes excise duty.

(b) Purchased from the collaborator in 1967 on a product loan basis; for simplicity, the transaction is treated as a straight purchase from the collaborator, effected at the world price.

(c) Estimated as 3% of value added after 1968, and as Rs 3.0 lakhs in 1967 and 1968.

(d) Some small items of expenditure for earlier years are either ignored or included in this year's figures.

(e) This column is estimated on the basis of full capacity sale of 22000 tonnes of HDPE p.a., compared to 1970 sales of 18100 tonnes.

Table 3 (a) Net of Indian taxes. Figures for 1972—81 are based on full capacity production; royalties end in 1977, that is, ten years after start-up.

(b) Net of Indian taxes.

(c) In converting to dollars, the post-devaluation exchange rate should be used throughout.

Synthetics & Chemicals Ltd. – Table 1

CAPITAL COSTS AND WORKING CAPITAL[a, b]

	1962 M	A_1	A_2	A_3	1963 M	A_1	A_2	A_3	1964 M	A_1	A_2	A_3	1965 M	A_1	A_2	A_3	1966 M	A_1	A_2	A_3
Imported plant & mach.	84.10	42.10	42.10	42.10	499	249.50	249.50	249.50	13.40	6.70	6.70	6.70	8.90	4.50	4.50	4.50	73.70	47.20	47.20	47.20
Indigenous plant & mach.	94.70	47.40	47.40	47.40	562.40	281.20	281.20	281.20	15.20	7.60	7.60	7.60	10	5	5	5	83	53.10	53.10	53.10
Land	4.70	3.10	3.10	3.10	0.10	0.10	0.10	0.10												
Buildings	39.80	31.40	33.40	31.40	86.60	68.40	72.70	68.40	2.40	1.90	2	1.90	0.60	0.50	0.50	0.50	8.70	7.30	7.70	7.30
Other Assets	90.40	71.40	75.90	71.40	4.60	3.60	3.90	3.60	1.60	1.30	1.34	1.30	0.30	0.20	0.30	0.20	5.40	4.50	4.80	4.50
Total Capital (Rs)	313.70	195.40	201.90	195.40	1152.70	602.80	607.40	602.80	32.60	17.50	17.60	17.50	19.80	10.20	10.30	10.20	170.80	112.10	112.80	112.10
($)	6.59	4.11	4.24	4.11	24.22	12.66	12.76	12.66	0.685	0.368	0.37	0.368	0.416	0.214	0.216	0.214	2.79	1.83	1.84	1.83

	1963 M	A_1	A_2	A_3	1964 M	A_1	A_2	A_3 (NPV)	1969 M	A_1	A_2	A_3	1971–81 M	A_1	A_2	A_3 (NPV)
Stock in trade	345.50	237.50	237.50	237.50	202.50	135.70	135.70	135.70	316.50	288	288	288	342.20	311.20	311.20	311.20
Stores & spares	69.50	46.60	46.60	46.60	108	72.40	72.40	72.40	189	172	172	172	204.30	185.90	185.90	185.90
Debtors – Cred. & Cash	28	28	28	28	56	56	56	56	122.50	122.50	122.50	122.50	132.40	132.40	132.40	132.40
Total Working Capital	452	312.10	312.10	312.10	366.50	264.10	264.10	264.10	628	582.50	582.50	582.50	678.90	629.50	629.50	629.50
Annual economic depr.[c]	118.31	61.73	61.87	61.73	118.31	61.73	61.87	61.73	118.31	61.73	61.87	61.73	118.31	61.73	61.87	61.73
I(r)	10%	51.24			10%	24.90	30.15	29.90	20%	43.60				25.98	26.21	25.98

153

Synthetics & Chemicals Ltd. — Table 2

ANNUAL REVENUE AND OUTLAYS[a]

	1963				1964				1965				1966				1967			
	M	A_1	A_2	A_3	M	A_1	A_2	A_3	M	A_1	A_2	A_3	M	A_1	A_2	A_3	M	A_1	A_2	A_3
Sales[b]	94	68.62	71.44	68.82	437	319.01	332.12	319.01	744	543.12	565.44	543.12	843	682.83	708.12	682.83	993	883.77	913.56	883.77
Other income	2	1.46	1.52	1.46	3	2.19	2.28	2.19	6	4.38	4.56	4.38	17	13.77	14.28	13.77	25	22.25	23	22.25
Raw material purchases	153	102.51	102.51	102.51	192	128.64	128.64	128.64	153	169.51	169.51	169.51	256	202.24	202.24	202.24	529	481.39	481.39	481.39
Utilities	48	38.88	40.32	38.88	36	29.16	30.24	29.16	56	45.36	47.04	45.36	54	45.36	46.98	45.36	80	69.60	72	69.60
Transport	6.60	5.08	5.28	5.08	8.30	6.39	6.64	6.39	10.90	8.39	8.72	8.39	11	7.81	8.14	7.81	22.70	18.84	19.52	18.84
Repairs[c]	2.01	1.59	1.69	1.59	2.53	2	2.13	2	3.34	2.64	2.81	2.64	3.38	2.84	3.01	2.84	6.98	6.14	6.56	6.14
Stores	43	28.81	28.81	28.81	39	26.13	26.13	26.13	40	26.80	26.80	26.80	33	26.07	26.07	26.07	56	50.98	50.96	50.96
Insurance	5.10	3.82	4.23	3.82	6.50	4.88	5.40	4.88	8.50	6.38	7.06	6.38	8.60	7.22	8.08	7.22	17.80	16.55	18.51	16.55
Land	0.75	0.50	0.50	0.50	0.94	0.63	0.63	0.63	1.20	0.80	0.80	0.80	1.30	1.03	1.03	1.03	2.59	2.36	2.36	2.36
Other expenditures[d]	9.10	6.82	7.19	6.82	11.40	8.55	9.01	8.55	15	11.25	11.85	11.25	15.20	12.01	12.46	12.01	31.32	25.68	26.94	25.68
Value added	−171.56	−117.93	−117.57	−117.93	143.30	114.82	125.58	114.82	362.10	276.37	295.41	276.37	477.52	392.02	414.39	392.02	271.60	234.50	258.32	234.50
Management[e]	0.92	0.74	0.74	0.74	4.30	3.44	3.44	3.44	7.29	5.83	5.83	5.83	8.26	7.60	7.60	7.60	9.73	10.22	10.22	10.22
Other labour	5.73	4.01	4.87	4.01	26.70	18.69	22.70	18.69	45.40	31.78	38.59	31.78	51.40	42.15	50.37	42.15	60.60	57.57	66.66	57.57
Operating surplus (Rs)	−178.20	−122.68	−123.18	−122.68	112.30	92.69	99.44	92.69	309.40	238.76	250.99	238.76	417.90	342.27	356.42	342.27	201.30	166.71	181.44	166.71
($)	−3.74	−2.58	−2.59	−2.58	2.36	1.95	2.09	1.95	6.50	5.02	5.27	5.02	6.82	5.58	5.81	5.58	2.68	2.22	2.42	2.22

	M	A_1 (NPV)	A_2	A_3
$S(r)-C(r)-M(r)-L(r)$ Discounted to 1962 — 10%	37.37	31.81	30.27	31.81
20%	17.38	14.84	15.84	14.84

Table 2 (continued)

	1968				1969				1970				1971–1981ᶠ			
	M	A_1	A_2	A_3	M	A_1	A_2	A_3	M	A_1	A_2	A_3	M	A_1	A_2	A_3
Sales	1210	1076.90	1113.20	1076.90	1392	1238.88	1280.64	1238.38	1373	1221.97	1263.16	1221.97	1484.30	1320.76	1365.28	1320.76
Other income	9	8.01	8.28	8.01	13	11.57	11.96	11.57	14	12.46	12.88	12.46	15.10	13.44	13.89	13.44
Raw material purchases	693	630.63	630.63	630.63	556	505.96	505.96	505.96	633	576.03	576.03	576.03	633	576.03	576.03	576.03
Utilities	90	78.30	81	78.30	69	60.03	62.10	60.03	88	76.56	79.20	76.56	88	76.56	79.20	76.56
Transport	29.80	24.73	25.63	24.73	23.77	19.73	20.44	19.73	27.40	22.74	23.56	22.74	27.40	22.74	23.56	22.74
Repairs	9.10	8.01	8.55	8.01	7.50	6.60	7.05	6.60	8.30	7.30	7.30	7.30	8.30	7.30	7.80	7.30
Stores	60	54.60	54.60	54.60	65.90	59.97	59.97	59.97	83.50	75.98	75.98	75.98	83.50	75.98	75.98	75.98
Insurance	23.30	21.67	24.23	21.67	19.60	18.23	20.38	18.23	20.40	18.97	21.22	18.97	20.40	18.97	21.22	18.97
Land	3.40	3.09	3.09	3.09	2.20	2	2	2	3.70	3.37	3.37	3.37	3.70	3.37	3.37	3.37
Other expenditures	41	33.62	35.26	33.62	30.08	24.67	25.87	24.67	40.41	33.14	34.75	33.14	40.41	33.14	34.75	33.14
Value added	269.40	230.26	258.49	230.26	630.90	553.26	588.83	553.26	482.30	420.34	454.13	420.34	594.70	520.11	557.26	520.11
Management	11.90	12.49	12.49	12.49	13.60	14.28	14.28	14.28	13.50	14.18	14.18	14.18	13.50	14.18	14.18	14.18
Other labour	73.80	70.11	81.18	70.11	70.40	66.88	77.44	66.88	83.80	79.61	92.18	79.61	83.80	79.61	92.18	79.61
Operating surplus (Rs)	183.70	147.66	164.82	147.66	546.90	472.10	497.11	472.10	385	326.55	347.77	326.55	497.40	426.32	450.90	426.32
(%)	2.45	1.97	2.20	1.97	7.29	6.29	6.63	6.29	5.13	4.35	4.64	4.35	6.63	5.68	6.01	5.68

155

Synthetics & Chemicals Ltd. — Table 3

FOREIGN FINANCIAL FLOWS[a]

	1960	1961	1962	1963	1964	1965	1966	1967	1968	1969	1970	1971	1972	1973	1974	1975	1976	1977	1978	1979	1980	1981
Fees for tech. assistance		28.13	18.75			7.50	20.62															
Disclosure & tech. know-how						18.23	18.23	18.23	18.23	18.23	18.23	18.23	18.23	18.23	18.23							
Equity	22.50	−112.50		−31.15																		
Dividends[b]											6.51	13.02	13.02	13.02	13.02	13.02	13.02	13.02	13.02	13.02	13.02	13.02
Loans[c] [incl. repayments]		−450	−316.73	−18	122.25	122.25	122.25	32.25	32.35	32.25	32.25	32.25	35.58	171.15								
Interest abroad			27	46	47.08	39.75	33.55	26.22	24.28	22.35	20.41	19.27	15.40	7.70								
Total outflow of funds (Rs)	22.50	−534.37	−270.78	−3.15	169.33	187.73	194.65	76.70	74.76	72.83	77.40	82.77	132.23	210.10	31.25	13.02	13.02	13.02	13.02	13.02	13.02	13.02
($)	0.30	−7.12	−3.61	−0.042	2.26	2.50	2.60	1.02	0.997	0.971	1.03	1.10	1.76	2.80	0.427	0.174	0.174	0.174	0.174	0.174	0.174	0.174

$F(r)$ 10% = −0.8907
20% = −5.2389

NOTES ON TABLES

Synthetics and Chemicals Ltd.

Table 1 (a) Some small amounts for later years have been added in to the 1966 column or omitted; but the 1966 column is so large because considerable expenditure was required after a fire at the plant in December 1965. The plant is expected to be worth operating until about 1981.

(b) Data for the above table are derived from the company's annual reports; for intermediate years linear interpolation is used, while for the period 1971–81, full capacity operation has been assumed, that is 30000 tonnes of synaprene rubber per year, as compared to 27749 tonnes in 1970.

(c) Estimated as 8% of the costs of plant and machinery, plus 2% of the cost of buildings.

Table 2 (a) Full data were only given for 1969 and 1970, so that the smaller items for earlier years had to be estimated.

(b) Including excise duty.

(c) Including repairs to plant and buildings, but excluding capital repairs needed after the fire of December 1965.

(d) Including overheads n.e.s., welfare and insurance of labour, etc.

(e) Estimated as 3% of value added.

(f) Estimated by assuming full capacity production and sales in 1971–81.

Table 3 (a) All data in foreign currencies were converted back to rupees at the post-devaluation rate of exchange; hence this same rate must be used to obtain the last row of the table.

(b) Net of Indian taxes.

(c) Loans were obtained from AID, U.S. Banks, and the Firestone Corporation.

Albright, Morarji & Pandit Ltd. – Table 1

CAPITAL COSTS AND WORKING CAPITAL [a,b]

	1966/67				1967/68				1968/69				1969/70				1970/71			
	M	A_1	A_2	A_3	M	A_1	A_2	A_3	M	A_1	A_2	A_3	M	A_1	A_2	A_3	M	A_1	A_2	A_3
Imported plant & mach.	27.36	21.34	21.34	21.34	26.06	20.33	20.33	20.33	1.94	1.51	1.51	1.51	1.55	1.21	1.21	1.21				
Domestic plant & mach.	73.78	57.55	57.55	57.55	63.70	49.69	49.69	49.69	4.76	3.71	3.71	3.71	3.80	2.96	2.96	2.96				
Land	5.24	4.77	4.77	4.77	2.77	2.52	2.52	2.52	1.06	0.933	0.996	0.933	0.57	0.502	0.536	0.502				
Buildings	19.95	17.56	18.75	17.56	3.17	2.79	2.98	2.79	0.09	0.079	0.085	0.079	0.32	0.282	0.301	0.282				
Other capital costs	6.20	5.46	5.83	5.46	7.94	6.99	7.46	6.99	7.84	6.23	6.30	6.23	6.25	4.95	5.01	4.95				
Total capital costs	132.52	106.68	108.24	106.68	103.64	82.32	82.98	82.32	34.44	31.34	31.34	31.34	30.74	27.97	27.97	27.97				
Stock in trade					17.22[d]	15.67	15.67	15.67	16.89	15.37	15.37	15.37	16.78	15.27	15.27	15.27	32.59	29.66	29.66	29.66
Stores & spares					8.45	7.69	7.69	7.69	12.38	12.38	12.38	12.38	12.58	12.58	12.58	12.58	16.84	15.32	15.32	15.32
Debtors – Cred. & Cash					6.19	6.19	6.19	6.19						50.59	50.59	50.59	50	50	50	50
Total working capital					31.86	29.55	29.55	29.55	53.71	59.09	59.09	59.09	98.12	93.83	93.83	93.83	99.43	94.98	94.98	94.98
Annual economic depr.[c]					10.15	8.14	8.15	8.14	20.30	16.27	16.30	16.27	20.30	16.27	16.30	16.27	20.30	16.27	16.30	16.27
Total (excl. some W/C, incl. in NPVs below) (Rs)	132.52	106.68	108.24	106.68	145.65	120.01	120.68	120.01	59.99	52.04	52.14	52.04	60.96	55.96	56.05	55.96	20.30	16.27	16.30	16.27
($)	1.77	1.42	1.44	1.42	1.94	1.60	1.61	1.60	0.800	0.694	0.695	0.694	0.813	0.746	0.747	0.746	0.271	0.217	0.217	0.217

	M	A_1	A_2	A_3(NPV)				A_3(NPV)		M	A_1	A_2	A_3(NPV)		M	A_1	A_2	A_3(NPV)		
I(r) 10%	5.89	4.83	4.86	4.83				4.83		4.14	4.14	4.17	4.14			4.14	4.17	4.14		
$I(r_2)$ 20%													5.03							

Albright, Morarji & Pandit – Table 2

ANNUAL REVENUE AND OUTLAYS

| | 1967/68 | | | | 1968/69 | | | | 1969/70 | | | | 1970/71 | | | | 1971/72–1981/82 | | | |
	M	A_1	A_2	A_3	M	A_1	A_2	A_3	M	A_1	A_2	A_3	M	A_1	A_2	A_3	M	A_1	A_2	A_3
Sales	136.84	74.30	74.40	121.80	190.73	107	107.20	169.70	333.02	180.70	181.10	296.40	480.60	261	261.40	427.70	474.33	257.50	258	422.20
Other income	1.20	1.07	1.10	1.07	5.16	4.59	4.75	4.59	7.82	6.95	7.19	6.95	11.18	9.95	10.29	9.95	11.37	10.12	10.46	10.12
Raw materials bought	81.70	63.70	63.70	63.70	84.12	65.60	65.60	65.60	146.31	114.10	114.10	114.10	209.52	163.40	163.40	163.40	212.92	166.10	166.10	166.10
Utilities	3.69	3.21	3.32	3.21	4.07	3.54	3.66	3.54	5.69	4.95	5.12	4.95	6.50	5.65	5.65	5.65	7.30	6.35	6.57	6.35
Transport	0.14	0.12	0.12	0.12	0.21	0.17	0.18	0.17	0.15	0.12	0.13	0.12	0.18	0.15	0.15	0.15	0.16	0.13	0.14	0.13
Repairs[d]	0.19	0.17	0.18	0.17	0.74	0.65	0.70	0.65	1.46	1.28	1.37	1.28	1.21	1.06	1.14	1.06	1.66	1.46	1.56	1.46
Stores	4.05	3.69	3.69	3.69	6.26	5.70	5.70	5.70	13.49	12.28	12.28	12.28	19.31	17.57	17.57	17.57	19.62	17.85	17.85	17.85
Insurance	1.56	1.45	1.62	1.45	1.32	1.23	1.37	1.23	1.34	1.25	1.39	1.25	1.34	1.25	1.39	1.25	1.34	1.25	1.39	1.25
Land	0.49	0.45	0.45	0.45	0.62	0.56	0.56	0.56	0.65	0.59	0.59	0.59	0.57	0.52	0.52	0.52	0.61	0.55	0.55	0.55
Other expenditure[b]	7.72	6.33	6.64	6.33	6.93	5.68	5.96	5.68	9.44	7.74	8.12	7.74	9.01	7.39	7.75	7.39	9.84	8.07	8.46	8.07
Value added	38.45	-3.75	-4.22	43.75	91.63	28.46	28.22	91.16	162.31	45.34	45.19	161.04	244.20	73.96	73.92	240.66	232.25	65.86	65.84	230.56
Management[c]	1.15	1.208	1.21	1.21	2.75	2.89	2.89	2.89	4.87	5.11	5.11	5.11	7.32	7.69	7.69	7.69	6.97	7.32	7.32	7.32
Other labour	8.98	8.53	9.88	8.53	9.18	8.72	10.10	8.72	8.41	7.99	9.25	7.99	6.88	6.54	7.57	6.54	8.73	8.29	9.60	8.29
Operating surplus (Rs)	28.32	-13.49	-15.31	34.01	79.71	16.85	15.23	79.55	149.03	32.24	30.83	147.94	229.96	59.73	58.66	226.43	216.55	50.25	48.92	214.95
($)	0.38	-0.18	-0.20	0.45	1.06	0.22	0.20	1.06	1.99	0.43	0.41	1.97	3.07	0.80	0.78	3.02	2.89	0.67	0.65	2.87

$S(r)-C(r)-M(r)-L(r)$

	M	A_1	A_2	A_3	A_3(NPV)
	10%	17.63	3.86	3.71	17.56
	20%	9.72	2.04	1.94	9.70

159

Albright, Morarji & Pandit – Table 3

FOREIGN FINANCIAL FLOWS

	1966/67	67/68	68/69	69/70	70/71	71/72	72/73	73/74	74/75	75/76	76/77	77/78	78/79	79/80	80/81	81/82
Loan (incl. repayments)	−10.76		1.08	1.08	1.08	1.08	1.08	1.08	1.08	1.08	1.08	1.08				
Interest		0.65	0.65	0.58	0.52	0.45	0.38	0.32	0.26	0.19	0.13	0.06				
Dividends[a] (& equity)	(−10.5)[b]		21.51	1.26	1.26	1.26	1.26	1.26	1.26	1.26	1.26	1.26	1.26	1.26	1.26	1.26
Technical fees[c]																
Total outflow (Rs)	−10.76	0.65	23.24	2.92	2.86	2.79	2.72	2.66	2.60	2.53	2.47	2.40	1.26	1.26	1.26	1.26
($)	−0.14	0.009	0.310	0.039	0.038	0.037	0.036	0.035	0.035	0.034	0.033	0.032	0.017	0.017	0.017	0.017

F(10) = 0.314

F(20) = 0.19

NOTES ON TABLES

Albright, Morarji and Pandit Ltd.
Table 1 (a) Some miscellaneous items were allocated to other categories.
(b) For 1972—82, working capital is estimated on an assumption of full capacity operation of the plant.
(c) Estimated as 10% of plant and equipment costs plus 2% of building costs.
(d) Working capital for this year is estimated as 50% of that for 1968/69.

Table 2 (a) Including repairs to both plant and buildings.
(b) Including overheads and other expenses on labour.
(c) Estimated as 3% of value added.
(d) Estimated by assuming continued full capacity production and sales.

Table 3 (a) Net of Indian taxes.
(b) The collaborator was credited with this value of shares as fully paid up, in exchange for technical assistance; no cash flow was involved.
(c) Fee payable on start-up of the plant to the satisfaction of the Indian partner.

PART FOUR

Aspects of Foreign Investment in Kenya

This part is based on case studies of foreign investment in Kenya. The first three chapters discuss the general features of the Kenyan economy, and foreign investment in Kenya, whilst the remaining chapters are concerned with the actual case studies.

This part is based on reports prepared by Jeffrey Thompson and Martin Cave. The data was collected and processed by them, and the results and conclusions presented in this part are due to them. The Appendix on the Industrial Estates Scheme was also prepared by Jeffrey Thompson.

IV.1 ECONOMIC STRUCTURE

Kenya is faced with a high population growth rate, increasing pressure on land, high urban unemployment, a low stock of skilled workers, and an inequitable distribution of disposable income and public goods between the towns and the countryside; between regions; and between races. We examine these principal development problems in greater detail below; clearly it is important to see how far this situation can be considered the responsibility of POI, given that Kenya has been experiencing high growth rates, usually considered to be due to large inflows of foreign capital.

Most African countries faced a transition problem after Independence, partly caused by uncertainty in the pre-Independence and the immediate post-Independence period. In Kenya, which became independent in December 1963, uncertainty of what the Government's development strategy would be led to a reduction in employment and output in the main sectors, though not uniformly, following the withdrawal of some of the Asian and European purchasing power, due to a large foreign capital withdrawal.[1] Clearly some part

---

1. See below, p. 183

of the economic policy of the early post-Independence economy was concerned with reviving the economy to its former level of activity.

The growth rate over the period 1964–68 was 6.3 per cent at 1964 prices, and this rate was achieved with little structural change in the economy. Agriculture, including subsistence agriculture, still employed in 1970 about 60 per cent of the labour force and accounted for around 40 per cent of G.D.P.; reflecting in part a dual economy difference in productivity, and in part the imposed terms of trade due to effective protection. Agriculture grew somewhat less than G.D.P. at 4.42 per cent p.a.; illustrative figures for other major sectors are manufacturing (5.70 per cent), transport etc. (11.37 per cent), and general government (8.45 per cent). Over this period government funds were placed mainly in non-industrial ventures, on the argument that new and existing foreign and non-Kenya citizen-owned enterprise could by itself sustain a high growth rate; investment in the public sector in commerce and industry amounted to K£5.1m. out of a total public sector investment of K£132m. i.e., 3.9 per cent. The economy-wide investment rate in 1970 was 20 per cent, but except for agriculture, capital-output ratios are rising quite fast.

The Second Development Plan, covering the period 1970–4, makes the following projections of sectoral growth rates:

Table 1 Principal Projected Growth Rates p.a.

	per cent
Rate of growth of G.D.P.	6.7
Gross domestic investment	9.1
Cash agriculture	5.1
Manufacturing and repairs	9.2
Building and construction	9.7
Transport and communications	9.4
Private services	9.0
Government services	8.0

Source: *Republic of Kenya Development Plan, 1970–4*, 1969, Table 5.1.

Public expenditure, during the Second Plan period, is biased towards agricultural projects, and rural development generally. We cannot of course discuss in full how successful the actual policy implemented to secure these objectives is likely to be. But the accelerated growth of manufacturing will depend importantly on foreign investment, and it is hoped that improved co-operation between the three East African countries will permit fast growth rates as scale-economies are exploited.

Kenya is heavily dependent on foreign trade. In 1970 imports were 26.4% and exports 17.5% of G.D.P. The trade balance has been in consistent and rising deficit, financed by a favourable invisible balance (largely due to the growth of tourism receipts), and by public and private inflows of long-term capital. Until recently Kenya has managed to maintain a high level of foreign reserves; in 1968 reserves were nearly one-quarter of the visible and invisible imports bill.

The trade imbalance will probably continue to rise. On the imports side, consumer goods imports rose by, for instance, 40% in 1968, probably due to higher levels of domestic income causing a level of demand which could not be supplied by Kenya's own consumer-good industries. Imports of intermediate and capital goods are also rising fast, often attributable to a few corresponding acts of foreign investment. Thus the 1971 *Kenya Economic Survey* (p. 35) reports: 'The major part of the growth in imports in 1971 was absorbed in the development of facilities for future production. Machinery for a new (foreign-owned) tyre factory account for 20% of the rise of these imports.' On the export side, Kenya is a small country, facing given but not necessarily constant terms of trade: export projections are lower than those for imports, under plausible assumptions.

Kenya devalued against sterling in December, 1971, but the previous dollar parity was maintained. During 1971, the import bill rose by 25% to nearly K£150m.; foreign exchange has been rationed for some luxury and agricultural goods and petroleum; a withholding tax on remittances was placed on foreign investment, and heavy credit restrictions were applied. Part of the balance of payments difficulty is the result of the current inflation in Europe and North America; but that inflation may not be a short-term phenomenon. Clearly, the growth strategy which Kenya has adopted, which places less emphasis on income distribution and employment goals, and which appears to require substantial amounts of foreign investment, is likely to be increasingly called into question; especially as Tanzania, her neighbour to the south, is pursuing a strategy which places more emphasis on the distribution and employment goals, and has a less welcoming attitude towards foreign (and local) private investment.

The total land area of Kenya is 220,000 square miles, but only 16% of this is agricultural land. The total population is over 11 million. Population predictions, under plausible assumptions, are not encouraging and there is a strong suggestion that estimates of land pressure have been underestimated in the past, as have estimates of current and possible future growth rates of population.

Land pressure has been underestimated, due to official calculations being based on allocating people and land to density categories according to the density of districts; the heterogeneity of land quality, important at the provincial and district level, is also important within districts. Cramer[1] finds that measuring population density in terms of sublocations (i.e. using data for the smallest units possible), some of the best-endowed rural districts have significant percentages of their population in areas with over 400 persons per square kilometre. These districts may not be the most worrying areas in terms of population pressure, since other areas may be potentially far less productive, but the land problem is likely to be an uneven fight between population growth and the dissemination of new strains of hybrid maize.

Cramer has estimated the current rate of population growth at 3.4% or even 3.5% p.a., rather than the usually accepted 3.3% p.a. While a few percentage points' difference in population growth rates might appear unimportant, these rates are important when viewed as actual population numbers, giving, say, an underestimate of the 1980 population by at least 250,000. Further, although projections of

1. J. Cramer, 'Notes on the Population of Kenya' (Mimeo, Nairobi, 1971) from which this section draws heavily.

future growth rates are always inexact, it seems likely that the possible future growth rate of population has been underestimated. Even the most successful practicable family planning programme can only slow down population growth, and will not make an impact on the labour market for two decades; indeed, it is unlikely to take place, since the current programme is a high-cost, urban and middle-class affair.

Percentage errors in population growth rates, now and in the future, are therefore important; a small underestimate in population growth rates may mean a large increase in the 'residual' category of those to be displaced by land consolidation, and those not employed and not in school. One important question is whether the population pressure problem is likely to become at some time in the future a marketable surplus problem.[1]

The discussion of population growth leads naturally to the discussion of projected employment growth rates. Again, this aspect of the Kenyan economy is doubly important when we recall the model of the dual economy and its treatment of unemployment and underemployment which is implicit in the *Manual*.[2] While the evidence on population growth suggests anxiety over employment, this has not always been the case. The *Development Plan for 1964–8*, published shortly after Independence, states that 'unemployment in 1970 therefore may be a less significant problem than it is today'. This inference is based on a severe underestimate of the population growth rate; a failure to measure urban unemployment, rural unemployment and underemployment correctly; and over-optimism concerning the number of jobs which could be created over the period. These last two classes of issues are examined now.

There is great unevenness in the quality and coverage of research on employment in Kenya. Certain important issues have been discussed: the magnitude, nature and determinants of rural-urban migration and its impact on the employment pattern; the behaviour and determinants of productivity and employment in the modern sector; and criteria for the

1. This has implications for shadow pricing — particularly of maize and labour. Thus, in the open economy, we may need to revise tax rates, and the correct pattern of international trade may also change.
2. *Manual*: Appendix for Professional Economists, pp. 251–67.

construction of an incomes policy. Some of this research material has even been watered down as textbook material; and the government has certainly taken some notice of this material in framing policy.[1] However, other priority questions do not appear to have been adequately dealt with; for example, employment relations in the small-scale urban sector, and employment relations generally in rural areas.

Estimated productivity growth (in the sense of the output growth rate less the employment growth rate) over the period 1964—8 was about 3% p.a., although there were the expected variations between sectors. Over 1964—8 estimated wage employment increased 3.8% p.a., and output grew at about 6.9% suggesting that about 15% of new entrants to the labour force were absorbed in some form of paid employment. However over one third of estimated wage employment in 1964 was based on unpublished and possibly unreliable estimates of rural unemployment, and 70% of the increase in estimated wage employment was unenumerated employment in the rural areas. Finally, many persons shown as family workers may have been unemployed or underemployed: the Plan is unhelpful on this point since its estimate of 'actively engaged' persons seems to be just the estimated total adult working population, with components wage employment, self-employment, and family workers.

The principal projected sectoral growth rates for 1968—74 are:

Table 2 Annual Rates of Growth 1968—74

	G.D.P.	per cent Wage Employment	Productivity
Agriculture	5.7	4.5	1.2
Building	9.7	10.0	−0.3
Manufacturing	9.2	4.5	4.7
Transport and communications	9.8	8.2	1.6
General government services	8.2	5.0	3.2
Total	7.8	5.1	2.7

Source: 1969 *Economic Survey* and 1970—4 *Development Plan.*

1. But perhaps implementation of the policy implications of this research has not been carried out with enough force, and some implications may have been accepted uncritically.

Very high output growth rates are therefore necessary for employment to increase significantly. The 1970—4 Plan predicts that only 25—28% of new entrants to the labour force will be absorbed in wage employment; further, few primary school leavers and, by 1974, not more than half the number of anticipated secondary school leavers can expect to enter wage-employment.

The principal features of the urban labour market in Kenya are the existence of a substantial excess supply of unskilled labour at the ruling wage rate and high rates of growth of wages despite high unemployment. The market for skilled labour will be looked at later. Consider first productivity growth as a factor in the urban labour market: Harris and Todaro[1] have argued that labour productivity (and so employment growth) are functionally related to the growth of industrial real wages, suggesting that for each one per cent rise in real wages, employment will be 0.76 less than what it would have been without the wage increase owing to the substitution of capital and managerial inputs for unskilled labour.

One could claim that little that is economically interesting appears from an ordinary least squares regression of value-added per African employee on wages per African employee;[2] but clearly even if their suggestion that productivity

1. J. R. Harris and M. P. Todaro, 'Wages, industrial employment, and labour productivity: the Kenyan experience', *East African Economic Review*, 1969.
2. The estimated equation is probably subject to both measurement and specification bias. Measurement bias occurs because the plausibility of taking wages and value-added per African employee as indicators of wages and value-added of unskilled labour changes over time; specification bias occurs because we would not express the relation hypothesised to be one of current changes in wages to current changes in value-added; as usual, even if we are confident about the direction of causation, a scatter diagram of two current variables tells us little. We would expect an adjustment process of the Brown-de Cani sort*. Any further analysis would have to take into account the historical uniqueness of the period (1955—66) for which Harris and Todaro made their test; productivity growth rates broken down by industrial classification (Development Plan, p. 314), which may not reflect a response to wage changes but rather the imposition of capital-intensive techniques; other possible partial explanations include the displacement of existing labour-intensive technologies (not so important in Kenya) the level of capacity utilisation, learning by doing, improved managerial practices (which would have occurred without the stimulus of higher wages), etc. (*) M. Brown and J. S. de Cani, 'Technological choice and the distribution of income', *International Economic Review*, Vol. 4, No. 3, Sept. 1963.

growth in industry and commerce (over the years 1956–66) is due to induced substitution caused by actual and expected wage increases, is not strictly correct, the causes do appear worth investigating. The results are clearly accepted by the Government. Thus:

> Taking the last three years as a whole, earnings in the modern sector are rising twice as fast as employment; the effects of this on slowing down employment growth need no emphasis.
>
> (*Economic Survey*, 1971, p. 163)

Further, a given increase in wages in the modern sector leads, through another well-known model by Harris and Todaro,[1] to an equilibrium increase in urban unemployment, due to rural workers maximising their expected utility by migrating to the urban sector and taking a chance of obtaining a relatively well-paid job. Again, the model can be criticised on grounds of over-simplicity,[2] but it appears to be broadly correct.

Bringing the two models together and assuming wage increases due to rises in the institutionally fixed wage, and to union bargaining power (see p. 175), we have the following simple trade-off for Kenya:

> A highly mechanised urban industrial economy, with a small, highly skilled and productive labour force with substantial and ever-increasing urban unemployment, or a less mechanized, more labour-intensive industry economy with a less skilled, less individual productive labour force, but one with more widespread human participation and lower levels of urban unemployment.[3]

1. E.g., J. R. Harris and M. P. Todaro, 'Migration, Unemployment, and Development: a two-sector analysis', *AER*, 1970.

2. A two-sector analysis may be an oversimplification since migrants are usually the younger, more able and more ambitious members of the rural community; on the urban side, there is probably some low productivity, low wage employment. Naturally proliferation of sectors makes tractability more implausible. To a lessening but still important extent, migrants retain their ties with the rural sector, although there are real flows in other directions also. Further it is an oversimplification to build a migration model in a static framework, however, there do not appear to be any successful attempts at dynamicising the relation.

We have seen in the Guidelines, that the decentralisation price of labour, in the face of a Todaro migration process should be set at the market wage (c). In more general treatments, which are not discussed in the *Manual* (where M ⩽ SWR ⩽ C), SWR > C is possible, and we have to pay more attention, for instance, to investment allocation between sectors.

3. Harris and Todaro, 1969, op. cit.

Clearly the employment, productivity, earnings nexus in Kenya is a substantial research topic in its own right, and we have presented here only the bare intuition of these two promising models. Nevertheless it should be clear that imputing responsibility for, say, urban unemployment should be done with some care: it may be that incomes policy has a comparative advantage in relation to alleviating urban unemployment compared to project analysis (and, more strongly, labour subsidies). Just as we have to distinguish between malconsequences resulting from foreign investment (which forms a significant part of the modern sector in Kenya), and those due to the government's protection policy, so we have to distinguish between consequences due to POI and those due to government's sectoral and incomes policies (see below).

Shortage of skilled labour is a common problem throughout Africa, and is thus not a special problem for Kenya. Success in Africanisation has differed among the States, and there has been more success in agriculture and in government services than in commerce and industry, thus suggesting that skills differ in the degree to which they can be provided locally by a country at Kenya's level of development.[1]

In many East African countries, tension rises between the desire to grow fast with the desire to Africanise quickly as many posts as possible. Further, most observers concur with the view that present educational policies are not providing a correct quantity and mix of skills. Largely due to the

---

1. In the private sector in 1967, 47% of all high and middle level posts (those requiring tertiary or higher secondary level education — the stock of administrators, managers, skilled technicians, and professional workers) were occupied by non-citizens; the figure for the public sector is 27%, giving an economy-wide weighted average of 40%. Many important occupations are almost completely dominated by non-citizens (see *Development Plan*, 1969, Table 4.4, p. 117). Generally the more training and experience required by an occupation, the greater is non-citizen participation in that profession. Kenyanisation has proceeded quite far in transport, construction and retail trade, aided by the Government through licensing, etc. The 1967 Kenya Manpower Survey predicts targets for Kenyanisation in middle and high level occupations which probably will not be met, thus requiring the recruitment of additional skilled non-citizen workers.

In 1968 over two thousand job permits were issued to expatriate craftsmen and artisans; and this shortfall will grow over the Plan period, given projected output growth rates.

retention, in very large part, of the educational system of the colonial period, there is now in Kenya an excess supply of primary and secondary school graduates while vocational training, especially if it does not require tertiary level education, has been underemphasised.[1]

Absence of skills can be quite important in preventing certain sorts of economic acticity being undertaken 'efficiently' in a less developed country. Baranson,[2] for instance, found in his work on diesel engine manufacture in India that the technology that took less than two years to transfer from the United States to Japan would take at least fifteen years to transfer to India, given the critical shortage in India of the necessary engineering and technical skills that are relatively more abundant in Japan.

This resource bottleneck could be partly alleviated by using the international labour market more fully; but the securing of skilled workers is not the only dimension of the problem. If we compare East Africa with some of the smaller Asian countries, we find that the human capital bottleneck is not only one of small quantities of skilled labour but also of skill cohorts which have not yet reached an acceptable level of discipline in dealing with machinery, and in accepting routine and punctuality.

For example, some urban workers are likely to be rural

---

1. For example, at the beginning of 1963 there were only 811 contracts of apprenticeship in Kenya; further the *Development Plan* (p. 112) reports that some of the twenty large firms who do undertake this type of training have tended to place more emphasis on production than on training. The Industrial Training Act has recently been amended to provide for an industrial training levy whereby employers' training costs are less likely to be lost due to 'poaching' of skilled workers by other firms. Private sector training programmes are considered by the Government to be an important part of the national training programme; for a description of such a scheme see p. 81 of the Plan. In the administration of work permits, the Government requires that applications for permits are accompanied by evidence of effort firms are making to Kenyanise positions for which permits are being asked.

The education authorities in Kenya provide trade courses for secondary technical schools; and the Mombasa Technical Institute and the Kenya Polytechnic, which together had 3,371 enrolments in 1970, provide courses in engineering, building and civil engineering, commercial and business studies. Of course, apprenticeships, for instance, may be inefficient training technologies for Kenya or elsewhere.

2. Jack Baranson, *Manufacturing problems in India*, Syracuse, 1967.

target workers, seeking only a fixed income from employment in the towns and then returning to the countryside. In so far as this phenomenon remains part of social life in Kenya, it produces a high rate of labour turnover. Thus assembly-line work, for instance, may be an inefficient technology when combined with a low personal efficiency of labour, and this factor may in part explain the lack of international competitiveness of some of Kenyan industry.[1]

However, we still need a distinction between skilled and unskilled workers; the economically relevant one for Kenya is between workers whose market is characterised by excess supply, and those whose market is not.[2] We cannot therefore accept, as a short cut, a cut-off rate below which a worker is considered unskilled, and above which he is considered skilled; instead, we should inspect the market, now and in the future, for evidence of excess supply, expecting that skilled labour is in more price-inelastic supply and demand relative to unskilled labour.

Great inequality of income distribution is a well-known fact of the Kenyan economy but it is difficult to find the correct numbers; for example, data for the determination of the Lorenz curve do not exist, though this may not be the interesting dimension of income distribution in the Kenyan

---

1. As argued by Bhagwati in Vernon, ed., 'The technology factor in international trade', N.B.E.R., 1970, pp. 362–3.

Human capital has been used for some time in attempted explanation of international trade. Note that neither of the two usual methods of taking account of this prima facie determinant of trade — either a measure of human capital or a measurement of skill (i.e. numbers in various job classifications) — serves to measure fully what we are suggesting may be true of the East African case, i.e. low personal efficiency of labour over a wide range of job classifications. A full treatment of the human capital factor in trade would however take us too far from our present brief.

But improvement in labour services is unlikely to be sufficient, without radical revision of the tariff structure, given typically low labour coefficients.

2. A skilled worker should be able to earn a marginal product elsewhere in the economy representing the costs to society of his being employed in a particular project. If the market for skilled labour is determined in part by trade-union bargaining, then probably no correction need be made, since his consumption represents a heavy cost to society; this is a double cost at the lower end of the skill spectrum, since we expect increases in compensation of low-skilled workers to pull up wages of the unskilled. One further difficulty in measuring human capital in Kenya is that the unskilled labour rate, needed to calculate the quasi-rents accruing to skilled labour, is not competitively determined.

context. Dimensions of particular interest are the differentials between skilled and unskilled urban labour, between unskilled urban labour and the peasantry, and between the regions; these categories are thought to be composed of unequal skewed distributions. If the differentials are large, then it appears that they have been increasing since Independence in 1963. Dharam Ghai[1] has argued that the benefits of growth since Independence have accrued to some businessmen, salary and wage earners and a few hundred thousand farmers. The rest of the population may have gained little or nothing — regional differences have at least remained constant and may have increased, and the urban areas, especially the capital, have gained relative to the countryside.

Some recent detective work by Maurice Scott[2] suggests that the data is too scanty to enable us to say anything very definite about the changes in rural incomes over the period 1964—8. Scott's procedure is to take the growth rate for small farmers' income, cash and non-cash, at current prices (5.3% p.a.) from 1964 to 1968, subtract the increase in numbers of families dependent on agriculture and then subtract the inflation rate as given by alternative price indexes, none of which is ideal but within which range of estimates the true rate is probably contained; and so arrive at an estimate of 0%—2%. This does not mean that wages of casual workers rose by the same amount: theory suggests that given the very high population growth rate, the increase might have accrued to farmers as land-owners rather than as farm labourers. Perhaps the most reasonable conclusion is that the real wages of casual workers remained roughly constant over the period 1964 to 1968. In contrast, Ghai estimates that the real income of unskilled urban workers rose about 8% p.a. over the period 1960 to 1963; that is, nearly double the G.D.P. growth rate.[3] 41,000 employees earning over K£600 p.a. representing 7% of recorded employment, received nearly 44% of total employment income in

1. Dharam Ghai, 'Priorities in economic research in Kenya over the Second Plan Period 1970—4' (mimeo, Nairobi, 1970).
2. M. Fg. Scott, 'Rural wages in Kenya' (mimeo, Oxford, 1970).
3. Ghai, op. cit., p. 4.

1964.[1] A conservative estimate of the rural household income-urban wage differential would be at least two.

In the urban economy, minimum wage regulations have substantially raised wages and improved conditions of work. The public sector has been a leading factor in wage increases — by paying its workers above the minimum wage and putting pressure on the private sector to increase wages similarly. In the private sector, there appears to be a group of firms with common characteristics[2] (high effective protection, low price and high income elasticities, capital-intensity i.e. mainly, but not exclusively, private overseas investment) which have forced the pace in wage increases. Employers accede to trade union demands perhaps because they perceive a change in the distribution of power between foreign investment and governments, or because the foreign investor is nowadays a timid and philanthropic animal,[3] in addition to economic reasons such as the high cost of training new labour.

Given the size and growth of the rural-urban differential, the Government could always adopt measures to contain a potential increase in this gap. While rural incomes can be increased by increased rural public investment etc., a suitably framed incomes policy could help to alleviate the gap. Although we have not presented a fully articulated model, it seems clear that, with present policies, income distribution will worsen. Incomes policy while still primarily concerned with employment and income distribution (for example, by keeping the growth rate of urban wages equal to that of rural incomes), may in the future be somewhat more concerned with the balance of payments. The task is complicated since trade unions in Kenya probably would not accept a moratorium on wage increases without a concurrent expansion of

1. Dharam Ghai, 'Incomes policy in Kenya: needs, criteria, machinery' (mimeo, Nairobi, 1968), p. 2. Skilled earnings in the public sector largely depend on the old Colonial scales; in the private sector, the wages of the managers, highly skilled workers, etc., are largely determined by contemporary developed-economy rates.
2. Dharam Ghai, 'Analytic aspects of an incomes policy for Kenya' (mimeo, Nairobi, 1967), pp. 19—20.
3. A. O. Hirschmann, 'How to divest in Latin America and Why', Princeton Essay in International Finance, No. 76, 1969, p. 7.

jobs.[1] While more moderate wage increases may be possible with the powerful set of tools[2] at the Government's disposal, the Government appears to give poor guidance to the Industrial Court, which is responsible for wage arbitration.[3] Certainly, as the Second Plan period has proceeded, the authorities are not making a determined attack on even public sector wage increases.

IV.2 POLICY FRAMEWORK

African countries South of the Sahara, aware of the observed correlation between POI and growth,[4] and embarking on a programme of industrial development must have a coherent policy of POI since they do not have, in general, the full resources necessary for indigenous development of this sector. Here we consider differential government policy towards POI as opposed to local investment, looking explicitly at the industrial sector.[5]

A common view[6] is that Kenya's position on foreign investment, which gives strong emphasis to the role of POI (i.e. accepts a large quantity of POI) is an extreme position in Africa, which she shares with Liberia, Ivory Coast and Nigeria, the other extreme being represented by Guinea, Mali and Tanzania. Of course placing heavy emphasis on the role of POI is not the same thing as having a 'soft' policy

1. The Tripartite Agreements of 1964 and 1970, between the Government, trade unions and employers, accepted a wage moratorium for a 10% expansion of employment in enterprises with more than ten employees. Note that Tanzania has imposed lower salary scales and national service to reduce the earnings of skilled workers; a loan scheme for education could also be introduced.
2. See the section on incomes policy in *Republic of Kenya Development Plan, 1970—4*, 1969, paras. 4.99—4.134.
3. See *Development Plan*, para 4.127. 'The Industrial Court will in general need very strong evidence for reducing or refusing a wage claim ... since the Government considers that most workers have a right to expect regular gains in real income.'
4. In Africa the relationship roughly holds after taking account of Independence and War periods; elsewhere, e.g., in Latin America, it does not. But such inferences have to be treated warily due to, for instance, choice of base — and end — years, and to overvaluation of industry's contribution due to effective protection — thus, we are talking of growth rates as *conventionally* measured.
5. In Kenya, foreign capital also remains important in the plantations sector; services and banking; transport and communications. Electricity is now largely publicly owned.
6. Pearson Commission, *Partners in Development* (Pall Mall, 1969), p. 164.

towards POI, although the latter may be a precondition of the former.

Measures to induce POI into a country and measures to protect POI resident in a country cannot be strictly separated because both form part of the government-imposed environment in which potential and existing POI must act; measures to protect POI are likely to encourage potential investors.

Measures we examine are: investment incentives, legal protection and tariff protection; we then look at some other measures (currency and immigration control) which impinge on foreign investment activities. We conclude by looking at joint ventures in Kenya.

Virtually all developed and less developed countries offer incentives for industrial investment; for example, grants, initial allowances, tax holidays, ready-built factories at low cost, cheap land, and rebates or reductions in local rates, rents or taxes. Kenya offers two incentives: initial investment allowances and cheap land on industrial estates. In addition to normal depreciation (wear and tear allowance), which enables an investor to write off 100% of his investment over varying periods, there is a 20% allowance on new industrial buildings, plant and machinery; so altogether a company can write off 120% of its taxable income over a number of years. These depreciation measures naturally bias POI towards greater capital intensity than would be the case otherwise, since they change the user-cost of capital,[1] and they are also an easy way to remit foreign capital. The elasticity of foreign investment with respect to depreciation allowances (and company taxation[2]) is very much an unexplored area. This

1. See Jorgenson's formulation of the cost of capital in, for example, 'Capital Theory and Investment Behaviour', *American Economic Review*, 53, May 1963, which also includes the influence of tax rates.

The *Development Plan* (para. 4.107) reports that the Government 'is considering whether a practicable plan for an employment allowance, to complement or substitute for the present investment allowance, can be introduced'. Depreciation laws are assumed constant in a recent study of company savings in Kenya. See P. N. Snowden, 'Preliminary study on company savings in Kenya' (mimeo, Nairobi, 1971).

2. Corporate taxation in Kenya amounts to 40% of net profits which, with surtax on distributed dividends, makes an effective rate of taxation of business profits exceeding 50%. The government thus benefits substantially from any rise in the profit share, and this social gain is measured in the detailed project analyses below. In the 1971 Budget, the Government introduced a 12½% withholding tax on dividends and interest payments overseas.

fiscal incentive is applied to all investment, both local and foreign, so POI does not gain or lose relative to local enterprise on this account. It might be noted that, generally, fiscal measures which encourage reinvestment are preferable to penalties for remitting, since such penalties defeat their purpose by discouraging new capital inflow; it may be that retained earnings are more sensitive to tax measures than new foreign investment.

The most commonly offered investment incentive in less developed countries is the tax holiday. Kenya did not offer such an incentive when its industrial boom started in 1949, because it was not felt necessary while Kenya was attracting most of the investment entering East Africa. The authorities have traditionally felt that a tax holiday would be ineffective, since, supposing the tax holiday is for five years, profits are rarely earned before the fourth year; this, however, is still an incentive, but it is doubtful whether a five-year tax holiday as opposed to a 20% investment allowance would prove a real attraction. Many potential investors visiting East Africa for the first time have expressed surprise at the lack of a tax holiday incentive. One important point is whether tax holidays could offset the effects of the transfer tax system; Article 6 of the East African Common Market Treaty states that the Partner States should attempt to agree to a common system of fiscal incentives towards industry.

The only other practicable incentive is ready-built factories at low cost, which could, if required, be used to encourage industry in less-favoured areas; the disadvantage with this policy is that finance would be required early on in the programme.

Legal protection of private overseas investment is given by the Foreign Investments Protection Act, 1964, which permits foreign investors, provided they possess a document called a Certificate of Approved Enterprise, to remit capital, profits and interest. The Act provides an indication of the Government's intentions towards foreign investment, but sums remitted are still subject to Exchange Control, foreign investment could still be nationalised (but only in the words of the Act if 'fair and prompt compensation' is given), and clearly foreign investors really base their views on the actual policy towards foreign investment rather than the guarantees given by an Act, which Kenya could always change. However possession of a Certificate is a necessary document for foreign investments' operations in Kenya, since if a foreign company does not possess a Certificate, it is likely to find its capital blocked when it tries to repatriate it.

In considering arguments for tariff protection (which a foreign investor often insists on before undertaking an investment) the Government pays regard not only to the profitability of the enterprise but also its costs and benefits to the economy as a whole, such as value-added in relation to loss of revenue to the exchequer, additional employment created, its balance of payments impact, the training provided by the company, its contribution to Africanisation, and any regional effects. But the actual criteria applied involve a two-stage process; first, whether the enterprise can 'pay reasonable wages, yield a fair profit, and charge "comparable" prices with international ones' (that is, roughly whether the private rate of return is adequate, given constraints on wages and the price of the enterprise's product), and then adding the 'social' effects listed above. Some of the 'social' costs and benefits mentioned here we do not value at all; the others can be weighted using the Guidelines, which have the advantage of providing a single criterion to decide whether or not to accept a particular act of foreign investment, rather than the Government's method of decision, which is simply an *ad hoc* checklist.

Further, every new project (including expansion of existing industry), which requires government financial participation is subject to examination by an interministerial Projects Committee, composed of civil servants from the ministries concerned and representatives of the two parastatal investment companies. The Committee advises the Government on the costs and benefits of each project, although no formal project analysis appears to be undertaken. There appear to be no restrictions on the industries which foreign investment can enter.

The Government also reviews existing protection arrangements. The Ministry of Commerce and Industry is responsible for such appraisals; and it performs this task in consultation with the other relevant economic Ministries through the Industrial Protection Committee.

An indication of the Government's attitude towards protection, which is also held by some aid agencies investing in Kenya, may be obtained from the following statement:

> It is essential to set up factories which will become viable economic units; a fairly high degree of protection in the earlier years of a project is usually necessary if industry in a developing country is to become established in the face of frequently strong competition from developed countries.
>
> (*Economic Survey*, 1969, para. 5—27)

We do not, of course, accept this view, and our disagreement is reflected in the Guidelines. If subsidisation is socially desirable, then tariff protection is not the proper way to provide it.

Industrial protection may be by means of import tariffs on commodities from outside East Africa (requiring Community approval), import licensing and quantitative restrictions, and by drawbacks of duty on imported inputs. Normally duty refunds for the home markets are granted only for a limited period and, in some cases, according to a sliding scale. Duty drawbacks on imported inputs are an important area for bargaining between the Government and foreign investor, both at the proposal stage and during the life of the foreign project.

Foreign investment resident in Kenya faces currency and immigration controls. All profit, interest and capital remittances, salaries, directors' fees, royalties, technical assistance fees etc., and inter-company transactions with a foreign-based company must receive exchange-rate approval. So even those items covered by a Certificate of Approved Enterprise are subject to Exchange Control approval. The Exchange Control is also responsible for regulating local short-term borrowing by foreign companies. Local bank overdrafts are limited to 20% of the foreign long-term liability where 50% or more of the equity is held by foreign nationals, and 40% of the liability where under 50% is so owned. A local overdraft is frequently the preferred method of finance by foreign investors, and it is easy to see why perceived political risk over the medium term should make this so. The banks are still mainly foreign-owned, and clearly this adds to local suspicion, but lending to foreign investors is probably more profitable for banks than lending to local investors. The suspicion of a close relation between domestic savings, the banks, loans to foreign investment, and repatriation of local savings to the developed world will remain until a less imperfect capital market appears in Kenya.

Concerning immigration regulations, every non-citizen must obtain a work-permit from the authorities, which in theory is granted only if the post cannot be filled by a citizen. Management posts are still mainly held by expatriates, and clearly one potential source of friction is the case of a citizen holding the necessary formal qualifications for an appointment but without sufficient practical experience.

Local ownership of foreign enterprise can be obtained by those companies selling equity on the Nairobi stock exchange, so involving a re-scheduling of outflow of foreign exchange resulting from an act of foreign investment, but such stock issues are, at present, often taken up by members of the non-African population. Joint ventures are more likely to satisfy local demands for some influence on the actions of foreign investors, and also to obtain some of the profits accruing to foreign investment; correspondingly, it is important to find the appropriate financial and institutional arrangement for joint ventures.

The two parastatal organisations which participate in joint ventures with foreign investors in Kenya are the Industrial and Commercial Development Corporation (ICDC), which began operations in 1954, and is wholly owned by the Kenya Government, and the Development Finance Company of Kenya Ltd. (DFCK) which was established in 1963 by agreement between the Governments of Kenya, U.K., and West Germany, the Netherlands becoming an investor in 1967. The Kenyan capital contribution to DFCK was provided through ICDC, thus providing a constraint on ICDC's activities, which was perhaps unfortunate since ICDC is also the principal body involved in the finance of small-scale indigenous commercial and industrial activity in Kenya. Although it accepts responsibility for aiding indigenous business, ICDC has always concentrated its resources in joint ventures with foreign investors; either new operations or, in the early post-Independence period, salvage operations to prevent the collapse of existing foreign and non-citizen investments. Thus in 1966, 88% of ICDC's assistance was to expatriate concerns, and only 9% to the Small Industries Revolving Fund, which is involved in aiding African business. Presently ICDC appears to be following a policy of securing participation in joint ventures, in the hope of obtaining high rates of return and, whenever possible, majority share-holdings.

ICDC is, however, a small operation compared with its counterparts in Tanzania or Uganda: the National Development Corporation (NDC) in Tanzania and the Uganda Development Corporation (UDC) in Uganda. Tanzania and Uganda are both poorer countries than Kenya, but their governments have pursued a more vigorous policy towards national control of industrialisation than has Kenya. For example, much of Uganda's basic industry (including textiles, cement, fertiliser plant, tea estates, tourism and urban property), as well as part of copper mining, grain-milling, fish and meat processing, and other enterprises, is owned by parastatal organisations.

DFCK is involved in over twenty large foreign investments, and even in this diluted form of Kenyan ownership and finance of foreign investment, there is clearly more scope for the Government's views to be presented than would be the case if the enterprise were entirely foreign owned and financed.

IV.3 FOREIGN INVESTMENT

Kenya is a classic case of foreign investment dominating the employment and investment picture of a less developed country,[1] and we shall be able, using the Guidelines, to capture the income and employment effects of specific projects which are especially important in Kenya since the social value of growth largely depends on the social value of a few large projects.[2,3]

1. However, unlike India, there is next to nothing in the way of official reports on government policy towards POI in Keyna.
2. See the list of projects given in *Republic of Kenya Development Plan, 1970—4*, p. 306.
3. In so far as this strategy is followed, project analysis is going to be important,

We discuss now the financial and technological contribution of private overseas investment to the Kenyan economy, and also whether, in the Kenyan case, foreign investment can be said to impede the development of local industry. Investment requirements over the second Plan period amount to K£440m., of which K£100m. is estimated to be placed in the manufacturing sector. There are insufficient domestic savings to finance this amount of investment. The government's total investment programme over the five-year period is K£100m., so clearly the Government's financial

Table 3 *Net Inflows of Long-term Capital Inflow and Net Outflows of Investment Income 1957—68*

| | K£'000 | | | |
	Net inflow of capital	Net outflow of income	Retained earnings after tax, foreign investment	Total net inflow
1957	1,119	5,360	—	−4,241
1958	650	5,450	—	−4,800
1959	375	7,016	—	−6,641
1960	5,642	7,283	—	−1,821
1961	−5,133	5,341	—	−10,474
1962	−2,696	4,845	—	−7,541
1963	9,800	9,843	3,514	−43
1964	10,800	8,665	3,546	2,135
1965	8,800	8,731	3,019	69
1966	2,100	8,750	2,800	−6,650
1967	4,100	9,170	4,400	−5,070
1968	9,000	9,590	5,000	−590

Source: East African Community Statistical Department and Central Bank of Kenya.
Notes: (a) net increase in long-term liabilities (represented by equity capital, loan and debenture capital, and retained profits after tax)
 (b) net outflows of dividends and interest, and retained earnings after tax.

and this must be done by the Government, since foreign investors are often, for instance, insistent on the presence of risk requiring 'high profits'.

In the *Development Plan, 1970—4*, p. 315, there is a statement of the government intention to play a 'more active role in the industrialisation process', by means of industrial surveys and promotion work, feasibility studies of single projects, industry and inter-industry studies rather than 'merely reviewing proposals submitted by private enterprise to determine their eligibility for protection'.

participation in industrialisation will be limited to a very small amount (estimated at K£1m.); although there are, in addition, the funds of the parastatal organisations, which are discussed above.

The recent financial contribution of private investment to Kenya is presented in Table 3.[1]

The fall in net liabilities in 1961 and 1962 reflects pre-Independence risk; in 1963 and 1964 we get unexpected results because there were large inflows into the electricity sector (which were later bought out). Retained earnings were

---

1. Needleman, Lall, Lacey, Seagrave (NLLS), in 'Balance of Payments Effects of Private Foreign Investment', UNCTAD, T.D./B./C/3 79 Add. 2 suggest that 45% of foreign long-term liabilities in Kenya are in manufacturing; 25% in trade and finance; 12% in construction and electricity (1960). Taking this 45% figure, then the contribution to capital expenditure in manufacturing by foreign long-term inflows is about 35% in 1966, 33% [1967], 42% [1968]; this is, of course, not the same as the 'contribution' to capital expenditure by POI as a whole.

These authors also present a table:

LOCAL AND FOREIGN-OWNED FIRMS IN MANUFACTURING
IN KENYA, 1968

	Number of 'foreign' firms	Number of 'local' firms
Food	23	6
Beverages and tobacco	11	–
Textiles (including clothing)	13	4
Footwear	3	*
Leather and rubber	6	3
Wood, paper, printing and packaging	27	20[a]
Chemicals, pharmaceuticals and petroleum products	18	*
Non-metallic minerals	6	–
Metal products	23	2
Transport equipment	6	17

*very large number of small local enterprises engaged in manufacturing.
(a) mostly sawmills.

Source: compiled from the Members' index of the Association of East African Industries; and from National Christian Council of Kenya, *Who controls industry in Kenya?* (Nairobi, 1968).

A foreign enterprise is defined as one in which a proportion of equity of the company is held by a non-resident institution. This definition would include enterprises where a large percentage of equity is held locally; more important, the 'local' column includes enterprises owned by European and Asian non-citizens. Such enterprises might manage to remit substantial funds abroad, although they do not enjoy the protection extended to POI.

more or less constant until 1967, when they rose by about 50%. Note that for some years retained earnings were positive, yet net inflow was negative. Of course, even in these years, some investible funds accrued to the Government (through tax payments).

Whitehead[1] has argued that the errors and omissions term in the balance of payments might be significantly negative in an economy accepting a large amount of foreign investment, perhaps as evidence that private overseas investment is remitting a larger sum to the developed world than is declared to the authorities. We have the following data:

Table 4 *Net Private Long-term Capital Flows, 1964—68*

			K£m			
	1964	1965	1966	1967	1968	Total 1964—68
Recorded flows in the balance of payments	Dr 15.0	1.5	1.0	7.9	10.5	5.9
Balance of payments errors and omissions	Dr. 5.1	Dr. 5.9	4.4	3.7	6.0	3.1
Totals	Dr. 20.1	Dr. 4.4	5.4	11.6	16.5	9.0

Source: *Development Plan, 1970—4*, 1969, p. 62.

reflecting the impact of the imposition of Exchange Control in 1965 until which private enterprises were sending out a significant proportion of their savings abroad. We should remember the microeconomics of this process; what these aggregate figures are reflecting is the typical time profile of an act of foreign investment, which is distorted by risk.

There has only been a small inflow of foreign capital over the period as a whole. Since 1965 there has been a recorded inflow of private capital, but including the errors and omissions terms, we get a total net inflow over 1964 to 1968 of K£9.0m.

1. In B. Ward, et al., eds., *The Widening Gap: Development in the 1970s* (Columbia, 1970), ch. 5.

But we should note that 'recorded flows in the balance of payments' in Table 4 includes net increase in foreign long-term assets held by Kenya residents, and this includes, importantly, intra-East African flows. Thus the 1967 and 1968 figures in Table 3 and Table 4 can be reconciled by noticing that nationalisation of Kenyan-owned assets by Tanzania in 1967 and 1968 led to credit capital movements of K£4.8m. (1967) and K£1½m. (1968). Thus the net inflow of private capital into Kenya from outside East Africa is substantially lower than appears in Table 4.

Data on POI flows for the period post-1968 is currently being assembled. We should however note that we should really be looking at the whole picture of aid, POI, and domestic savings, but this is a very large research topic in its own right. Some relevant data is, however, shown in Table 5.

Table 5   Some Economic Ratios

	1964	1965	1966	1967	1968
$\dfrac{\text{Gross investment}}{\text{GNP}} \times 100$	13.6	14.8	18.9	21.8	20.4
$\dfrac{\text{Gross national savings}}{\text{GNP}} \times 100$	15.8	14.0	17.2	17.6	16.2
$\dfrac{\text{Gross domestic savings}}{\text{GDP}} \times 100$	17.4	15.5	18.5	19.2	17.0
Gross capital inflow K£m	–	–	7.4	11.1	13.2

Source: *Development Plan, 1970–4*, 1969, p. 61.

Foreign investment makes a difference to the nature of debates on choice of technique since its presence affects the timing and size of the reinvestible surplus. But the direct effects on surplus generated are not the only ones worth mentioning; we have seen that Harris and Todaro argue that Kenya's choice is between an economy characterised by high productivity, low employment, and a poor income distribution, or one characterised by lower productivity but higher employment and an improved income distribution. 'Local' labour-intensive enterprises, with lower wages, and perhaps a greater surplus for reinvestment, might be possible. For this to be true, certain assumptions have to hold about the existence of alternative techniques, about savings behaviour, and about the nature of productivity growth.

We consider here technology. We were not able to test the technological epoch hypothesis for Kenya. This hypothesis asserts that when there is a (statistically) significant change in factor shares and a change in the aggregate elasticity of substitution then we pass from one 'technological epoch' to another. Increasing foreign investment may result in Kenya switching from one technological epoch to another. Econometrically, the task is too time-consuming, and anyway, there is a lack of suitable data. It may be the case that the technology used by foreign investors in some cases dominates any possible 'local' techniques; that is, these technologies may be more efficient than 'local' techniques at any factor-price ratio.

Of course, the decision on choice of industries to be established is probably more important with regard to employment and growth than the decision on the choice of capital-intensity for a particular industrial process. There appears to have been little feasibility analysis on small industries, with a total fixed capital of, say, K£50,000, where there are not already existing competitors elsewhere in East Africa. Existing industries producing elsewhere in the East African Community and protected by internal tariffs, may sell in Kenya, and a small Kenya industry may have great difficulty in selling in these countries. So labour-intensive industries may satisfy the whole of the present East African market, leaving Kenya to industrialise through more capital-intensive techniques, if she cannot find small industries of her own. Kenya's present experience with small industries (usually smaller than the ones we have in mind here) are described below in the Appendix. The argument is, of course, that Kenyanisation, small industry and rapid labour absorption could proceed hand in hand; such industry is unlikely to be of interest to the private overseas investor.

Returning to choice of technique for foreign investment ventures, there is a good deal of evidence both on technological flexibility and on industries which, although not very flexible in technique, are fairly labour-intensive.[1] It is clear, however, that not too much weight should be placed on this sort of evidence which is usually presented in the form of cross-country comparisons of factor intensity at a point in time. Much depends on the nature and completeness of the industrial classification. Further, the figures given are historical figures, whose valuation is sometimes doubtful, and, if the data is grouped on a country basis, they often represent a variety of techniques. The only way to identify choice of technique in practice is to examine existing and potential blueprints of machinery and plant. We briefly review two possibilities: second-hand machinery and capital-goods production.

In terms of vintage capital theory, there is a *prima facie* case for the use of second-hand capital equipment in Kenya, since quasi-rents of old machinery will still be relatively high in a country with a low wage-level. Clearly the stream of quasi-rents is reduced if the second-hand machinery is wasteful in the use of raw materials, requires a heavy complement of skilled (i.e. maintenance) workers, and has a short physical life; but this machine is still preferable to a new machine if the saving in investment cost is greater than the loss in discounted quasi-rents. Both inflation in developed countries and developed countries' treatment of depreciation allowances for tax purposes (for example, if the second-hand machine is sold to Kenya at its depreciated price in the developed country) make second-hand machinery relatively more desirable. Second-hand machinery sold by a parent company to its associate in Kenya naturally offers an opportunity for transfer-pricing; correspondingly, there is no easy rule for the Government when bargaining with a foreign investor for goods in which markets are thin.

Production of capital goods might be considered plausible in Kenya, since she already has a wide range of consumer goods industries, and it is not clear what she should import-substitute against next; Howard Pack and Michael

1. See the list of industries in R. B. Sutcliffe, *Industry & Underdevelopment*, (Addison-Wesley, 1971, pp. 149–55).

Todaro[1] have provided some figures suggesting some capital goods may be rather labour-intensive in production. The remarks we made above about the usefulness of such figures of capital-intensity of course apply here; and the existence of particular techniques does not say very much about their social profitability, for which we must employ project analysis.

Does foreign investment in Kenya significantly inhibit the growth of local enterprise? This could be the result of foreign investment forcing up the wage level, securing finance from the banking sector and hence making it unavailable to the local enterprise, and, through greater efficiency, forcing out or preventing the entry of local producers. Financial institutions (including commercial banks, finance houses, and bank development corporations) seem to find it more profitable, after taking account of risk, to lend to large foreign companies than to (especially the smaller) local ones; but at the moment, commercial banks' loans could be increased, given the present level of deposits. Since even the East African market is small, scale considerations in many cases prevent new companies, foreign or local, entering Kenya, and, for many commodities imported into Kenya, there are no domestic producers. Given the whole Kenya market, efficient Kenya producers can in many cases sell over the internal tariff barrier; this appears to be rarely possible where the Kenya market is divided across several producers, even though there may be complete protection against imports.

Kenya has, in African terms, an extensive spread of industry, although the individual industry in Kenya has a smaller market than those in, say, Nigeria. Most of the easier (in terms of market, not technology) industries were established in Kenya before independence and were usually based on the whole East African market. Before the Kampala Agreement in 1964, and the imposition of import licensing by Tanzania and Uganda, Kenya's established industries tended to expand in step with the growth of the whole of the

---

1. L. H. Pack and M. P. Todaro, 'Technological transfer, labour absorption and economic development', *Oxford Economic Papers*, 1969.

East African market. Then followed a period in which the large existing consumer-goods industries either established associated projects in Tanzania or Uganda, or deferred expansion until Kenya's market merits it. The East African Community came into being in December 1967 with the signing by Kenya, Uganda and Tanzania of the Treaty for East African Co-operation, and replaced the previous trading system, characterised by heavy quantitative restrictions, by an internal tariff system; this is discussed below.

Despite well-known limitations, effective protection is useful in analysing the effects of trade policy on resource allocation and factor pricing, the international un-competitiveness of particular processes, and in separating out consequences of foreign investment which are its responsibility and those which are the government's responsibility.[1]

Richard Reimer[2] has charted the structure of effective protection for particular industries in Kenya — his estimates range from very high (916.7) to relatively high negative rates (—46.3). As one might expect, final consumption goods, and food processing in particular, are more heavily protected than intermediate and capital goods. Phelps and Wasow find no strong evidence for Kenya satisfying the Stolper-Samuelson theorem, i.e. that the structure of protection encourages capital- and skill-intensive industries, but this is perhaps partly due to Phelps and Wasow[3] not excluding some capital-intensive industries which can be protected by transport costs rather than by tariffs.

The existence of foreign investment strictly represents a departure from assumptions of the effective protection model, but clearly taking account of this departure would involve a good deal of work, without perhaps changing results too much. Another problem with measuring effective protection in an economy containing foreign investment is that although we may appear to be measuring efficiency losses of a process, we may in fact be measuring the effects of transfer

---

1. Not a completely strict separation due to tariff bargaining by foreign investors.
2. Reimer, I. D. S. Staff Paper, 1970. Note that duty drawbacks, when granted on imported inputs, raise the effective rate of protection.
3. Phelps and Wasow, op. cit., p. 14.

pricing at work. This may mean that an activity is worthwhile in itself, but its value is outweighed by the investor's monopoly power.[1]

Kenya is passing the stage of easy import substitution, and will now turn to more sophisticated consumer goods and intermediate and capital goods. Because of limited markets, this stage of import substitution should be contingent on planned specialisation[2] between the three Partner States of the East African Community. Hence, analysis of effective protection rates in East Africa is incomplete without an analysis of the degree of protection given by the Transfer Tax system.

The 1967 Treaty banned most quantitative restrictions and substituted transfer taxes, which are internal tariffs based on trade within East Africa, levied at the value of the commodity on the border of a taxing country, less any duty paid on imported inputs which are subject to duty on entering East Africa. The intention is to give some protection to Kenya in partner states' markets relative to foreign firms while also giving Tanzania and Uganda some protection relative to Kenya (and also to minimise these countries' trade imbalances with Kenya). The transfer system applies only to a limited list of manufactures, and a transfer tax for a particular commodity can only be imposed by a partner state in overall deficit in manufactures with the state against whose commodity the tax is imposed.[3] Since Kenya has the widest range of industries and is the country which foreign

1. Bhagwati and Chakraverty, 'Contributions to Indian Economic Analysis: a survey', *American Economic Review*, Supplement, 1970, p. 63.
2. As in the Andean group of countries in Latin America and the Regional Cooperation for Development scheme (Pakistan, Turkey, Iran).
3. Other principal conditions are: 1. goods of similar description to those taxed should be made or going to be made within three months of imposition of levy by the taxing state; 2. national production capacity for these goods must not be less than 15% of domestic consumption, or not less than £EA100,000 ex-factory; 3. the rate of transfer tax on any one good may not be more than half the rate of external duty on the same good; 4. imports from another East African country may only be taxed up to the value of the deficit in manufactured goods with the importing country; 5. a levy may not be imposed on a commodity of which 30% or more of the production in the state imposing the duty is exported to other states; 6. the sum of transfer tax and excise tax cannot exceed the external tariff; 7. any commodity can be subject to transfer tax for no more than eight years.

investment usually prefers,[1] it is against Kenya that most transfer taxes are levied.

Because imported inputs are subject both to a tariff and a transfer tax, Kenya may, for some values of tax rates and import contents, be at a disadvantage in relation to foreign firms in Tanzania and Uganda.[2] Further, because the taxes that Kenya producers must pay when a Tanzanian competitor is in business must be discounted over time, and because the present value of the protection afforded to the Tanzanian producer accrues largely in the early years of a project, the rule that no commodity can be transfer taxed for more than eight years is not likely to be important. Paradoxically, however, it is unlikely that the transfer tax system will switch new large-scale investments from the presently preferred location to Uganda or Tanzania. Consider a foreign investment project large enough to satisfy the whole East African demand for its product. The costs facing the Kenyan firms will be the direct costs of the transfer tax when exporting to Uganda and Tanzania, plus the indirect costs of the transfer cost decreasing the size of this project's market, due to the incentive given to, say, a Tanzanian competitor. Unless the East African countries are so irrational as to welcome large projects being reproduced in triplicate, all operating far below capacity, it is unlikely that Tanzania will start such an industry for quite a few years, in which case the present value of the disincentives to investing in Kenya will be rather small.

Soon after the Treaty was signed, Tanzania imposed transfer taxes on a wide range of manufactured goods. An examination of Kenyan exports to Tanzania over the period 1960–70 suggests that a rising trend was broken after 1967, although we should remember that the 1964–7 period was disturbed by quantitative restrictions, and the pattern of trade would have been different if the Kampala Agreement had not taken place. For Uganda we have the following (only suggestive) data:

1. Because of better transport and communications, financial and industrial services, more welcoming government policy towards POI, and, most important, Kenya's larger internal market.
2. See P. A. Diamond, 'Effective Protection of the East African Transfer Taxes', *East African Economic Review*, 1968, upon which this paragraph largely draws.

Table 6 Trade with Uganda: Annual Rates of Growth 1960–70

	Rates of growth %	
	Imports	Exports
Before Treaty	9.8	9.6
After Treaty	13.8	9.3

Source: *Republic of Kenya Economic Survey 1971*, Table 3.22.

It should be noted that intra-Community trade has been subject to quite wide fluctuations. Disaggregating, total Kenya exports since the Treaty to the partner states have grown at a faster rate than have those subject to transfer tax.[1]

IV.4 CASE STUDIES I: NATIONAL PARAMETERS
The next few chapters present our case studies of POI in Kenya, based on the Guidelines of Part II. Certain parameters are common to these studies, and these are discussed below, after a brief recapitulation of the basic formula for calculating the return to the host country from the operation of POI.

Using the Guidelines, it is possible to evaluate, in addition to the 'standard' Little-Mirrlees net present value of the project an extra figure showing the net present values of the overseas financial flows associated with the project – typically, capital inflows, loan repayments and dividends, and occasionally, licence fees or fees paid under technical and management agreements. Using the notation adopted in Part III, the total return, at discount rate r, of the project to 'host country capital' is given in the following expression:

$$N(r) = S(r) - C(r) - M(r) - L(r) - I(r) - F(r)$$

where

$N(r)$ is net present value of the project as a whole
$S(r)$ is present value of sales revenue
$C(r)$ is present value of costs other than labour and materials

1. As reported in *Economic Survey*, 1971.

M(r) and L(r) are present values of material cost, and of labour costs

I(r) is present value of capital costs

and F(r) is present value of net cash flow abroad associated with the project

In the studies below, net present values are calculated on the basis of market prices and of 'world prices' under various assumptions. For market price calculations units are Kenya pounds (K£); for 'world price' calculations units are K£ of uncommitted foreign exchange.

Before going on to consider the shadow wage, a word may be said about externalities. The present study was intended to focus on externalities, particularly the effect of private overseas investment on technique in the host country — technological externality — and the labour-training effects of the projects under consideration.[1] To deal with the latter first, it may be said that the labour market in Kenya is so slack that few unskilled or semi-skilled workers would be in a position to take the benefits of their training elsewhere and thereby to represent an external economy for the training firm. As far as skilled workers are concerned, there is no evidence from either of the projects considered here of any labour-training external economy. It is even more unlikely that any data on technological transfer would be collected. In short, the present study gives no ground for dissent from the remark in the *Manual* that 'there is little chance, anyway of measuring any of these supposed external economies'.[2]

The Shadow Wage
The basic expression for the shadow wage rate (SWR) is:

$$SWR = c - \frac{(c - m)}{s}$$

where c is workers' consumption evaluated at border prices, and $(c - m)$ is the increase in consumption generated by the employment of an additional worker. The value of m is, therefore, consumption, at accounting prices, of the worker's

1. See Guidelines, Chap. II.5.
2. *Manual*, p.37.

previous occupation, which is conventionally taken to be in agriculture.[1] The number s expresses the value of one unit of savings relative to one unit of consumption; its excess over unity indicates the extent of deviation of actual from optimal savings. The shadow wage, then, consists of the actual consumption of the worker, minus a factor reflecting the weight attached to the improvement in consumption he enjoys compared with his previous conditions; for s = 1 (optimal savings), the SWR = m. For s = → ∞, SWR = c.

In the calculation of s, the present study uses the formula:[2]

$$S_1 = (1 + \tfrac{1}{2}(r_1 - i_1))^T$$

r_1 is the accounting rate of interest in the initial period; i_1 is the equivalent consumption rate of interest. T is the period of years at the end of which a unit of savings and a unit of consumption will be considered equally valuable. In making the short-cut from the more direct method of calculating described in Chapter 13 of Little-Mirrlees, we are obliged to assume a steady closing of the gap between r and i over the T years. As all the numerical calculations are highly speculative, the marginal cost of this assumption seems minimal.

In assigning values to the parameters we shall follow the work of N. H. Stern[3]; r is, in principle, the internal rate of return of the marginal public project. A value of 10% will stand as a proxy for this figure, on the argument that the Government of Kenya can, if it chooses, borrow abroad to finance a marginal project at an interest rate of 10%. The value of T, the number of years to elapse before the sub-optimality of savings is eliminated, is very hard to estimate. In N. H. Stern's study, a value of 30 years is adopted, yielding 1997 as the year in which optimality is achieved. The same value is adopted in this study, though it is largely

---

1. This is a simplification; the employment afforded by a project may cause a chain of job changes from one sector to another. The value of m is the value of consumption of the worker at the end of the chain, in his previous occupation. See F. Seton, *Shadow wages in the Chilean Economy* (OECD, Paris, 1972), and Part II, above.
2. *Manual*, pp. 178–9.
3. N. H. Stern, *An Appraisal of Smallholder Tea in Kenya* (OECD, Paris, 1972).

chosen at random, and we fear that the target date may recede into the future as it is approached.

The estimation of the consumption rate of interest requires some sort of social utility function. Without too much loss of generality we may take a constant elasticity utility function, dependent on consumption:

$$u'(c) = kc^{-e}$$

As we are for the moment concerned with the distribution of consumption over time, and not its distribution at any point in time, c may be taken as average consumption per head; k is a scale factor. Obviously a high value of e will reflect concern for a more equal distribution of consumption over time. With these assumptions the value of i is given by:

$$i = \left(\frac{Ct + 1}{Ct}\right)^{e} - 1$$

Taking the rate of growth of incomes and of consumption to be 4% per annum, this reveals the following value of s for the two values of e to be used in this study:

$$e = 1 : s = 2.421$$

$$e = 2 : s = 1.318$$

On the assumptions made by Stern (that c = 3750 k. sh. p.a. and m = 400 k. sh. p.a.) we have, that, for e = 1, SWR = 63% of the market wage; for e = 2, SWR = 36% of the market wage, before multiplication, in both cases, by the standard conversion factor.

To take account of income distribution at a given time, the Government would, in principle, be able to design welfare weights to benefits accruing to different sections of the population, in the style of J. S. Meade,[1] as it will do implicitly in making policy decisions. However, the information obtained in these weights will be approximate at best, and in any case, not available to the investigator. The constant elasticity utility function:

$$u'(c) = kc^{-e}$$

has two parameters, the rate of change term 'e' and the scale

1. J. S. Meade, *Trade and Welfare* (Oxford University Press, 1955).

term 'k'. For any e, the scale term k is obtained as in Chap. II.6, as $\bar{C}C^*_{(e-1)}$ where $\bar{C}$ is mean consumption and $C^*_{(e-1)}$ is the harmonic mean of degree $e-1$ of the distribution of consumption. The following values are obtained for the shadow wage:

$$e = 1 : SWR = c - \frac{k_1}{s_1} \log\left(\frac{c}{m}\right)$$

$$e = 2 : SWR = c - \frac{k_2}{s_2}\left(\frac{1}{m} - \frac{1}{c}\right)$$

where k_1 and k_2 are the scale factors for their respective values of e:

$$k_1 = \bar{C}$$
$$k_2 = \bar{C}C^*_{(1)}$$

An entirely analogous procedure may be used to take account of differences in average incomes in different regions.

The difficulty in putting the above method into practice lies in finding the required data. For regional income distribution the most recent available data for Kenya was published in 1962, and includes money incomes only, as the following table indicates:

Table 7 Distribution of Monetary Income in Kenya, 1962, by Old Province

Old Province	Population '000's	Per Capita Monetary Product K£
Nairobi EPP	315	252
Coast	728	39
Rift Valley	1049	23
Central	1925	12
Nyanza	3013	6
Southern	1014	5
Northern	590	3
Total	8634	21
Total excluding Nairobi and Mombasa	8139	9

Source: *Republic of Kenya Development Plan 1966–70* (Nairobi, 1966), p. 29, Table 15.

Calculations with this data will be to little purpose. In recognising this necessity we may take comfort from the fact that the effects of regional income disparities will partly be taken into account by calculations using national income distribution data. The government may be equally dissatisfied by a random distribution of income over the entire country and rigid segregation of rich and poor in different regions. To take into account regional as well as national income distribution may lead us to favour the rich in poor regions or to disparage the improvement in the position of those poor living in relatively well-off regions. The condition which justifies regional income weights — immobility of resources from one region to another — does not seem to be operative in Kenya.

National distribution of income data is for Kenya nearly as inadequate as the regional data. The data available in the Statistical Abstracts 1970 is segregated by race, with over-lapping intervals for the different races and no averages available for income receivers in each interval. Even more serious is the absence from the coverage of rural labour and the urban unemployed or casual labourer.

In these circumstances it was considered best to adopt from another country the income distribution parameter in ques-tion: the ratio of the harmonic mean of degree $e - 1$ to the arithmetic mean. Dr. Seton[1] has calculated this statistic for Argentine in 1961, for the United Kingdom in 1959 and 1966, and for the USA in the mid-thirties and in 1959. In Part III, the equivalent statistic for India was calculated for 1955/56. The range of variation for $e = 2$, is from 0.6729 for India to 0.548 for USA in 1959. In the present study we have adopted an intermediate value 0.6300, that of Argentine, as a proxy for Kenya's income distribution, in the belief that the comparatively small variation shown over a range of widely differing economies will prove this assump-tion to be not unreasonable.

Having determined the variation, we must now estimate the mean. The information required — total consumption

---

1. F. Seton, *The Shadow Wage Rate in Chile* (OECD, Paris, 1972).

and number of persons actively engaged — is taken from the *Kenya Development Plan 1970–74,* tables 2.24 and 2.41. For 1968 we obtain an estimated K£90 p.a. as consumption per worker. Of course, data on total consumption, including as it does consumption in the non-monetary sector, is open to some doubts; and difficulties and discrepancies in the data on persons actively engaged (incomplete coverage, double counting etc.) are outlined on page 68 of the Development Plan.

We may now proceed to numerical estimates of the shadow wage, bringing together the threads of the previous discussion. Hitherto consumption and income have naturally been distinguished, but in the calculation below, and in the case studies, the difference between them, savings, is ignored. The effects on income distribution are shown in the following table. Throughout m is taken as K£20 p.a. and values of s and k as summarised here.

$$e = 1 \; : \; s = 2.42 \quad k = 90$$
$$e = 2 \; : \; s = 1.32 \quad k = 5103$$

Table 8 Shadow Wage Rates

| | $e = 1$ | | | | $e = 2$ | | | |
| | Distribution accounted | | Distribution ignored | | Distribution accounted | | Distribution ignored | |
Market Wage	SWR K£	SWR as % of market wages	SWR K£	SWR as % of market wage	SWR K£	SWR as % of market wage	SWR K£	SWR as % of market wage
100	30	30	67	67	−55	−55	39	39
150	75	50	96	62	−18	−12	51	34
200	114	57	126	63	26	13	63	32
250	154	62	155	62	72	29	75	30
300	199	66	185	62	119	40	88	29
400	289	72	243	61	216	54	112	28
500	380	76	302	60	314	63	136	27

A curiosity of the results is the negative sign of the shadow wage of low income groups when e = 2. However this need not cause surprise: the very high value attached to the increase in income achieved by the lower-paid (relative to

their previous assumed consumption level of K£20 p.a.)
outweighs the nominal cost to the economy of this extra
consumption.[1] Different values of m have been tried
experimentally. For e = 2, the shadow wage of a man
earning K£100 p.a. is zero at an m value of only K£27. Thus
the results are sensitive to small absolute changes in m.

We were able to collect data on income levels in the firms
studied in sufficient detail to apply the above table. Indirect
labour inputs are a problem though. In the study of firms in
India in Part III, it was assumed that the income distribution
in firms supplying the chemical factories was the same as that
of the factory employees. For the case of Kenya, we are
making no such correction. This amounts to the assumption
that the sum of indirect inputs going into the firms analysed
in this study are produced under income distribution
conditions representative of the economy as a whole. This
doubtful assumption is made more respectable when we
remember that the average consumption figure used in this
study is average per persons actively engaged, and not average
per head of population. Of course, any government committed to the methods outlined in the Little-Mirrless Manual
and wishing to incorporate income distribution considerations on the lines of the Guidelines in Part II, will be able to
dispense with this and other cavalier assumptions of the
present study, at the cost of a little research.

The rest of the analysis follows the standard form. Maurice
Scott's[2] extremely useful input-output tables for non-

---

1. As a check we calculated what government-supported income level would yield
the same result. In countries where the government is committed to maintaining a
minimum level by welfare payments, Maurice Scott suggests evaluating k by
putting the marginal utility of consumption at that income level equal to the
value of uncommitted government resources channelled to consumption. This is
done by solving for c the equation:

$$u'(c) = \frac{K}{c^e} = s(e)$$

where s is a function of e, as shown by the expression in the text. The results: for
e = 1, c = K£37; for e = 2, c = K£62.

2. Maurice Scott, 'Notes on the Estimation of Accounting Prices for some
non-tradeable and tradeable goods in Kenya'. Mimeo, 1970, to be included in Scott,
MacArthur and Newbery, *Project Appraisal in Practice* (Heinemann), forthcoming.

tradeable goods have been used where possible. A standard conversion factor of 0.75[1] has been used in all calculations.

IV.5 CASE STUDIES II: FOOD PROCESSING

(i) Pineapple canning

Our study began with a decision not to examine smallholder or plantation activities but in a predominantly agricultural economy such as Kenya's, we find agricultural processing to be a very important industry. Thus, in Kenya, agricultural processing is the second largest industry after motor repairs. We will not, however, discuss agronomic questions except in so far as they affect the viability of a processing plant.

Urban middle-class populations in the less developed world tend to consume more 'European' fruit and vegetables as their income rises, but, if a food goes to a market where the majority of consumers are rather poor, there is little point in expenditures to improve quality or secure uniformity of the product. Hence, in the industry we examine – pineapple canning – most producing countries trade a large proportion of their production. Processed produce now accounts for 10% of total consumption of fruit and vegetables and as much as 30% in the U.K. and Northern America (somewhat less in Europe). Of the canned fruits, pineapple is the second largest (after canned peaches) in international trade. Market analysis[2] of the world pineapple market suggests that the three major importers – the U.K., U.S. and West Germany – are near saturation level, in part because canned pineapple is often somewhat more expensive than canned peaches (for which pineapple is a close substitute) and in part because of increasing popularity of fresh produce and exotic canned fruit, such as papaya, mango, passion-fruit and guava. Parts of Europe other than West Germany appear to be the only remaining market growth areas; it is generally believed, for instance, that the French market is capable of considerable expansion, since pineapples there have been subject to a

1. As calculated by M. Scott, op. cit.
2. United Kingdom Tropical Foods Institute, "A Review of world production and trade in canned pineapple", 1965.

heavy import duty and to a value-added tax, calculated on duty-paid value, in order to protect high-cost producers in the French Community.

In the 1950s and 1960s the producing countries had to face a period of adjustment to lower market prices (South African prices, for instance, fell from £162 in 1954 to £80 in 1962; there has been some recovery since then), and, therefore, rationalised their production, both in the field and cannery. Hawaii, with its high labour costs and freight costs to its major markets is facing strong competition from low-cost producers such as Taiwan, Malaysia and South Africa. There has been a very large increase in production in South Africa; and, in this period of world over-supply, many countries' trade was threatened.

It is difficult to forecast future production in pineapples since the fruit is yielded rather quickly (usually 18–24 months after planting), there is a large supply of land throughout the world suitable for pineapple production, and most of world production takes place on smallholdings. As the growth in the pineapple market has slowed down, the brand image and the label, associated with high-quality fruit, has become more important. Uniform fruit is rare even under ideal growing conditions; however, for most export markets high-quality produce is required.

The present trade is increasingly characterised by direct selling by exporters to wholesale traders in the developed world; making it more essential for producers to offer a continuous supply and high quality. One difficulty is whether these marketing arrangements encourage the attainment and maintenance of the competitive solution in pineapples. Rather little work appears to have been done on the social value of alternative marketing arrangements. If, as appears to be the case, the world pineapple market (like that for other food products) is becoming increasingly determined by large selling organisations, who are often producers and processors of the raw product, then if the farm-gate (or, in the case of a processed food-product, the factory-gate) price is determined by fixed margins (percentage or absolute) for other services (transport, wholesaling etc.), unless rather stringent conditions are satisfied the competitive solution is not obtained.

An international company decides to locate, or continue to locate, in a particular country if its presence there is justified by the long-term comparative advantage of that country. Companies with interests in high-cost locations, such as Hawaii, are likely to want to enter potential low-cost areas, of which Kenya may be an example. In a static market where quality and brand names are considered important, there may be little chance of breaking into a market without established markets; if so, the choice is not whether a country should 'employ' the services of an international company for processing and marketing, but the terms and conditions on which it should do so. The host country should, for example, examine the margins which a vertically integrated canning and marketing operation takes, remembering that cross-country comparisons are unhelpful since they represent a combination of differing technologies and factor costs. Certainly producers do not necessarily receive a higher proportion of retail price under an 'advanced' marketing system, and transfer pricing could occur at several stages — at the plantation, the factory, the importing port, or the wholesaler. Speaking rather generally, there are two views about transfer pricing — the first, that it is an important element in the costs of accepting private overseas investment; the second that its relative importance recedes when compared with other costs and benefits of POI. Our method can capture transfer pricing, but the quantity and quality of information required is rather high. In some cases, however, the effort should be made.

At several stages of a canning operation, machines and manual workers are interchangeable; however, sometimes attempts to reduce initial capital requirements have raised processing costs more than they have saved on borrowed capital. Small-scale enterprises are also possible, since a fruit-canning plant is based on little more than a boiler and simple can-closing equipment. Such small plants operate in Tanzania and Ethiopia, serving domestic markets.

Costs of production typically depend on production coefficients of the order: raw materials (pineapples and sugar): c.31%, packing (cans, labels, corrugated and board paper): c.47%, salaries and wages: c. 13%, and direct costs:

c.10%. The last two figures refer to production costs only. So the prices charged for pineapples, sugar, and packing materials are very important for the profitability of the enterprises; and if, say, the domestic metal can industry is heavily protected, then the social profitability of a pineapple cannery tends to exceed its private profitability. The obstacles to the development of canned fruits in India, for instance, during the mid-1960s were sugar costs well above the world price and the use of domestic tinplate protected well above world prices, and poor in quality. A number of pineapple canning countries (not Kenya) subsidise the price of sugar to canneries. Pineapple supply, prices and quality are highly important, but the extraction rate of usable pineapple is only about one-third of the crop.

Most pineapple producers — except Hawaii — depend heavily on international trade, but Kenya depends on foreign trade more than most. While an average of 50% of the product enters the international market, in Kenya 90% is exported, so Kenya is more vulnerable than most producers to world price fluctuations, and is herself unable to influence these prices, producing only about 2% of world output.

The Smooth Cayenne pineapple is grown in Kenya, and the fruit grown in the Kiambu/Thika area is very suitable for processing. However altitude is very important — the best altitude for fruit for canning is 4,500—5,500 ft., above which height the fruit is pale in colour and has a weak flavour, and below 4,500 ft. the fruit is often insipid. The industry has been handicapped in the past by a high proportion of fruit grown at altitudes exceeding 5,500 ft., so reducing the proportion of first-grade fruit.[1]

1. There is a report of a possible K£5m. scheme near Thika to expand pineapple production and processing. 'Back of the envelope' calculations suggest that such a scheme would have a very large impact on the economy of the host region, which is subject to heavy population pressure; illustrative figures include a full-capacity export production of K£13m., with a payroll of over 15,000 workers. The 1969 population of Thika was 19,000; the scheme would have, say, 45,000 workers and dependents. Such an export value would make Kenya a 'large' pineapple producer.

Thika is a 'designated growth centre' (*Development Plan*, p. 86). Designated growth centres are intended to relieve congestion in Nairobi and slow down its growth. Calculations of the SWR should include regional corrections on the lines of the Guidelines to take account of the project's favourable regional impact.

While sales are made in world markets where Kenya has no control over the prices obtained, the purchase price of raw pineapple (roughly one-third of the cost of production) is fixed by Government and in the past has not been directly related to the prices obtained for the raw product. Foreign investors seeking entry into the Kenyan pineapple industry have usually sought guarantees on price and quantity produced, to relate the selling price of canned pineapples to the growers' price. Government-fixed prices vary very greatly, according to the grade of fruit, naturally with the intention of raising the proportion of first-grade fruit. Pineapples have been declared a 'Special Crop' so that the Canning Crops Board has authority to control pineapple movement into the domestic fresh market which has been growing rapidly.

The Kenyan pineapple industry began in 1950 when canned pineapple was extremely scarce, particularly in the U.K., the principal market for Kenya's produce, and one protected by Commonwealth preference. Throughout its life the industry has been considered one of major development significance in view of its foreign-exchange earnings, the labour-intensity of its production, and the incomes accruing to smallholder producers.

Kenya has faced most of the production problems discussed in the analysis of smallholder pineapple, although some observers feel that tight organisation coupled with technical assistance could make smallholder pineapple a success for Kenya in the same way that smallholder tea is a success.[1] The profitability of the canning industry has been threatened by years of drought interspersed unevenly with years of overproduction exacerbated by smallholders growing up to 3rd to 5th ratoon crops. In addition to government research the private sector has attempted to inject its agricultural knowledge into the outgrowers' operations, and one large company in the 1960s took over a derelict sisal estate to make trial plantings and select areas for expanded plantation production of pineapple.

It should be made very clear that the project we examine

1. See N. H. Stern, *An Appraisal of Smallholder Tea in Kenya* (OECD, Paris, 1972).

does not represent any existing company's operations in Kenya. The project examined is a feasibility study of a project considering the possibilities of modernising and expanding an existing small pineapple-processing plant. The mechanisation proposed included the provision of conveyors and belting. It was felt that too many operations in the production lines were carried out by hand, the operatives not being able to operate at the same rate as the mechanised sections: the reduction in wage costs (due to paying workers for evening and weekend work) to achieve the desired throughput was considered to be more than the increase in capital required. In addition, machinery would be installed to pack vegetables during the slack season for pineapple deliveries, so reducing overheads and maximising capacity utilisation.

This project, owned by a group of local non-citizen firms, had been experiencing technical and financial difficulties for some years; members' interest had become considerably less than the net value of fixed assets necessitating long-term borrowing for working capital. There had been some injection of ICDC loans, finance houses and public development corporations were unwilling to take a financial interest in the project unless technical and marketing services could be obtained from an established international canning organisation (an ICO). However, companies approached appeared to demand an option to secure control; indeed such companies would plausibly seek to control as much equity as possible, in order to avoid interference by minority share-holders.

Therefore it is assumed that an agreement was signed giving the ICO an option to purchase a majority of equity after five years; during those five years, the ICO would provide management and technical services, and would market the output of the project through its international sales organisation. The ICO would take over all management in the initial five-year period, controlling all production operations and the pineapple-growing expansion programme and purchase of raw materials; the company providing a General Manager (i.e. in U.K. terms a Managing Director), a Financial Manager and possibly one other executive, and some technical personnel. For these services the ICO would receive an annual fee of 3% of annual sales (the usual way of evaluating a managing agency and technical service fee is to base it on the gross profit margin). Concerning the marketing agreement, the vast bulk of the sales would be made against the ICO's label. It might be noted that one machinery-exporting firm offered to manage the project (and sell probably an excessive amount of machinery); the offer was refused because it did not have access to the world market, even though it was willing to hire the services of a selling organisation.

In the appraisal below we assume that production targets are met; although we should recall that the pineapple industry in Kenya since the assumed inauguration of this project has been subject to severe production difficulties, due to very low deliveries to the canneries. The ICO is assumed here to hold no equity for the first five years, although it provides some loan capital; thereafter the ICO has a majority shareholding.

Results. Foreign cost of capital, as explained above, came out at 8.1%.

	IRR	NPV at 10%	NPV at 20%
1. Little-Mirrlees prices e = 1; SCF = 0.75; domestic-financed	14%	K£89,000	−K£183,000
2. Little-Mirrlees prices e = 1; SCF = 0.75; foreign-financed	21%	K£111,000	K£27,000
3. Little-Mirrlees prices e = 2; SCF = 0.75; domestic-financed	16%	K£110,000	−K£132,000
4. Little-Mirrlees prices e = 2; SCF = 0.75; foreign-financed	24%	K£135,000	K£76,000

These results would be considerably modified if we had been able to take into account the conditions under which inputs are produced.[1] Note that while the capital-labour ratio is quite low, labour input is also low, due to the heavy weight of the raw crop in cost of production at domestic prices.

1. See Stern, op. cit., on the importance of revaluation of the main input, tea labour, in the determination of the social rate of return in Kenyan smallholder tea.

(ii) Cocoa Processing and Soft Drinks

The second food-processing venture we examined was a joint cocoa processing and soft drinks plant. Cocoa beans can be processed into cocoa powder, used in the manufacture of chocolate and chocolate-based drinks and cocoa butter; another by-product is cattle-food produced from the discarded shell of the cocoa beans. Until the building of the new plant, the object of our study, the company owning the new plant packed cocoa from bulk supplies of cocoa powder imported from West Africa, employing eleven men and, in 1971, importing 400 tons of cocoa, on which about K£17,000 was paid in duty.

As part of the new project producing both soft drinks and cocoa-based products, the new K£1.2m. plant will turn Kenya from a cocoa powder importer to an exporter of cocoa powder and cocoa butter, in addition to manufacturing chocolate and cocoa-based products. Cocoa beans requirements in the first year of operation will be 1,200 tons, most of which will have to be imported from West Africa, since East African production is limited to a CDC project in Tanzania producing about 200 tons. The parent company of the Kenya operation has agreed to accept all the Kenyan production of cocoa butter, giving a large foreign-exchange 'saving'.

The social advantage of this project depends on the social cost of transforming the raw food product in Kenya, as opposed to importing it from West Africa. At the present moment, cocoa beans are subject to a 30% tariff and cocoa powder to a 15% tariff. The company sponsoring the project, which has substantial interests in the cocoa industry in West Africa and hence a wide knowledge of the technology of the industry, argued that the tariff on cocoa beans should be removed since the project would turn Kenya from an importer of cocoa powder into an exporter of cocoa powder, chocolate-based products, and cocoa butter, the last source of export receipts being guaranteed by the company; these receipts would cover the 'loss' due to the tariff on imported beans. With a 30% duty on beans, the cocoa products side of the new project would be privately unprofitable. Agreement has, in fact, been reached with the Government to provide a customs drawback on imported beans; the tariff on cocoa powder and chocolate, etc. (at a higher rate than that on cocoa powder) remains. It should be noted that the cocoa market has fluctuated widely in recent years, reaching prices of between S£200—S£500 per ton on the London market; an international cocoa agreement may be in the offing. Coffee and tea price movements have been small by comparison.

The soft drinks market in East Africa, and especially Kenya, is growing rapidly (at about 10% compound p.a.), but the share of this company was limited by a production bottleneck which it was felt could only be eliminated by the purchase of a new production line. The initial choices facing the company were making use of existing plant in Nairobi and Mombasa; purchasing an additional plant and running it alongside the present plant; purchasing a new plant capable of meeting future requirements on one shift, for which a number of suitable pieces of equipment were already available in the old Nairobi plant. It was felt that the first possibility was impracticable because, even running with two shifts, the Nairobi plant would be unable to cope with late 1971 and onwards market demand; the second possibility was uneconomic because the relatively small saving in capital outlay would be outweighed by extra operating costs (two production teams, extra maintenance, power, planning and quality control) and loss of revenue from sale of the existing plant and land. The third possibility would cope with 'foreseeable' future demands on one shift, together with the Mombasa plant being run on a no-profit no-loss basis, with no major capital injection.

The present products sold by the company will be produced by the new factory, and it was felt that later on the project could produce sugar confectionery and jams. The factory is capable of considerable expansion; there has been enough space left for another production line.

Production labour requirements on the cocoa products side is low (about 22 people, in contrast to soft drinks which is much more labour-intensive); in the early years, there will be a substantial excess capacity on this side — the cocoa-making plant will be quickly utilised for 8 hours a day, but machinery for some products (for example, chocolate manufacture, the machinery for which is quite complex) will be operated at only 30% given reasonable sales projections. Second-hand machinery (from the parent company's stock of old machinery in the U.K.) is extensively employed, on the argument that employing new capital would substantially affect the company's return on capital. On choice of technique, we have seen that the decision to cut down on shift working marks an increase in capital-intensity, but even with the labour crew chosen it is uncertain how much of the labour force is simply overmanning, i.e., the 'observed' choice of technique may not be optimal. However, the company did believe that the supervisory content of the labour force was substantially greater than in the U.K. No formal training is undertaken.

The company's products are sold in Kenya through a well-developed distribution system down to the duka level. In the project analysis below, we have netted out the social costs and benefits of distribution, and therefore final products are valued at Nairobi c.i.f. cost.

On finance, the local company follows the parent company's world-wide investment policy of financing projects out of local sources and retentions. This project is financed by retained profits and depreciation, and borrowed money in Kenya to obtain benefits of gearing and enable the company to repatriate its outstanding loans.[1]

For the combined project we see immediately that since the internal rate of return of the domestically financed project is, for both values of the SWR, less than the foreign cost of

---

1. In July 1971, the Kenyan Government imposed credit restrictions in a bid to reduce the balance of trade deficit; how long these restrictions will last is not known. The subsidiary legislation introduced probably should not be interpreted as an attack on the privileges that foreign investment enjoys since it affects local capital as well, but as a predictable reaction to short-run difficulties. The subsidiary legislation laid down restrictions on hire-purchase business (which could finance e.g. machinery imports), reductions in advances to importers of consumer goods; factoring arrangements (banks and other financial institutions undertaking factoring requested not to enter new commitments and to eliminate those outstanding within five months); these arrangements could again finance borrowing for capital expenditure by foreign investors.

Thus local financing of foreign investment extends beyond bank overdrafts, the controls on which were described on p. 180.

Table 9 Cocoa Processing and Soft Drinks
Results: Foreign Cost of Capital: 8.2%

	Domestic finance 'low' SWR/C	Foreign finance 'low' SWR/C	K£ Domestic finance 'high' SWR/C	Foreign finance 'high' SWR/C
NPV at 5%	116,702	82,135	44,018	−25,259
NPV at 8%	0.0089	−5,772	−60,761	−94,840
NPV at 10%	−61,452	−52,227	−115,728	−132,062
NPV at 20%	−245,946	−199,677	−279,108	−246,571
Approximation to NPV is	−0.0088068130	−0.0044026942	−0.0391546451	−0.0040945518
when rate of return is	8.00%	7.78%	6.16%	4.08%

capital, the domestic alternative is less costly than foreign financing of the project, although neither alternative should be undertaken with plausible values of the ARI (see for instance, present values [NPVs] at 10%).

The cocoa side fails completely, failing to give a positive NPV at any positive interest rate; the soft drinks side performs quite well, since soft drinks face a high excise tax, which is levied on the producer, together with high tariffs on inputs. According to Reimer, op.cit., the effective rate of protection is 20.5 per cent.

In Statistical Appendix 2, we show that the soft drinks component of the 'combined' project should be undertaken, preferably financed by foreign capital.

IV.6 CASE STUDIES III: TOURISM

General

World tourist movements and expenditures are expected to rise in the reasonably near future at rates about twice those for commodity trade, and tourism is subject to less fluctuation around trend than most internationally traded commodities.[1] Kenya has fully participated in this growth, which is due mainly to rising incomes in the developed world, together with a high income elasticity of demand for tourism; and to reductions in air travel costs.

Between 1950–1961, total visitor arrivals rose at a rate under 5% p.a., over the period 1961–7, at 18% p.a.; and the projected rate of growth over the 1970–4 Plan period is 20% p.a. Gross product, i.e. value-added and gross foreign exchange earnings, were expected to develop as follows:

	Gross product in tourism, K£m.	Gross foreign exchange K£m.
1968	9.0	15.0
1974	22.0	36.5

Source: *Republic of Kenya Development Plan, 1970–4,* 1969 Table 16.1.

1. Fluctuations are significantly dependent on recessions in the important developed economies, and controls by these countries on foreign tourism expenditures.

However estimates of total visitor arrivals give an incomplete and in some cases inaccurate measure of the growth rate of expenditure in tourism, and the corresponding investment required. The number of visitor arrivals projected should be broken down by purpose of visit (since tourists demand a different vector of goods from that demanded by foreign businessmen), by origin of visitors (Asians and British often do not stay in hotels, but with relations or friends; few Americans go to the beach), by class of tourist (the package tourism business in Kenya only really got under way in the late sixties). We next need to calculate the average number of bed nights per visitor/tourist, expenditure per day on hotel accommodation, food, drink, travel, National Park entrance fees, other goods purchased (different classes of tourists purchase different vectors of goods).[1] The growth rate of expenditure is thus the product of expenditure per visitor day of various classes of visitor/tourists, the length of stay of the various classes and the growth rate of visitors of a particular class. Some of these classes should include local residents. Similarly, we can easily calculate aggregate investment required by the tourist industry; this will depend on changes in the average length of stay, and the stay at different locations, on national and class composition of tourist flows, on occupancy, rates, and on the utilisation of hotel space by domestic tourists. We cannot expect these relations to be stable over time; they are likely to be quite sensitive to price.[2]

The case for expansion of the tourist industry which was accepted by the Kenya Government and is reflected in the current (i.e. 1970—4) *Development Plan* is based on favourable estimates of expenditure flows, a calculation by Frank Mitchell[3] of the national income benefits of existing

1. We cannot include in this figure tourist expenditures syphoned off by foreign carriers and travel agents; travel agents outside Kenya are obliged by law to remit prepayments, i.e. payments made to travel agents outside Kenya on inclusive package holidays to cover travel and accommodation in Kenya. Such remittances (totalling nearly K£3m.) are probably an underestimate given the growing proportion of package holidays (*Republic of Kenya Economic Survey, 1971*).
2. Optimal tax rates will also differ.
3. F. Mitchell, 'Costs and benefits of tourism in Kenya', *East African Economic Review*, June 1970.

(i.e. 1967) tourism in Kenya, and favourable results generated by some simple sectoral analysis. These measures are discussed below. The execution of the revised tourism development plan for 1970–4 was vested in the Kenya Tourist Development Corporation (KTDC).[1]

As usual in Kenya, the target increase in capacity is composed of a limited number of large projects, some of which were appraised and finalised rather late; however, a substantial proportion of international class beds, in Nairobi, the game parks, and at the Coast, were completed early in the Plan period. Overall the Plan implies a near doubling of hotel capacity over the period 1968 to 1974; finance required to meet the hotel development programme is K£10.5m, of which K£3m. is from the public sector.[2,3] The execution of the Plan has been troubled by construction costs above estimates, and receipts below estimates. As the Plan period proceeds, a switch in markets is already apparent. Tourist receipts have fallen behind the target 15% p.a. growth rate, and estimated expenditures per visitor day (including prepayments) have fallen from Ksh. 135 in 1969 to Ksh. 120 in 1970; this is in part due to decreased expenditure by Americans, following the recession in the U.S., but also to the increasing proportion of receipts being generated by mass tourism. This reduction in expenditures per visitor day is probably a trend, and not one likely to be reversed. Hence, more visitors are needed for constant receipts; this does not of course, necessarily imply that either the social or private rate of return to tourism in Kenya will fall over time.

Kenya's attractions are principally her game areas and beaches; and near the Ocean, it is often easy to combine the two. The Coast is the most important tourism area in Kenya, stretching some two hundred kilometres from Shimoni in the south to Lamu in the north, and is centred on Mombasa.

1. See p. 219.
2. A large proportion of these government funds have already been committed to international-class projects. Hence the importance of determining the social value of such a project in a coast location. This we do in the detailed project analysis below.
3. In addition infrastructural requirements of K£3m. are required over the Plan period.

The trade is not yet an all-year-round one, although the government would clearly like to see it so. The seasonality of the trade is determined in part by vacation habits in Europe and America; and in part by the weather. Peaks occur in December to March and July to September, with low points in April to June and in November, the periods of the long and the short rains. Total visitor arrivals are typically half in May (the lowest point) what they are in January (the peak), although arrivals in eight months of the year vary little from the mean. The promotional activities of the government, tour operators, and hotels have not yet had time to convince the tourist and business markets that Kenya has even a ten-month season. Further, seasonality varies with the location of a project; game areas are also subject to more seasonal variations than units at the Coast. Kenya is facing competition in both these markets; several countries are making an energetic bid to capture some of the safari market with new lodges and hotels. Concerning beach holidays, Kenya faces competition from elsewhere in East Africa, from islands in the Indian Ocean, and the Caribbean; but it does have the advantage of being a country where such a holiday can be combined with game-viewing.

The air travel component is a heavy proportion of cost for tourists visiting Kenya, and one which is determined in an imperfect market.[1] Since Kenya has an interest in the airline business, we ought to include with any gains from lower tourist prices due to reductions in the air travel component, a possible loss of revenue accruing to the East African airline.[2] Substantial reductions in the air fare might do much to boost tourism, although Kenya will have to match carefully the facilities provided to the new set of tourist demands; for example, emphasis on medium-class accommodation might improve Kenya's competitive position, particularly in the European market.

1. For example, scheduled airline passenger rates to East Africa are higher per mile than for routes of simiiar length elsewhere.
2. This calculation, of course, would not give social net benefits to a reduction in, say, the Frankfurt—Nairobi scheduled air fare. Nevertheless, revenue changes should be estimated since they are required to determine social net benefits.

We now consider the world price of tourism. Most tourism projects in Kenya operate in the international tourism market, and prices in, say, Europe must be such that there is some rough comparability with prices charged in the Indian Ocean area and the Caribbean.

But this does not mean that tariffs should be set as low as possible. The relevant case has been discussed by Peter Diamond.[1] In an economy where lump-sum redistribution and price discrimination against tourists is impossible, production efficiency should be preserved, but prices should be set so that we trade off tax revenue from raising the tax with the cost to individual consumers, weighted by their social marginal utilities of income giving a zero weight for tourists (domestic consumers of goods purchased by tourists generally have low social marginal utilities). Thus the result for tourism follows immediately from the well-known Diamond-Mirrlees[2] theorems on optimal taxation: we tax relatively highly those goods demanded by those we wish to redistribute income away from and tax relatively lightly goods demanded by those towards whom we wish to redistribute income. To get beyond first-order conditions and look at the actual optimal prices we need to look at tourists' and domestic consumers' utility functions; nevertheless, there is no presumption that the world price is a low price. The analysis also suggests use of monopoly prices to ration limited capacity during peak periods. The case of tourism is analogous to that of a primary exportable in which a country has monopoly power; following the *Manual* we use marginal export revenue as the appropriate output price in project analysis for if the tax on tourism is properly set, it represents a pure tradeable gain due to tourism.

Mitchell[3] has provided such an estimate of the gains from tourism, with the existing tax structure (which may not be optimal), on the worst possible assumptions: labour is fully

1. P. A. Diamond, 'On the economics of tourism', *East African Economic Review*, Dec. 1969.
2. P. A. Diamond and J. Mirrlees, 'Optimal Taxation and Public Production', Parts I and II, *American Economic Review*, March and June, 1971.
3. F. Mitchell, 'The value of tourism in East Africa', *East African Economic Review*, 1969.

and efficiently employed, there are no intra-marginal rents earned on factors working in tourism, or pure profits earned in tourism and accruing to residents, and the exchange rate is optimal. Mitchell finds on these assumptions, that the net gain (in 1967) from foreign tourism to East Africa as a whole amounted to between 5 and 10% of tourist receipts. In so far as the Kenyan economy is not optimal, additional gains will accrue, though a national income measure is useless for saying how much and in which direction tourism should expand.

Sectoral analysis of tourism in the past in Kenya has been conducted in terms of finding foreign-exchange earnings, income per worker generated and incremental-capital output ratios (ICOR), and comparing these numbers with values obtained for other sectors. Thus Mitchell[1] finds the ICOR in tourism to be in the range 2.5 to 3.0 (this figure includes infrastructure, hotel construction, and training costs), as compared to the monetary economy as a whole (3.0), to agriculture (2.7), and manufacturing (4.4), and direct employment generated (in 1966/7) of 10,000, together with indirect employed of 7,000. K£1,500 of visitor expenditure yields one job in direct employment and 1.7 jobs in total employment, thus giving an employment projection of 23,000 in direct employment and 40,000 in all for 1974. This employment measure is not here, of course, given by value-added per worker, which is another item of interest in determining sectoral choice. But note that none of these measures should be given too much weight, the ICOR for instance, is a suggestive partial indicator, which may give hints to policy but should not itself be used to determine sectoral choice.

Another way of making much the same point is that we cannot expect sectoral analysis of this sort to do the same work as project analysis, given the heterogeneity within the sector (including differential timing of net social benefits). Further, if we examine a certain sort of project, which performs well, we cannot state that the sector as a whole will do correspondingly well. But we can say that since tourism is

1. Ibid.

an exportable we shall not obtain biased upward estimates of national income due to effective protection, although tariffs on imports can affect the international competitiveness of the industry. This absence of effective protection is an *a priori* point in tourism's favour, which has nevertheless to be corrected for the social value of resources absorbed and this is especially important when, as in Kenya, the labour market is imperfect and the currency is overvalued. These factors can only be satisfactorily handled in project analysis, but, as stated above, we cannot generalise from experience in the project examined to tourism as a whole.

Raising the degree of foreign financing tends to lower GNP as a percentage of tourist expenditures (due to increased dividends, interest payments and fees); so it is important to consider the differential social value (discounted at the ARI) of modernizing and extending medium-class accommodation compared with investing in new first-class hotels.

Lack of data for medium-class operations prevented such a calculation but it should be noted that the Kenyan government is considering emphasising this latter sort of operation, which in the past has been locally owned. Foreign investors may not find it worthwhile, or be willing, to finance such expansion. Thus, varying the proportion of tourism financed locally may vary the portfolio of hotels of different classes in Kenya.

We have seen the nature of optimum government policy towards tourism: here we look at some features of actual policy. The industry is predominantly privately-owned, a high proportion of it by non-citizens. As in the industrial sector, substantial quantities of foreign investment are required to meet Plan targets; this finance appears forthcoming from both public and private foreign sources. There is a suggestion that the constraint on accepting more projects, especially joint ventures, has been in finding acceptable financial terms and management. There is no special government aid to hotel and lodge development in Kenya; this is in contrast to the policy of many O.E.C.D. countries. Foreign investment in tourism faces the same laws and regulations as foreign investment in other sectors; receiving, for example, the same depreciation allowances as foreign investment elsewhere. Construction and machinery for the tourism industry is classified as industrial buildings and machinery. These fiscal incentives mean a bias towards greater capital-intensity, but not a discriminatory bias facing foreign investment in tourism as opposed to foreign (or local) investment in other sectors.

The organisation of the public sector in tourism consists of, at the government level, the Ministry of Tourism and Wild Life (concerned with policy, promotion, and co-ordination with other government departments) and at the parastatal level, K.T.D.C., which is involved in joint venture financing with foreign investors;[1] it receives all its funds from the Ministry and has to submit all its investment proposals to it. Government finance has in the past had some unfortunate experiences, especially with Safari lodges, in all the East African countries, with capital cost per bed higher than what is considered to be reasonable for a given class of accommodation.[2] Unfortunately the relevant problem is not a cost-minimisation problem to obtain minimum capital requirements for a given tourist market.

Joint ventures' boards frequently include high-ranking civil servants and Government ministers; it is not clear whether this is due to power-building or is a symptom of the scarcity of high-level manpower, but clearly the bargaining power of foreign investors vis-à-vis the other investors is affected.

In interviews with foreign investors, it became clear that they do not welcome the Government's desire to influence their choice of location, and they resent the uncertainty caused by sudden changes in taxation (e.g. in 1971 the 10% tax on hotel beds), and by the imposition of price controls.

1. With C.D.C., D.E.G., I.F.C., and Pan Am, K.T.D.C. embarked on a programme totalling £1¼m. to build a 2 x 100-bed game lodge in Tsavo National Park, and a 200-bed beach hotel. In Nairobi, the Hilton and Intercontinental hotels are joint ventures. All these units are international class.
2. Mitchell, op. cit., pp. 19−20, 'while government lodges in all these countries are costing between K£2000 and K£3,500 per bed installed, it is possible to erect extremely attractive and comfortable facilities for K£1000 per bed' (Mitchell's study refers to 1967 prices).

They are also perturbed by trade-union pressures, and feel
that the pace of Kenyanisation is sometimes too fast.[1]

Project I

The project under consideration is a proposal, which has not
yet been carried out, for a two hundred bed low-rise hotel of
a standard suitable for the luxury charter market in a bay in
the Watamu area of Coast Province, some seventy miles north
of Mombasa. Watamu is one of the three main areas on the
Coast (the others are the Kilifi-Mtondia and the Kongo-Diani
areas) which the Kenyan government is anxious to develop for
tourism. Being relatively isolated, infrastructure would generally have to be provided in this area (and so would represent a
social cost) for the proposed project.

The infrastructural requirements for the proposed project
include a complete staff village, housing all except the
management staff; water supply, treatment and storage;
electricity supply and access roads. However, if the project is
located in the Bay, these infrastructural requirements will not
have to be provided, since there is already an existing project
in the Bay for which infrastructure was provided. The pro-
moters of this earlier project were obliged to build a murrum
road to Public Works Department requirements from the end
of the existing tarred road leading to the main coastal road
from Mombasa to Malindi. The proposed project would be
given direct access by this murrum road. Water and electricity
services already exist in the Bay, but the existing 2" main
would have to be increased to serve an additional hotel of
200 beds. No estimates have been made for the increased
social cost of infrastructure resulting from the proposed
project being carried out (except for the staff village), in part
because insufficient data was available, and in part because
the social cost due to this project would be rather small (wear
and tear of the murrum road and other roads, expansion of
water supplies). While such infrastructure would be rather

---

1. Mitchell calculates potential private returns before tax on capital invested in
game lodges and beach hotels of 21 per cent and 17 per cent respectively,
assuming capital investment per bed of K£2000 and K£1000. It is however
not clear what measure of the rate of return is used.

important for a game lodge, at this site at least the net infrastructural requirements would be small but, again, considering placing this project elsewhere on the Coast would probably require us to consider more explicitly the infrastructural requirements.

The proposed location of this project invites us to consider the relative social gains of placing this project in an isolated, rather low-income area of the Coast rather than, say, on the outskirts of Mombasa. In part, such a comparison is illegitimate in that we would expect construction and other costs to be somewhat higher seventy miles from Mombasa rather than, say, five miles from Mombasa, and the market which the two alternative projects could serve, would be rather different, as we see below. Nevertheless a comparison of the relative social gains of placing the hotel in the Watamu area does seem worth investigating, and we use the method of income distribution weights of Part II to measure such effects.

One division of the international tourism market is between the package tourism market and the more exclusive charter tourism market, in which small groups of say a dozen, travel by scheduled airlines; a market where higher prices can be charged but the standard expected is correspondingly high. It may also be true that demand is more price-inelastic for luxury tourism than it is for mass-tourism — it still appears that to a large number of people the most expensive is best.[1] The project we are examining is geared towards this market and it is important to consider the consequences. For example in any tourism project a major uncertainty is the number of rooms sold. This uncertainty can be lessened by orienting one's project more to the mass charter market, on the assumption that the host government, and the governments of tourist-sending countries do not impose arbitrary restrictions on charters. This can be especially important in the first few seasons, when, if the project is directed towards the luxury market, liquidity is often low. Penetration of the

---

1. This may mean that private (and social) profitability may not be raised by changing prices in line with or a little below competitors; it would not justify fixed-cost pricing, which is practised by some hotel operations.

mass tourism market does however require careful planning; for example, it is desirable to start marketing a project before it is ready to open, since it takes four operators up to twelve months to market a tour programme and confirm reservations.

The demand for a hotel serving the international tourism market is also likely to be influenced by other markets, such as that generated by businessmen in commercial centres. Thus a project within twenty minutes' distance of Mombasa may be at an advantage vis-à-vis projects such as the one we are considering, which is far from the largest town on the Coast, and which cannot draw on this market to lessen fluctuations in demand.

One important issue concerning the market for a particular hotel project is whether the standard of the hotel, and so the class of customer the project can expect, is or is not fixed fairly clearly by the standard of its fixed capital. Once fixed capital is in place, it is argued, the decision on the standard of the hotel is largely made. Capital required per bed can generally be expected to rise as a hotel 'changes its standard'. This capital required for the luxury charter market may be expected to differ from that required for a new charter market in that the former, but not the latter, may require a larger public area, higher quality finishes to construction and some specialised public rooms (for example, a night club or a private parties room). But the standard of food and service (floor service, ambitious menus, etc.) could be varied.

It proved difficult to find hard information on the optimum size of this project: it does not seem unreasonable, however, that a hotel could be larger than the hotel discussed here without damaging its exclusive position, that is, the limited number of people who are prepared to stay there provided that the two projects provided the same services. The interesting question is what are the relative valuations by tourists of different services provided. It may be possible to lower capital costs per bed, by increasing the number of beds, accepting a lower public area per guest, but compensating for this reduced area, by adding a night-club; and we could calculate the net social rate of return of this alternative project of say, 200 rooms, taking account of any revenue change that would take place after a perceived change in standards of the hotel. It is not necessarily desirable that the expansion should take place subject to the constraint that the project caters for the same market as before the expansion. Basic data on the capital costs involved are presented below:

Estimated capital costs: 100 room expansion	*1969 costs K£000's*
Add 100 rooms (including structure of night club)	300
Extension of kitchen and restaurant	44
Night club (furniture and fittings only)	3.5
	347.5

Capital costs before and after expansion would be:

K£000's	*Existing*		*Expanding*	
	Total	per bed	Total	per bed
	555.600	2.778	979.500	2.499

There appear to be significant scale-economies and com-plementaries between hotel projects; there are scale-economies for instance in promotional and advertising activity both in Europe and Africa; and one hotel can create demand for another. These cost savings can result in a balanced circuit of city (Nairobi), beach, and game lodges being the most efficient arrangements; these units can obtain advantages of centralised accounting, bulk purchasing, company secretarial, and reservation services. Exactly how many units of particular sizes should be grouped together is a matter for detailed, specialist research. One view put forward by tourism consultants in Kenya was that a hotel complex of 200 rooms in three units (a beach hotel of 100 rooms and two lodges each of 50 rooms) was too small; and larger units could better serve the demands for larger package groups at a fairly low tariff. Certainly the difficulties due to there being long distances between units should be carefully examined, and are important for ensuring that, for example, the units' managers are accountable to central management. If a circuit is controlled by one company, and if marketing the circuit does not go ahead as planned, then some units may be able to take advantage of other markets; those that cannot will reduce the overall attractiveness of the company.

The typical history of a tourism project involves the build-up of occupancy levels as the particular demand for that project's services is created, and, depending on the relation between fixed costs[1] and variable costs, if reasonably high occupancy levels are not achieved relatively soon, the project may make a heavy loss, thus requring a restructuring of the finance of the project.[2] This risk is, of course, less if the project is directed towards the mass charter market, and is successful in obtaining contracts in that market.

Analysis of the short-run cost behaviour of this project remains a lacuna because it proved difficult to distinguish fixed costs from variable costs in the original project appraisal; further, we cannot give too much weight to estimates of particular items of cost from other projects, unless these projects are comparable in terms of market, size, and factor-intensity. Yet we should expect that administration costs, for instance, expressed on a per head basis, should be smaller for a larger than for a smaller project. This issue of short-run cost behaviour is important, since compared with hotels catering for luxury charters, the lower-priced hotels on the Coast have achieved higher occupancy levels; and, generally, fixed costs appear to be a large proportion of total costs in tourism projects. The choice of technique in the operation of this project has, too, been troublesome; we have therefore imposed a technique which may be feasible but may not be optimal (in the sense that there could be a shrinking in of the isoproduct surface at near zero cost).

But besides considering the choice of technique in the operation of the project we have to consider the choice of technique in the construction of the project. The principal issue here is whether more traditional, 'African' building would allow more labour-intensive construction, and perhaps, a higher social profitability. But it seems that if traditional

1. Including 'imposed' fixed costs which result for example if it is policy on 'development' grounds that a certain labour force is to be employed throughout the year.
2. Perhaps finance conditions should initially be arranged to take account of this risk. Difficulties of this sort can lead to scepticism on the part of the Government as to the desirability of accepting further projects of this sort. At least, the Government will want to know the reasons for a project's short-term difficulties before sanctioning further projects of a similar sort.

construction is employed, it will have to be modified to accommodate amenities which tourists characteristically demand. It is frequently asserted that tourists coming to Africa would like to experience African conditions, but it is not clear how they can do this if they also want the services of an international-class hotel. There are some hotels on the Coast with a traditional appearance, but they hardly reflect local conditions of life; further they are older units, and it is not clear that how much more cheaply they could be built now. Bandas, for instance, could be built instead of bedroom wings; say square clusters of four with bathrooms in the middle. But such an arrangement would entail a larger site and the lengthening of services — water, electricity, and telephone, which raises costs above those in a compact bedroom wing; because of the simpler construction of the bandas, the overall cost of bedrooms would be reduced. Similarly, one could use more traditional materials for floors, roofs, and walls both in the public areas and the bedrooms, but such savings, in reducing the standard and practicability of finishes, would increase maintenance costs.

The architects and quantity surveyors of one of the international class safari lodges suggested that savings on the lines above could reduce the cost of builders' work by one-third. The builders' work generally represents only about two-thirds of the building contract, the remaining one-third being specialist work which can hardly be reduced at all; the maximum saving would thus be about 22% of the cost of construction. This calculation does not give us the resulting change in labour-intensity,[1] and it does suggest that if standards drop too much, the hotel will find itself in a different market. The older hotels (and lodges) were built at a time when building costs were much lower, and running at present tariff levels, these units are able to give reasonable rates of return to their operators.

1. We were not able to obtain estimates of labour-intensity in construction for either the large Asian or European contractor or for the new breed of small African contractor sponsored by the National Construction Corporation for a tourism project. Further, it has not proved possible to reconcile Mitchell's estimates of capital per bed (see p. 220) with the estimates presented here; even given reported estimates of cost inflation in construction.

It has been assumed that the firm which manages this project is a firm of specialist tourism consultants, with offices both in Europe and Africa, which provides management, accountancy, staff training, marketing and promotional services. The company could manage, say, twenty similar projects in East and Central Africa, and draw from its experiences in other parts of the world features which may distinguish the demand and cost structure of projects in East Africa from those, say, in the Caribbean. With such a management company the project may well be able to draw on expertise which could not be obtained, say, from a hard-loan agency, and thus could be rather important if large private investors, specialists in the tourist business, perceive a low rate of return in a project such as we are examining.[1] However, such a management company is likely to be responsible for a wide range of activities, and if a number of units are to be managed by one company to take advantage of scale-economies in management, accountancy, etc., problems might well arise about the allocation of the company's resources between, for example, tightening management control in a particular project and engaging in new project feasibility studies. Indeed experience with some recently established projects in Kenya suggests that a high quality of management accountancy (as opposed to financial accountancy, which is also important), is crucial, especially in the first few years of a project. Even in developed countries, management accountancy methods are not used as frequently as they might be, and, with the shortage of accountants trained in management accountancy techniques in Kenya, it may be worthwhile to search for an accounting technique which, while capturing features of a project likely to offset profitability can still be used by low-grade staff in fairly small operations incapable of paying the costs of advanced methods.[2]

1. But note that I.F.C. is increasing its tourism expertise, as it finances more projects in this area.
2. This remark clearly has an implication for the cost of Kenyanisation, and on the determination of the marginal product of an expatriate, although it should be remembered that an expatriate accountant who does not know the appropriate techniques may still be able to extract a high reward, and, further, whatever this marginal product is, it does not mean that on social grounds Kenya would wish to pay that amount to a Kenyan with equivalent skills when the expatriate is replaced.

If the management company cannot effectively perform this function, the investors may have to use their own resources;[1] this may be particularly difficult if the project is financed in the way we posit,[2] where there are a large number of participants of various nationalities, each perhaps with a different view as to the cause of the project's short-term difficulties. It has been assumed that the project shares with three other projects (totalling 400 beds) a General Manager, an Accountant/Company Secretary; and that the managing company provides an expatriate manager for each unit; and is organised with those three projects in one company.

Similar projects to the one under consideration have been financed by a rather large group of investors of different nationalities, and these investors would normally be expected to follow different investment criteria. The degree of local participation in the project's company is largely a function of the amount of capital provided by KTDC. This local component attributable to KTDC, which comprises roughly 33% of the equity and 29% of the debt of the project, is supplemented by the local component in a hotel-owning company (Company A), whose investors include private foreign investors, private and public development corporations, and KTDC. The local component in company A is only 7.6% of the equity and none of the loan capital of the project's company, and since company A only provided some 22% of the equity and 21% of the loan capital of the company, it is clear that the degree of local participation is not raised significantly by the addition of the local component in the project's company. It is also assumed that the National Park Trustees held 0.003% of share capital, but no debenture capital.

The other investors in the project are foreign investors of two classes: hard-loan agencies and private foreign investors (airlines and hotel groups); Both classes of investors hold equity and debt, and together provide 44% of share capital

1. It is assumed that the management company has no direct financial interest in the company — the payments it receives for the various functions it performs are described in the Statistical Appendix.
2. See below.

and 48% of loan capital. The overall debt-equity ratio is 73.3 :
26.7; and this debt-equity ratio is roughly the same for all
investors (DFCK's policy is to hold a 3-1 ratio). In sum, this
project is financed in a rather complex way, rather different
from the usual picture of foreign investment. It proved
difficult to obtain judgments as to whether the debt-equity
ratio chosen, and other components of foreign financing cost
vis-à-vis local financing cost, were optimal for the various
participants. But we can say that debt-equity ratios found
when projects run into loss conditions (as has happened with
some existing tourism projects in Kenya financed on the lines
above) do not represent, except by chance, the optimal
debt-equity ratio, when the project fulfils its profitability
estimates; further, when loss conditions have arisen, changing
the debt-equity ratio held by each investor was not considered.

Results:
We recall that we are calculating:

(1) $NSB_n{}^A = R_n{}^A - M_n - L_n{}^A - F_n{}^A$

where: $R_n{}^A$ is the value at accounting prices of the
foreign-financed project in year n.

$M_n{}^A$ is the value in accounting prices of inputs other
than labour in year n.

$L_n{}^A$ is the value at accounting prices of labour of
various categories in year n.

$F_n{}^A$ is the value of the net cash flow abroad
associated with the project.

We seek the NPV of (1) over the economic life of the
project. If we exclude the last term — $F_n{}^A$ — we have the
domestic project valued in Little-Mirrlees terms, on the
assumption that exactly the same physical project could be
reproduced.[1]

---

1. Remember that if the cost of foreign finance [the internal rate of return of the
F^A terms] exceeds the ARI, domestic financing is preferred. This is not
immediately obvious if we merely find the value of (1) above at the ruling ARI,
for with a reasonable cost of foreign capital, foreign capital appears to give a
'small contribution' to net social benefit.

The principal features of this project we wished to examine were:

(1) NPV of the present physical project, present foreign finance conditions, and the original feasibility study's estimate of tariffs, occupancy rates, etc., with SCF = 0.75 and e = 1 generating the SWR.
(2) (1) with alternative values of SWR and SCF.
(3) (1) with different (lower) tariffs.
(4) (3) but with an expanded project (p. 223).
(5) (1) with SWRs generated by income − distribution weights.

The number of possible combinations is rather large. Some summary results include:

	IRR	PV at 10%	PV at 20%
1. Shadow prices; e = 1 SCF = 0.75; domestic-financed	22%	K£489,161	K£35,000
2. Shadow prices; e = 1, SCF = 0.75 foreign-financed	61%	K£535,020	K£255,650
3. Shadow prices; e = 2; SCF = 0.75 domestic-financed	29%	K£920,770	K£269,620
4. Shadow prices; e = 2; SCF = 0.75; foreign-financed	109%	*PV at 70%* K£50,360	
5. Shadow prices; e = 2; SCF = 0.85; domestic-financed.	26%	*PV at 10%* K£750,580	K£177,050

Since the ratio of construction to plant and machinery in tourism projects is much higher than that for the average industrial enterprise, capital costs, which can strongly affect the IRR, are rather low when revalued in social terms (see Scott's breakdown (for construction)), especially when the SWR is low. In such a case, especially, lowering the degree of foreign finance lowers the IRR considerably. Preliminary estimates are that the IRR is also, as expected, quite sensitive to early period losses.

It might be thought that we have spent rather too much time discussing markets, choice of technique, short-run cost behaviour in tourism projects. Yet it should be clear that these are important questions in practice. Tourism projects are nearly always going to be successful in a Little-Mirrlees world. Certainly the Kenya Government, following a method of project appraisal (particular for joint ventures) of looking at the private profitability of projects, and then, in an *ad hoc* way, adding balance of payments, employment, and so on, effects, might feel dubious about investment in certain sorts of tourism project. The project analyst, equipped with the *Manual*, might argue that the social rate of return is good enough, but forget that with a heterogeneous commodity like tourism, social gains may be higher.

Project II: Safari Lodge (SL)

The origin of Company X, of which Safari Lodge is part, is in a report prepared by the Commonwealth Development Corporation hotel consultant and submitted to the Kenya Government in November 1965. The recommendations in Phase I of the report for two game lodges in Tsavo National Park and a beach hotel, were accepted and in October 1966, the KTDC registered a company to build lodges and hotels. After a series of complicated negotiations, involving the right to participate in other hotel projects as well as in Company X participants in the project emerged as: KTDC and National Parks Trustees, CDC associated with a BOAC subsidiary company, DEG and DHG (respectively the German Development Corporation and a German hotel company) and Kenya Hotel Properties Ltd. (owned by the Intercontinental Hotel Corporation, the International Finance Corporation and other organisations). In the final capital structure of K£1,125,000, 67% of equity and 71% of debenture loans come from organisations outside of Kenya (including KHP in this category) and will be treated as foreign participation.

Safari Lodge comprises one quarter of the hotel beds of Company X, but for reasons given above, it has seemed worthwhile to obtain separate estimates for a game lodge. But the advantages SL enjoys as member of a hotel group should not be glossed over. They include: a discount in the contract price from the building firm, if it was given the right to build the other lodge in the company: buying and management facilities centralised over the whole company: common booking facilities which make it possible for visitors to the beach hotel directly to book accommodation in the group's game lodges (the management company set considerable store by this external economy to the beach hotel's operation). However, any game lodge constructed in the future will probably be part of a group, and hence will enjoy the same advantages in this respect as does SL.

Safari Lodge opened for business at the end of 1969. Original expectations of occupancy rates and hence of income and cash flow proved to be optimistic, with regard to SL and to the other hotels in the group. A part of this shortfall has been attributed to inadequate promotion, especially overseas. The importance of this factor is hard to assess, but it is worth mentioning that individual companies acting separately are unlikely to provide the optimum level of promotion in view of the difficulty of differentiating their product sufficiently to distinguish it from their competitors. The management company take the view that an average annual occupancy rate of 50% is unlikely to be exceeded by a game lodge, in view of the seasonality of the trade. (This figure is based in part on experience in game areas with a bed shortage.) Only by extending the season will this figure be exceeded. The government and private investors are likely to make efforts in this direction, but it seemed reasonable to adopt the 50% occupancy figure for SL in the years after 1975 for the following reasons: extending the season will require a heavy investment in improving the all-weather standards of roads to and within the parks, and the SL area stands to get only a small fraction of government infrastructural tourist investment: secondly, competition in the SL area will be provided by the two lodges under construction for Hilton Hotels.

There is some difficulty in establishing a 'world price' for the services provided by the lodge. A comparative analysis of tariff levels in game lodges in Kenya was carried out by Company Y, the company managing Company X. This revealed that SL's tariffs are among the lowest, in spite of its modern construction, its comfort and its large range of facilities. The report acknowledges that monopoly rents inflate the tariffs of lodges in particular sites. However some have discerned a desire on the part of the government to keep tariffs down so that as many Kenya citizens as possible may enjoy the facilities available to the foreign visitor. A possible way to achieve this end is a tariff system differentiating between Kenya residents and others: such a system already operates for admission to game parks, and is analysed from a theoretical point of view by P. Diamond.[1] If its administrative difficulties proved insuperable in the case of hotels, then seasonal price variations could go some way towards achieving the same end.[2] Furthermore, SL's prices, if maintained at their present level, will compare very favourably with those of its rival Hilton lodges, from the inflation in construction costs if for no other reason. However, we have maintained the actual tariffs, or tariffs projected until 1975 as 'world prices' in the expectation that the substantial increases — in the region of 20-40% — which some consider practicable will not materialise.

Before the results of the analysis are presented, it is worth considering the possibilities of alternative technical variants in lodge design. SL and its sister lodge in Company X are of solid two-storey construction; an alternative is to build a lodge of reduced specifications, with banda (chalet) — type accommodation for bedrooms instead of conventional bedroom wings, and with other economies. Company Y have estimated the resulting savings in building costs to be a maximum of 18%, at market prices. The only increase in running costs, if it occurs, will be caused by the greater difficulty in enforcing guest and staff discipline. If, as the

---

1. P. Diamond, 'On the economics of tourism', op. cit., pp. 53—62.
2. See F. Mitchell, 'The Value of Tourism in East Africa', op. cit., p. 11.

argument of the previous paragraph suggests, the same tariff would have been charged as in the lodge as built, the present value of the alternative variant will be the higher, but by a comparatively trivial amount. But this alternative may be worthy of consideration in the future, not least because of its special features which may make it more attractive to some visitors than a conventional lodge.

The results of the study are given in Table 10 (p. 234) and are summarised in the accompanying graph. Net present values are worked out at discount rates of 10% and 20% p.a., using four sets of prices:

1. Market prices.
2. Little-Mirrlees or world prices, ignoring income distribution at a given time, but using a value of 1 to evaluate S.
3. Little-Mirrlees prices, but with direct labour inputs of different income groups evaluated using an e value of 1.
4. The same as 3 but with an e value of 2.

Before remarking on the results it should be noticed that the accompanying graph shows only rough linear approximations of the relationship between NPV and the discount rate for the various prices. The level of the internal rate of return is doubtful, though we may have more confidence in the difference between internal rates of return calculated for various prices. Bearing in mind this qualification the following conclusions are presented:

1. Market prices: the rate of return is fractionally greater than 10% (this conclusion is relatively certain, as may be seen from the graph). This is not a high rate of return in the Kenya context.
2. At Little-Mirrlees prices the project is highly profitable, with an internal rate of return in the region of 23%. This is as you would expect in a highly labour-intensive industry when shadow and market prices diverge as much as they do in Kenya.
3. At a discount rate of 10%, taking income distribution into account with e values of 1 and 2 raises the NPV above the standard Little-Mirrlees level by respectively K£28,754 and K£125,422. This represents an increase in internal rates of return of approximately 0.4% and 1.2% p.a. Though considerable in themselves, these figures may well have been increased had we been able to take into account the income distribution conditions under which indirect inputs were produced.

Safari Lodge Results

Table 10 *Net Present Values as of 1968–9 in K£*

(1)	(2)	(3)	(4)	(5)	(6)
Discount Rate	Prices used	Revenue – current costs	Capital costs	Foreign financial outflows	Total (3)–(4)–(5)
1.	1. Market prices	286,595	270,057	11,414	5,124
	2. Shadow prices e = 1; no distributional weights	603,192	208,004	11,414	383,744
10	3. Shadow prices e = 1; with distributional weights	631,916	208,004	11,414	412,498
	4. Shadow prices e = 2, with distributional weights	728,484	208,004	11,414	509,166
2.	1. Market prices	104,412	281,714	−74,531	−94,809
	2. Shadow prices e = 1; no distributional weights	226,252	216,964	−74,531	83,819
20	3. Shadow prices e = 1; with distributional weights	239,658	216,964	−74,531	97,225
	4. Shadow prices e = 2; with distributional weights	284,774	216,964	−74,531	142,342

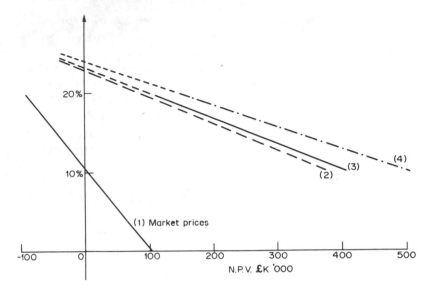

N.P.V. £K '000

IV.7 Case Studies IV: Cables

1. East African Cables Ltd.
The manufacture of cables in Kenya by East African Cables Ltd. began in 1967. Before this date, demand for cables in Kenya was satisfied by imports, the predominant part of which came from E.A.C. Ltd.'s parent company, Enfield Cables Ltd, of Middlesex, England, itself a wholly owned subsidiary of The Delta Metal Company Ltd.

A special interest of the present project is that it produces behind a tariff wall an output embodying a large import content; in other words, the processes involved enjoy, potentially at least, a high degree of effective protection. The value of imported raw materials alone, as a percentage of the values of output was in 1970, 61.1. These materials would, of course, have to be imported under any proposal to manufacture cables in Kenya. Thus a very crude calculation of the rate of effective protection, ignoring imported capital inputs, let alone substitution effects, gives a maximum potential rate of 77%. To bring out most clearly the consequences of this feature of the firm's operations, we shall try to establish what level of excess of Kenya prices over world prices is compatible with the enterprise's continued social profitability in the Little-Mirrlees sense. That, together with a calculation of the break-even commercial price level (including normal profits) will indicate the area of surplus to be shared between the country and the firm. It should be strongly emphasised that although care has been taken to make the figures used as accurate as possible, much of the underlying data, in particular the projections stretching to 1990, can only be considered approximate. The purpose of this study is only to illustrate the potentiality of the method. On no account can it be used for drawing any conclusions about the particular firm.

The major processes carried out by East African Cables Ltd. are the following:

1. Drawing copper rod to medium and fine wires, and annealing.
2. Bunching and stranding of wire.
3. Covering bunch or strand with PVC insulation.
4. Laying up of insulated cores.
5. Covering cable with PVC bedding sheath.
6. Steel wire armouring of cable.
7. Covering armoured cable with outer PVC sheath.
8. Shaping of conductors for larger armoured cables to ½, ⅓ or ¼ segments (since October 1970).

Before the establishment of the Company, the parent Company sought an undertaking from the Kenya Government that a degree of protection should be provided. This protection was seen as a deterrent to the 'dumping' of imported cables at unrealistic prices by outside low-cost producers. Although low wage-costs in Kenya would tend to permit cheap production, the ratio of labour to material cost is low and the cheap labour factor is counterbalanced by low efficiency; high training costs; high overheads and the short runs possible.

Originally a tariff level of 15% was established in Kenya and Uganda with Tanzania holding the duty in suspense. Later, the tariff was increased to 30% in Kenya and Uganda and, at the same time, Tanzania adopted a 15% tariff.

The range of cables covered by the tariff was widened when the Company expanded its range of production to more sophisticated cables.

A transfer tax of 15% exists in Uganda, where there is a competing cable factory.

Prices in the three countries are generally kept identical by a varying discount system.

The method of establishing prices is as follows:

Copper is bought on the London Metal Exchange, converted into wire-rod in the U.K. and shipped to Nairobi, the journey taking about two months. (Some copper rod is imported directly from Zambia but, for the present purposes, this is ignored.)

The firm establishes an average price for copper consignments in store and in transit and, on this basis, price lists are issued. Prices vary with copper but efforts are made to keep price lists stable for as long as possible and small variations in the price of copper are ignored.

Thus prices in Nairobi tend to lag behind world prices by two or three months' travel time, a circumstance that makes detailed price comparisons difficult. In net present value calculations we have chosen, after consultations with staff of East African Cables to take prices charged as world prices, with the calculation of the effects of price variation as described above. Fortunately the pricing system adopted makes NPV calculations independent of future fluctuations in the copper prices, except insofar as demand is affected by the resultant variation in cable prices.

Demand for the product is obviously closely related to the electricity industry, though not so much to the quantity of electricity generated as to the number of new connections made. In addition there is replacement demand. But prediction is made difficult by the considerable fluctuations in the composition of sales by country.

The factory was designed to be able to supply the combined requirements of the three East African countries for the range of cables manufactured. The virtual failure of the Kampala Agreement, the establishment of a competing factory in Uganda, and political and economic considerations in Tanzania have all tended to change this concept.

The Kenya market accounts for approximately 62% of the Company's sales and the balance is made up of exports to Tanzania, Uganda and the other neighbouring countries.

Since exports are largely unpredictable, calculations as to the annual rate of increase of sales are based on Kenya only where the best-guess for the rate of increase lies between 8–11% p.a. In the calculations we have used 9% p.a. With this rate of increase, capacity of the present plant will be reached in about 1974. In the circumstances, it seemed specially hazardous to make capital projections; the market is not large enough and the runs are too short to justify use of the most fully automated equipment, yet new capital equipment will probably embody new technical processes, as successive vintages are imported from the parent company and some modern equipment is installed. We have therefore limited the project to the firm as it will have expanded by 1974, using 'realistic' depreciation rates to establish current technique replacement demand for capital goods until 1990, when the project is assumed to end. Of course this is not very satisfactory, as the firm will expand beyond 1974, and the costs and benefits of this expansion will be profoundly affected by the existence of the project analysed here.

The equity capital is owned entirely by the parent company, and equity capital is treated as an inflow. A long-term loan of K£90,000 was provided to E.A.C. Ltd., by the Development Finance Co. of Kenya. DFCK is owned equally by the state-owned Industrial and Commercial Development Corporation, the Commonwealth Development Corporation and Dutch and German banking groups. Transactions between DFCK and E.A.C. Ltd. have not involved foreign exchange, and therefore do not enter the foreign payment flows calculations.

A balance of payments element in the project is the Agreement for Technical and Management Assistance made between Enfield Cables Ltd. and East African Cables. The agreement provides for a percentage of the value of cable sales of E.A.C. to be paid in return for technical assistance (choice of equipment, engineering design, introduction of techniques, etc.), and a further percentage for management assistance (selection and training of staff, advice to and supervision of management personnel, recruitment of additional personnel, etc.). The management assitance is to last for 25 years from the beginning of the company's operations. In practice the services of the parent company are described as being used every day by correspondence and personal visits, training of E.A. Cables staff in the U.K., recruitment of Kenyan graduates in the U.K., etc.

In the course of a year, they consisted in visits from Enfield Cables Ltd. directors and senior executives, the provision of spare parts, help in overcoming the problems of metrication, and assistance in developing exports markets. Part of the machinery used in the Nairobi plant is imported as fully reconditioned equipment from the parent company. This creates a problem in pricing these imports since the world market for reconditioned cable-making equipment — extruders and the like — is necessarily limited and comparison prices are, therefore, unavailable. Since the equipment is valued at 'market prices' by the parent company, those prices are used in this study.[1] The use by an overseas subsidiary of less fully automated machinery shipped free from the parent company's chief theatre of operations is a source of intermediate level technical equipment which may repay examination in other industries. The chief disadvantage seems to be the limited choice of potential investing firms available to the host country.

In summary, the degree of dependence of East African Cables Ltd. on its parent company is very high. Management and machinery are of parent-company origin; sales have displaced imports from the parent company, and the parent company has exercised general supervisory functions. This degree of dependence makes it unrealistic to look separately at the net present value of the manufacturing project and the net present value of the foreign payment flows necessary to sustain it.

The results of the study are given in the next table, and are summarised in the accompanying graph. Net present values at a discount rate of 10% p.a. are worked out using four sets of prices:

    1. Market Prices.
    2. Little-Mirrlees or world prices, ignoring income distribution at a given time, but using an e value of 1 to evaluate S.

1. Furthermore, the Kenya Government requires valuation certificates from independent valuers for items of second-hand and reconditioned capital equipment.

3. Little-Mirrlees prices, but with direct labour inputs of different income groups evaluated, using an e value of 1, briefly, Little-Mirrlees Guidelines prices.
4. The same as 3, with an e value of 2.

East African Cables Ltd. Results

Table 11 Net Present Values as of 1966 in K£

(1)	(2)	(3)	(4)	(5)
Prices used	Revenue – current cost	Capital costs	Foreign financial outflows	Total (2)–(3)–(4)
1. Market Prices	1,799,004	662,687	513,405	622,912
2. L–M Prices e = 1	2,850,511	576,512	513,405	1,760,594
3. L–M–G Prices e = 1	2,803,681	576,512	513,405	1,713,764
4. L–M–G Prices e = 2	2,908,096	576,512	513,405	1,818,179

The graph shows the effect on net present value of changes in the world price as a percentage of the actual price. At a value of 100% on the vertical axis, world and actual prices are identical, and net present values are shown in the table above. Before drawing any conclusions from the graph it is as well to repeat the necessary caveats about the accuracy of the data. Nevertheless, the following conclusions are tentatively presented.

1. Market prices: To obtain a rate of return of 10%, the company would charge its output at 92½% of actual prices.
2. At border prices, the net present value of the project would be zero if domestic prices were 27% in excess of border prices.

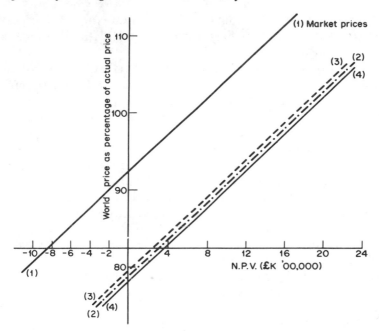

3. The income distribution factor makes little difference (for $e = 1$, excess of domestic price over border price giving a zero Net. Present Value is 26%; for $e = 2$, 28%). This is hardly surprising. Domestic value added is low as a proportion of price, and in any case only direct labour inputs have been revalued.

IV.8 CASE STUDIES: CONCLUSIONS

Kenya is a dual economy — both technologically and socially. In our introductory discussion on the Kenyan economy, we tried to show how malconsequences resulting from POI could be separated from those due to other factors. This is especially important in Kenya's case since her whole economy would be substantially different in the absence of foreign investment. It is for this reason, and because the Kenyan economy is less complex than India's, that we presented (Chapter IV.I) a review of Kenya's development problems and policies.

We recall that while foreign investment in India has concentrated on the transfer of advanced technology (and it was for this reason that case studies of chemical plants were undertaken), the constraint that foreign investment is usually expected to weaken in East Africa is that of the shortage of human capital.

The problem is complex,[1] but we perhaps need not be dismayed by our apparent failure to measure labour-training externalities. The extent of 'poaching' is often remarked on in Kenya. Some firms raised compensation, often consider-able, to discourage workers from leaving, and perhaps the foreign investors we visited were just reticent about this feature of their operations. On Kenyanisation, the overall speed and the specific areas in which this should take place are obviously emotional topics; we did not feel qualified to appraise postulated cases of over-rapid Kenyanisation.[2]

Yet it should be clear that, at least in part, some labour requirements (including, of course, managerial skills) can only be obtained by learning and by doing. Provided one is not 'too sociological' about the origins of entrepreneurship, an entrepreneurial class in industry could develop if local staff are hired, although perhaps not in the jobs they will eventually occupy, but ensuring that they are trained by the day of independence from foreign capital for the enterprise.

We also wished to examine the industrial choice of technique likely to be available to a country such as Kenya.[3] To some foreign investors we visited the notion of choice of technique appeared alien, suggesting that a search for alternative technologies, either by the planners or by poten-tial investors, might be socially worthwhile. If a choice of technique was considered by foreign investors, it was that between new and old vintages of machinery, although some foreign investors believed they should remain silent about their use of old machinery, since they felt its use might be construed as an insult to the host economy!

There is no doubt that the methods of evaluation adopted here are more complicated than those for the determination of present values using market prices. But the information required is no more than the information which a sensible

1. See, especially, pp. 172–3 and the Appendix on the Industrial Estates scheme.
2. See, for example, p. 171, although many foreign investors would criticise the Government for the current speed of Kenyanisation.
3. See, for example, pp. 186–9.

planning commission should seek anyway. One advantage of using shadow prices is that their use forces us to think about the determination of actual prices and the justification for these prices, e.g., for tourism. Actual values of the planning parameters should be known by a planning commission aware of the long-run possibilities open to the economy, and aware also of social preferences.

There are some very obvious 'dodos' in the portfolio of foreign investment in Kenya, and, indeed, the engineering and marketing side of project appraisal is of the greatest importance, but experience suggested that it was not sufficient just to test for the expected private return of a project, and accept the project provided it made some contribution to 'social' objectives.[1] The economic costs of industrialising behind high tariff walls are now so well documented that it is rather sad that Kenya does not appraise projects by a method specifically designed to pinpoint these costs. This is especially so since the benefits to growth will probably continue to be distributed very unequally, and since a rational programme of industrialisation requires far greater co-operation with neighbouring states.[2]

Statistical Appendix to Part Four

We present below further explanation of the results in Tourism Project 1; and some more results on Food Processing Project 2.

APPENDIX 1: TOURISM PROJECT 1

A. Labour Costs

1. It was assumed, rather arbitrarily, that skilled workers are those earning in excess of K.sh.600 per month (including an

---

1. See p. 179.
2. This is difficult, one reason being that Kenya's Partner States have different, and vacillating, attitudes to POI.

implicit housing allowance); but observers report an important scarcity of skills at rather low levels in this industry (e.g. cooks); this is in part reflected by the very wide differential between different job descriptions.

2. *Percentage labour costs by group*

	Expatriates	Skilled	Unskilled	Total
Numbers	4	16	162	182
K£ Total Cost of Group	7749	10677	24900	43326
K£ Average cost per group	1935	667	154	238
% Labour costs	17.9	24.6	57.5	100
% total current costs	4.1	5.2	12.9	22.2

3. In contrast to usual practice, labour is assumed to be employed throughout the year; on the grounds that since this is a 'development' project, labour should not be laid off during slack seasons and that training can take place at such times.

4. It is assumed that staff are recruited locally, sent to Mombasa and Nairobi for training, and receive further training on the site. There are two management trainees understudying the (expatriate) assistant manager; the chef's responsibilities include those of instructor. It is assumed that all training costs are included elsewhere in the estimates, e.g. in the salaries of those who do the training.

B. Capital costs

1. Total project cost is K£691,000 at local prices, which is broken down:

	% total costs	Accumulated total
1. Building costs (including land-scaping and staff village)	49.64	49.64
2. Plant and machinery	5.07	54.71
3. Air-conditioning	7.35	62.06
4. Professional fees	9.22	71.28
5. Furniture and furnishings	3.36	74.64
6. Vehicles	0.81	75.45
7. Operating equipment	4.05	79.50
8. Development costs	10.58	90.08
9. Working capital average	3.36	93.44
10. Contingency	2.33	95.77
11. Land	4.34	100.00
	100.00	100.00

2. Shadow cost of construction: we wish to divide costs of construction into four components: 1. unskilled labour; 2. skilled labour; 3. tradeables; 4. residual (taxes, tariffs, etc.). We multiply each component by appropriate conversion factors. Thus the unskilled labour component is multiplied by the ratio of shadow wage to actual wage; similarly for skilled labour; tradeable costs are valued at unity, and the residual is not valued at all. Scott ('Non-traded Goods and their inputs in Kenya,' mimeo, 1970) finds (breakdown 3) the inputs into construction in Kenya as: unskilled labour 0.243; skilled labour 0.206; tradeable 0.473; residual 0.078; comparison of breakdowns of other items of capital expenditure show that construction is quite heavily taxed in relation to e.g. industrial machinery. Further, construction gains heavily due to its high labour component, as compared with, say, industrial machinery (Scott, op. cit., breakdown 27). This feature alone goes a long way to explain the high IRRs obtained from tourism projects, as reported in the text; often countries with different technologies and tax systems will have different responses.

3. Building costs include cost of buildings, including plumbing, sanitary and electrical installations, all built-in furniture and fitments, including site works, car park, swimming pool (inc. filtration plant) and access road from site boundary to project entrance, and staff village for 175 staff. Thus Scott's breakdown here is not ideal, but data available from architects and quantity surveyors was not suitable for our purposes.

4. Note the low proportion of costs due to plant and machinery compared with the 'typical' industrial project i.e. only 5.065% of capital costs.

5. The cost of land is the capitalised value of its marginal product in alternative uses. Due to its small weight, we need not be too careful about ensuring that the reported cost of land is the true social cost. Note that Scott's breakdown 3 includes land already. Here the local cost of land is converted to world prices using alternative SCFs.

6. Contingencies are broken down in the same proportion as the other capital items combined.

C. Financing and management services
1. Management fees are taken at 3% of revenue and sales promotion fees at 2% of revenue.
2. The private IRR on capital employed is 10.25%.

D. Current costs at 60% capacity

	Percentage
1. Salaries and wages (including leave pay and provident funds)	22.4
2. Staff expenses (staff meals; entertainment; medical; personal accident insurance; workmen's compensation; general manager's subsistence, housing allowance)	4.8
3. Staff travel (local passages, transport allowance, leave pay and provision, head office travel)	0.8
4. Property upkeep and expenses (rent, rates, insurance, building maintenance, garden and landscaping)	1.5
5. Repairs and renewals (equipment, plant and vehicles)	2.1
6. Operating costs (fuel, electricity, water, material, licences)	12.7
7. Administration expenses (bank and legal charges, audit fees, management fees, bad debt provisions)	3.7
8. General charges (commission, advertising, subscriptions and donations, decorations, sales promotion)	12.3
9. Office expenses (telephone and cables, postage, printing and stationery, booking office, head office)	4.3

Thus most of the items are small; we have used Scott's breakdown 5 for Miscellaneous Office Services; breakdown 6 for post, telegraph and telephone; breakdown 14 for furniture; breakdown 19 for stationery; breakdown 21 for vehicles; breakdown 22 for electricity; breakdown 24 for uniforms.

E. Revenue
Tariff rates are set at the levels of the highest tariffs on the Coast, which concurs with the consultants' views.

Current costs in local prices are based on the consultants' report, and allow a return on capital of the size reported in section C. Unease about costs appropriate in an expanded project other than fixed capital costs, prevented a calculation of the social cost/benefit of the expanded project. Occupancy levels have been set at levels considered plausible for the luxury charter market, viz. 1st year of operations 45%; 2nd year of operation 55%; 3rd and subsequent years 60%; these rates should be considerably improved if the mass charter market was exploited. A 10% discount for group bookings has been assumed; this discount applies to 50% of bed-nights.

Tourism projects sell not just accommodation but other items as well. Food and drink are quite heavily taxed (see Scott, 'Accounting Prices for goods and services in Kenya,' mimeo, 1972), and therefore raise the social value of the project.

APPENDIX 2: FOOD PROCESSING PROJECT 2

K£

1. **Soft drinks alone:**

A. *Domestically financed:*	*'low' SWR/C*	*'high' SWR/C*
NPV at 10%	244,570	167,100
NPV at 20%	−85,700	−76,900
IRR Approximation	16.75%	13.5%

B. *Foreign-financed:*		
NPV at 10%	274,700	209,500
NPV at 20%	−33,400	−66,350
IRR Approximation	18·25%	14·7%

(N.B. Rather more approximate methods of calculation were used in calculating the above results than elsewhere in project analysis.)

2. **Cocoa alone:**

A. *Domestically financed:*	*'low' SWR/C*	*'high' SWR/C*
NPV at 5%	−213,675	−220,100
NPV at 10%	−213,506	−218,275

B. *Foreign-financed:*		
NPV at 5%	−234,121	−240,628
NPV at 10%	−218,074	−222,907

Appendix to Part IV
Industrial Estates — an Alternative to Private Overseas
Investments?[1]

African entrepreneurship[2] in Kenya is not a recent phenomenon restricted to the urban sector. However, in industry, as
opposed to the government administration and agriculture,
Africans still play a relatively minor role (although even in
agriculture Africans were not allowed to grow tea or coffee,
Kenya's most valuable export crops, until 1952). Again, both
local and foreign industrial firms recruit and train African
managers, and although Africans are appointed to their
boards of directors, the locus of decision and responsibility is
now in non-African hands. Until very recently the small
enterprise (including for the moment retail and wholesale
establishments) has been dominated by the Asians. Peter
Marris and Anthony Somerset[3] report that, in 1967, there
were 'scarcely two hundred African businesses in Kenya
larger than a country store or a craftsman's shop . . . and
only three African firms in Nairobi's industrial area'.

We want to consider here the possibility of industrial
estates as a means of helping African businessmen. But it may
be recalled that one traditional view was that African
entrepreneurship should only be encouraged around the
circumference of industry — producing raw materials, in
transport and in distribution — rather than in industry itself,
in part because of doubt of the existence of appropriate

1. It is sometimes argued that POI may impede the development of local
entrepreneurship. It is often not clear what supporters of this view would count as
evidence for this proposition and, more importantly, what should count as
evidence. But note that Hirschman, op. cit., is talking about an economy
somewhat more developed than Kenya's; nevertheless we can still ask what policy
should be adopted now to develop a strong entrepreneurial class by the time the
dangers to which Hirschman refers, occur (see also Chapter II.5 in Part II).
2. The term 'entrepreneurship' is multivocal; for our purposes we need not
explicate the term fully. All we want to discuss are the constraints and
opportunities facing the small African businessman so that within a reasonable
period, a class of independent businessmen, not requiring concessional support,
can establish itself. It is therefore important that entrepreneurs on an industrial
estate should not be 'hand-fed'; they should be able to survive by themselves after
a reasonable period.
3. P. Marris and A. Somerset, *African businessmen: a study of entrepreneurship
and development in Kenya* (London, 1971), pp. 1 and 12.

technology. This and other problems of small African businesses are reviewed below, but some of the other problems (finance, marketing, transport, training) have been handled in two quite successful examples of African business — smallholder tea and construction. In tea there is centralisation of those activities offering scale-economies. In construction, while the bulk of the industry is still in non citizen hands, a National Construction Corporation (NCC) was started in 1968, with the aim of assisting African contractors to enter the industry and to make loans available to overcome what was considered to be the main handicap to African enterprise — a shortage of working capital. During 1968, NCC with financial assistance from ICDC, granted loans of K£146,000 to African contractors. Such loans were found to be, however, a necessary but not sufficient condition for the development of African contracting: supervision of the contractors was seen to be necessary, and there was a shortage of trained supervisors. NCC therefore decided to act as main contractor, and sublet part of the contracts to African contractors financed by it, but retaining some supervisory functions. So the present responsibilities of NCC encompass three main functions: financial assistance, subcontracting, and training.

How do the problems of fostering entrepreneurship in industry differ from those found in other sectors? Scale-economies in industry are likely to exist for a wide range of commodities; this will be important because finance will present a limit on the size of enterprise that a small businessman can operate. Marris and Somerset[1] argue that small business is unlikely to be successful in manufacturing a standard product (e.g. saw mills, bakeries, canneries) where scale-economies exist. Plausible areas for small business include items of austere mass consumption (e.g. cheap furniture and clothing), and also simple construction materials and tools. Marketing problems are generally likely to be more complex than with construction or a smallholder crop.

Consider now factors of production. Qualified skilled

1. Marris and Somerset, op. cit., pp. 164—70.

workers (e.g. even motor mechanics) are quite hard to find in Kenya and command a substantial premium over the unskilled wage. With lower productivity techniques than foreign enterprises the small businessman has to watch this element of cost carefully. The entrepreneur may be willing to see his income fall, when he leaves a large local or foreign enterprise, or government service, to start his own business, but his employees will not.

The cost of capital is likely to be a strong constraint on the small businessman; we have already seen that commercial banks are still resistant towards financing small indigenous enterprise. Failing action by the commercial banks, ICDC has played a major role in financing small industry; Marris and Somerset report that ICDC financed nearly all the small African industrialists they contacted, contributing 76% of capital to firms established with less than K£2,500 initial capital; 50% for firms with initial capital exceeding K£5,000, and 53% in the middle range.

Loans from the Small Industries Revolving Fund, together with the industrial estates scheme, are the two principal ways in which ICDC has attempted to encourage African industrialists.

But ICDC is charged not only with aiding local business, but also with buying interests, and making loans to profitable, or potentially profitable, foreign investment. The 1966—70 *Development Plan* provided K£4½m. of state capital for local business promotion, i.e. K£½m. less than ICDC spent on promoting joint ventures. Further, 80% of the ICDC budget was allocated to industrial estates. Therefore, it may be questioned whether ICDC's budget was too small, whether too little of the budget was allocated to local industry, and whether too much of the 'local' budget was allocated to industrial estates. Besides personal savings, government loans [not ICDC], bank loans, the principal sources of finance include the entrepreneur's own savings, contributions from partners, and the issue of shares. Consider partnerships, which are usually unwieldy instruments. The principal problem is to decide who should be the working partners, employed full-time in the enterprise, for the remaining partners will receive no return on their investment for several years, and so there is a tendency for most partners to work part-time on a salary basis. It is rarely possible to do this with small-scale industry; a large number of partners reduces the surplus for expansion.

Small African industry in Kenya is usually so small that the manager/owner has to involve himself with a wide range of responsibilities — understanding machinery, appraising workers, estimating costs, undertaking accounting, marketing, distribution and transport. To relieve the burden of his being fully responsible for all these functions in an environment where it is difficult to obtain finance from the normal market, the industrial estates scheme, to which we now turn, seems a plausible way of lightening the small industrialist's load.

Kenya Industrial Estates Ltd. (KIE), a wholly-owned subsidiary of ICDC owns a system of industrial estates which are intended to make 'a genuine offer to local people with initiative' by providing factory buildings of standard types flexible enough to be extended as required. They also provide industrial infrastructure: water and electricity supply, sewage, access roads and rail, a technical centre and advisory services. The advisory centre provides advice on the selection of machinery, equipment and raw materials; production planning, and the preparation of the layout of the factory; and on management and accountancy. All these services are provided free of cost. The technical centre's services include installation of machinery, running-in tests, repairs and maintenance (dies, tools, fixtures and other services are charged to the enterprises). The standard factory buildings are let to the enterprise; this saves the small entrepreneur the cost of financing his own factory building, and relieves him of the business of securing title to the land, building the factory, and providing services. Technical assistance is provided by the Indian and West German government in the form of technical officers, and part of their function is to train Kenyan officers who will in the future replace them. Up to 100% loans for the purchase of machinery and equipment (usually over 8–10 years at an 8% interest rate) are provided. Working capital has to be provided by the entrepreneur himself. Apart from examining ideas put forward by the entrepreneurs themselves, ICDC has conducted a number of feasibility studies itself.[1] The assistance provided is thus all-embracing, both in the initial stages of a new project and in the day-to-day running of the enterprise. The screening of potential entrepreneurs suggests that only established businessmen are considered.[2]

The original first-phase of the scheme (1967–1970) proposed to establish five industrial estates at Nairobi, Mombasa, Nakuru, Eldoret and Kisumu, but this proved too ambitious — and efforts were restricted to Phase I of the Nairobi estate to gain experience. Phase I of the Nairobi estate[3,4] was set up in the industrial area of Nairobi, 3½

1. The ICDC list of market surveys, as of 1970, provides a list of industries of which 'preliminary indications suggest that most of these either single or in combination, could be economically manufactured in Kenya'. The list includes tea-chest fittings, plaster of paris bandages, wooden rulers, bifurcated rivets, elastic tape, spectacle frames, wheel-barrows, umbrellas, metric weights and measures, cash boxes, locks and padlocks, knitwear, paper cups and cartons, iron tower bolts and cotton thread.

The project reports, as distinct from the market surveys, include: a statement of the nature of product; demand estimates; projected production programme; estimate of capital requirements, foreign and local; financing of project; cost of products in breakdowns for each year; profitability estimates; loan repayment schedules; and a conclusion giving recommendations. All prices are local (though estimates of 'required' tariff rates are made), and choice of technique appears to be largely unconsidered.

2. As can be seen by looking at the questionnaire which potential entrepreneurs have to fill in: 1. Name, 2. address, 3. present occupation, 4. give in order of preference the industries in which you are interested, 5. have you handled any of these items either as a dealer or as a consumer? 6. have you made enquiries about present demand for these items in the country? 7. name the bulk consumers of these items, 8. What is the investment required for starting this industry? Give as much information as you may have, 9. How much of your savings/assets can you invest in this industry?

However, experience required is *not* necessarily industrial experience. It is for this reason that aid donors have criticised the sort of person selected to start small industries in Kenya; the reluctance of private financial institutions to lend to potential industrialists with no industrial experience compounds the still general reluctance of these institutions to lend to Africans.

3. Present projects in Phase I can be classified: Group 1: Hinges and assembly of balances; Group 2: wire products — 1. pins and paper clips, 2. paper pins, 3. wire nails; Group 3: apparel: 1. handbags, 2. ready-made garments; Group 4: printing press and litho plates; Group 5: miscellaneous, including wooden clothes pegs. Note that Group 2 projects are automatic processes, recalling Hirschmann's suggestion that such machine-paced operations might be more suitable for a country such as Kenya than skill-intensive industries.

4. The West German government provided a loan to finance Nairobi Phase I. The terms of this loan appear not to have been disclosed, so in detailed calculations we have assumed a typical 'hard' rate.

miles from the centre of the city, and, apart from an administration block (which also serves some of ICDC's general functions) and a technical centre, the estate has 25 factory buildings of different sizes, varying from a covered area of 625 sq.ft. to 3,750 sq.ft.

Phase II of the Nairobi estate, over the period 1970–2, was intended to provide a further 24 factory units of covered area between 1200 and 5400 sq.ft. and also an extension to provide special plots for larger industries (Phase II Capital cost K£530,000). Over the period 1971–2, the Nakuru estate was scheduled to provide 15–20 units (total capital cost K£505,000); and over 1972–5, the Mombasa estate was expected to provide 25 units (£610,000). Probably over the same period, the Kisumu (K£305,000) and Eldoret (K£105,000) schemes were to be developed. Total capital cost of the programme was thus K£2.2m.

The industrial estates scheme has been slow in developing. As early as 1967, ICDC stated that the principal constraint was not finance but suitability of applicants for financial aid. In 1968, it was reported that only 10 out of 200 applicants had been selected, so in Nairobi Phase I buildings were taken up much later than expected.[1] A scheme which has to accept Asian citizens (the scheme is restricted to citizens) does not look too healthy when it is supposed to foster African entrepreneurship. Marris and Somerset suggest that industrial estates were built for firms which could not hope to succeed without substantial tariff protection, and this the Government was not prepared to give.[2] Of course, other countries have had difficulties with industrial estates.[3]

Jorgenson[4] suggests that industrial estates succeed where

1. *Republic of Kenya Economic Survey*, 1969, p. 91.
2. Marris and Somerset, op. cit., p. 230. Marris and Somerset say rather little about the *economics* of African entrepreneurship, particularly with regard to the Industrial Estates scheme. Compare lists given in footnote 1, p. 197, and footnote 2, p. 198. Rather trivially, only project analysis can tell us about the viability of such projects.
3. 'Both the Indian and Nigerian experiments have failed to attract the right kind of entrepreneur, the technical assistance is ignored, rents – even when subsidised – are too high, and frequently unpaid, and the estates are not fully occupied.' Marris and Somerset, op. cit., p. 170. See also R. W. Davenport, *Financing small manufacture in developing countries*, 1967.
4. N. O. Jorgenson, 'ICDC: its purpose and performance', I.D.S. Discussion Paper No. 47, 1967.

there is a tradition of small entrepreneurs in industry, and where small enterprises could be run more efficiently when concentrated in one place, where both market and infrastructure are available. Jorgenson argues that in Nairobi industrial infrastructure is available anyway — if one cannot accept this judgement, then it is still true that more labour-intensive construction could have been used. Clearly in a developing country, we would not want to value attractive facilities highly,[1] rather, we would want to ask whether under-utilised infrastructure and premises exist, and whether if new construction has to take place, we could use a different technology.[2] Further, the economies of concentration of services should be carefully investigated.

Due to its slow start, inability to find suitable entrepreneurs, and the failure of any of the aided entrepreneurs to move elsewhere, the estate as a whole must be held to have failed in its objective of providing a continuing flow of indigenous business; rather at the moment it is just a means of subsidising a limited number of existing businessmen.[3]

1. The estate is a well-laid out collection of low-rise buildings of modern constructions and good finishes, with metalled roads and pavements between the factories. Kenya has made other excursions into the area of investing in attractive buildings, e.g. the shopping centres, intended to replace open-air markets. Jorgenson argues that cost of goods would rise 25%–50% if African traders used these facilities.

2. Jorgenson suggests that support given the small-scale enterprise by industrial estates is fifteen times as expensive as loans to small industries; this conclusion is based on a comparison of the capital requirements required by ICDC to support an entrepreneur on the estate, compared with an average figure for the loans given to small enterprises through the ICDC Revolving Fund. The number is unimportant since it neglects scale factors; but it does say something about the relative gains from different projects financed by ICDC. It also has an implication for decision of aid-donors' governments as whether to finance industrial estates as opposed to, say, some other form of technical assistance; a decision to lend for industrial estates, through, say ICDC, would be reflected in the opportunity cost of ICDC finance.

3. One suggestion for further research is to find the social costs of the ICDC rural industrialisation and small-scale industrial programme, to be located in small towns and rural areas. Industries considered include (*Development Plan*, p. 318) saw-milling, wood-working, shoemaking, leather processing, clothing, vehicle repairs, and manufacture of simple building materials. An *a prori* social advantage from these schemes would be their influence on regional distribution. During the 1970–4 Plan period, the schemes include K£234,000 for the establishment of rural industrial centres, grants to the small-scale and cottage industries programme (K£52,000), and loans from the Small Industries Revolving Fund. This programme, too, is partly financed by foreign aid.

Nairobi Industrial Estate 1970

1.	Total cost of Phase I including Administration block and technical service centre (building and civil works)	K£190,000
2.	Number of factories in full commercial production	16
3.	Capital investment:	
	i) Fixed capital (machinery and equipment)	K£110,950
	ii) Working capital	K£84,000
4.	Number of workers employed — 250 persons	
5.	Total capital	K£384,950
6.	Capital — labour ratio	1 : K£1,500
7.	Value of output	K£200,000
8.	Value-added	K£74,600
9.	Value-added as percentage of total value of output	37.3%
10.	Value-added by Estate as % of total value of output — national industrial output	0.136%
11.	Value-added per employee	K£298
11a.	Value-added per employee, average Kenyan industry 1967 —	K£651
	projected 1974—	K£803
12.	Wage-bill per employee (Nairobi minimum wage)	K£180
13.	Annual foreign exchange savings approx.	K£107,200
14.	Value of experts to Uganda, Tanzania, Malawi, and Zambia	K£6,600

Items 1, 3, 5, 6, 11—14 are all in local prices, while we ideally want measurements in border prices. For some items, especially 11 and 12, this should, however, do no more than second-order harm.

Our discussion of whether to accept foreign investment is important, since the Nairobi estate is financed by a foreign aid loan (footnote 4, p. 252). The present social value of the estate might be positive at the ARI only if the foreign loan is included; if the present social value of the same project (i.e. same technical coefficients) was positive when financed domestically, it will be preferable to finance it by foreign funds provided the cost of foreign funds is not too high. But we have to take into account the social costs of capital-intensive construction and excess costs due to tying the project to foreign imports of capital goods. If the foreign loan was untied but fixed in amount, then a different capital formation bill would be faced, perhaps giving investible resources to be used elsewhere in the economy; if the foreign loan could be obtained at less than the ARI (which is plausible with typical 'hard' rates), then it would be better to accept the foreign loan rather than finance the same somewhat more labour-intensive construction technique and untied capital goods domestically. Thus the present estate as a whole may be socially profitable given its method of financing, but it could be more profitable.

The particular enterprise in the estate for which we did a project appraisal was the rather unglamorous example of a factory producing hinges. Various sizes of butt type and 'T' type steel hinges are used in houses and other building, wooden furniture, steel and wooden boxes, and suitcases. On the basis of the market survey conducted by ICDC – the estimated consumption in Kenya of various sizes of butt and 'T' type steel hinges in 1966 was:

Butt type hinges	Size	4″	45,300 dozen pairs
		3″	63,000 dozen pairs
		2½″	68,600 dozen pairs
		2″	68,600 dozen pairs
		1½″	13,300 dozen pairs
		1″	27,500 dozen pairs
'T' type hinges	Size	12″	20,300 dozen pairs
		10″	20,300 dozen pairs
		8″	28,600 dozen pairs
		6″	28,600 dozen pairs

The future demand for steel hinges, except for the smaller sizes of butt hinges used in steel and wooden boxes, can be directly related to future building activity in the public and private sector. According to the 1966–70 *Development Plan*, expenditure on low-cost housing and more expensive housing was likely to increase by 171% and 196% respectively during the Plan period, i.e. demand for steel hinges was likely to increase at a yearly rate of 45–49% over the 1966 consumption. This rate of increase continued in the 1970–4 Plan period. In 1967, there was no factory manufacturing this item in Kenya, the demand being met by imports from Mainland China, England, Germany, and Sweden. For a time, a 15% customs duty was imposed on the import of this item, which has now been removed. Mombasa CIF cost per dozen pairs of various size butt-type hinges in 1967 was:

	Chinese	English
4″	sh. 7.80	sh. 8.82 – 11.82
3″	sh. 3.60	sh. 4.75 – 5.62
2½″	sh. 2.40	sh. 3.00 – 4.25
2″	sh. 1.80	sh. 2.25 – 3.32
1½″	sh. 0.84	sh. 1.75 – 2.75
1″	sh. 0.72	sh. 1.20 – 2.10

The actual price paid is a function of size of order. It was suggested that the Chinese price is a dumping price, and that the Chinese raise prices when they have captured a market. Thus it is not clear that export markets e.g. Zambia would be lost to a Kenyan producer.

The parties sponsoring the project felt that in the first stage machinery should be installed having an annual capacity to produce the full 1966 Kenyan demand for butt type hinges. The machinery proposed will be automatic and, assuming a working efficiency of 80%, the blanking and cranking machines will have to work eight hours a day and the assembling machines sixteen hours a day to meet the production targets. Production of the item started in June 1968, and full capacity working was reached by the end of that year. Production of 'T' type steel hinges and suitcase locks started later, and the project examined is on the assumption that this second phase has not been carried out. No provision for additional capital expenditure and maintenance has been made. Maintenance services for both stages of the project are provided by the Common Facility Tool Room on the Estate.

Capital requirements involve a number of small items, all new.

Machinery and tools at f.o.b. prices Hamburg

1. One automatic blanking and perforating power press, with complementary equipment: K£6,461.
2. One automatic cranking initial rolling, finish rolling and milling machine with complementary equipment: K£8,485.
3. One automatic hinge parts assembling machine with complement equipment: K£6,460.
4. Tool sets for above: K£6,000

Local capital costs are minor items, including workshop and office tools, and two locally manufactured tumbling barrels with motor and starters. Estimates of transport cost from Hamburg to Mombasa, clearance, duty, forwarding and transport to Nairobi raise fixed capital costs to K£31,700, at local prices. These items were broken down, and their social cost evaluated in terms of Scott's breakdowns. Working capital is calculated on the basis of three months' recurring expenses.

Other expenses include rent for a 2,500 sq.ft. shed, say K£700, electricity, water, office and selling expenses; raw materials and packing materials include cold rolled mild steel strips, cold drawn mild steel wire, and cartons.

The financing of the project involves a loan from ICDC equal to the fixed cost of the project at local prices; the loan is at 8% interest p.a. for eight years, to be recovered in fourteen equal half-yearly instalments after a grace period of one year. The entrepreneur is expected to provide a contribution equal to projected working capital; say, K£11,000.

The following labour crew appears the most reasonable for the operation of this set of equipment:

1. Manager at K.sh. 3,500/— per month.
2. Secretary-cum-telephonist at K.sh. 900/— per month.
3. Foreman-cum-tool-setter at K.sh. 2,000/— per month.
4. One skilled worker (Grade 2) at K.sh. 600/— per month.
5. Five skilled workers (Grade 3) at K.sh. 450/— per month.
6. Twelve unskilled workers (Grade 9) at K.sh. 260/— per month.
7. Watchman at K.sh. 260/— per month.

to which are added medical expenses, overtime payments, and contributions to workmen's compensation, say K£300 p.a. Total labour remuneration is thus K£8,829. In the present company, with stage II in operation, there is an expanded labour force; in addition casual labour is employed at K.sh. 7/— per day (the Nairobi minimum wage), but very infrequently (for rush orders). The above labour cost is re-estimated in social terms at various SWRs and SCFs. The grades (of skilled worker) are based on Government classification, but for the project analysis below, we again take skilled labour to be labour earning in excess of K.sh. 600/— per month.

Workers are employed casually to begin with; of these the best are selected for monthly engagements. About two weeks is required for the workers to develop an aptitude for working the machines. Skill requirements are, therefore, relatively low; only industrial discipline and the ability to operate simple machinery are imbued. No labour-training externalities, as measured by the Guidelines, were measured, in part because this is a machine-paced, low-skill operation, and it is doubtful, given the short training period required, that we would want to count Grade II and Grade III workers as skilled; and in part, because according to the management, no workers have left of their own accord; many, however, have been sacked owing to their low personal efficiency.[1]

Some questionable assumptions have been made about allocation of common costs but we have acted on the

1. Since the project being examined has a rather low skill-content, we describe the training programme of a large foreign investor operating in Nairobi and Thika. This firm launched a training programme in 1966, to train technician apprentices (who would be trained to install and maintain machinery, specialising in either the mechanical, engineering or the electronic sides for eventual appointment as departmental superintendents) and craft apprentices (who would be trained as toolmakers, maintenance fitters, electricians, fitters and turners; for eventual appointment as chargehand or foreman). Both technician and craft apprentices are recruited at about 19 years from the Vocational Secondary Schools, where they obtained pre-craft or pre-technician certificates after three years' study. All the apprentices are enrolled at the Kenya Polytechnic for further training, either on a sandwich or day-release basis; the company paying all tuition and examination fees. For the first two years of the five years' apprenticeship all the apprentices receive practical training from the Company's Apprentice Training Centre. The third year is spent in the Toolroom and Maintenance Department, and the fourth and fifth year on the production lines; there are also opportunities for further training in the U.K.

A technician apprentice's rate on satisfactory completion of his training is at least K£900 p.a., and for a craft apprentice K£810 p.a. Note that these rates are far above Scott's cut-off rate for skilled labour (K£250 p.a.). Some foreign investors go to quite some length to provide training but even in the absence of a fuller study of Kenya's manpower needs, we can surely say that while legislation is welcome, the Government itself should orient its educational expenditures more towards vocational training.

For large industry it may be preferable to instruct the foreign enterprise to train local managers and higher technical grades for the day of independence from foreign capital; it will be important and difficult to ensure that during this time period firm-specific and industry-specific technology is transferred to local staff. We should really attempt here an analysis of the cost of training by different 'agencies' and an analysis of the optimal use of legislation and taxation in a situation where the market mechanism alone is unlikely to produce the correct amount of training.

assumption that it is better to be explicit especially about the questionable. We took the percentage-covered area of this project to total area of Nairobi Phase I times total construction cost of Nairobi Phase I, as construction cost of the hinges project. Discussion of present values and internal rates of return generated should proceed while remembering that very probably a more labour-intensive technology in constructions exists.[1]

Results	IRR	PV at 10%	PV at 20%
Little-Mirrlees prices;			
e = 1; SCF = 0.75	10.5%	K£829	−K£17,630
Little-Mirrlees prices;			
e = 2; SCF = 0.75	13%	K£13,676	−K£21,900

1. As usual we were defeated in our quest for actual numbers regarding choice of technique in construction! We are, of course, not arguing against capital intensity as such, which could be optimal depending on the value of the SWR, but against capital-intensive techniques yielding no corresponding increase in investible supplies.

PART FIVE

Passion, Politics and Power

This part provides a highly selective account of the non-economic aspects of private foreign investment. Many of these aspects involve deep and complex problems in ethics, politics and law. It is clearly beyond the scope of this book (and my competence) to do full justice to this important area. Nevertheless as in many ways the problems to be discussed in this part are considered by many observers to be the most crucial for the future role of private foreign investment, and in particular of the multinationals, in the world economy, it is important to know what the problems are, and how (if at all) they can be mitigated. The first chapter in this Part, deals with the problems, and the second with their mitigation.

V.1 PROBLEMS

The previous parts of this book have been exclusively concerned with the economic aspects of POI, and have shown how the host country can determine the net economic gains to itself from such investment, as well as the divergent net social benefits in fact achieved in the small sample of case studies we conducted. We have emphasised the importance of social evaluation of each act of POI, and of the bargaining process in which the host country should obviously try and maximise the net gains to itself. Given this it is platitudinous that POI can be an important aid to development.

Nevertheless POI arouses fierce passions and opposition in most developing countries (as it has too in developed ones). It is easy, but in my view facile, to dismiss (or at least diminish) the importance and relevance of these passions, as some economists have done[1] as a non-economic collective consumption good 'which the polity may choose to buy,

---

1. Kindleberger, *Power and Money* (Macmillan, 1970); Johnson in Kindleberger, ed., op. cit.,

giving up economic advantages afforded by foreign investment'.[1] This formulation is unhelpful as an aid to understanding the nature and sources of these passions, as well as
to devising means for mitigating them (to the extent to which
this is desirable).

Much of the passionate resistance to POI can be looked
upon as a subjective fear of being violated. This could be a
fear of violation of the country's sovereignty, and/or of its
cultural and moral values. The past history of colonial rule,
moreover, tends to aggravate this fear, especially if colonialism was seen to have been linked (whether or not this was
the case) to foreign commercial interests. Moreover this fear
of violation must ultimately depend upon the perceived (or
imagined) threat inherent in differentials in power between
the host country and the foreign investor (and/or his parent
country). POI is then seen as the Trojan horse which
diminishes the power of the host country. But power to do
what? A study by David Vital is particularly useful in
answering this and other questions connected with the
inequality of states. Vital states that:

> The measure of state power is the capacity of a government to
> induce other states — or governments — to follow lines of conduct or
> policy which they might otherwise not pursue; alternatively, it is the
> capacity to withstand the pressure of other states — or govern-
> ments — which are intent on deflecting it from a course which the
> national interest — or the interest of its leaders — would appear to
> require. For the great state it is the first aspect of power that is of
> highest and most immediate importance; for the small state it is the
> second. It may also be said that what characterises the middle power
> in this respect is its indeterminate position between the two.[2]

Most developing countries would fall into the small and a few
into the middle power category. Of the small power Vital
correctly observes that 'its major problems (in its external
affairs) are how to avoid situations where its weaknesses will
be exposed and exploited and how, on the other hand, to
make the most of its limited resources'. The latter aspect
obviously gives it an incentive to use foreign trade and
investment to further its development, but this also opens it

1. Kindleberger, op. cit., p. 188.
2. David Vital, *The Inequality of States* (Oxford, 1967), p. 5.

up to the dangers of coercion. It is the form which economic coercion could take, and the conditions for its success which are of particular interest to us.

Again Vital is useful and succinct. He distinguishes between the external face of the state, whereby 'it presents itself . . . as a corporate body whose authority cannot openly be questioned, whose decisions and internal processes are privileged, and whose actions in the external sphere are, within very broad limits indeed, unbound by law'[1]; and its internal face where there is a well-understood distinction between 'the state and those who rule it'. He then argues that, normally, in international relations it is the *external* aspect of the state, in which its rulers are customarily treated as the state, which is considered relevant, and a 'foreign move to weaken the rulers' domestic authority or interfere with the link between them and the machine runs against the grain of all peaceful and proper international relations. Yet where one government desires to impose its wishes on another and has exhausted those means which are commonly permissible within the framework of orderly relations, an obvious course is to consider action within the domestic sphere of the second government where it is both actually and conceptually more vulnerable'.[2] The most obvious form of such coercion is subversion, which seeks (or threatens) to weaken the internal hold of the rulers over their subjects. 'Economic pressure pursues essentially the same aim by attacking at the same point. Only its concrete means, and of course its ambience, differ. It does not attack the government as such, it attacks the governed'.[3]

Political fears of host countries about POI, moreover, relate not only to the possibility of economic pressure exercised by foreign powers through their foreign companies, but equally to the fear of the possibility of direct subversion by foreign powers to protect the local interests of their companies in the host country. It is in large part this fear of direct and indirect subversion which in my view accounts largely for the fierce passions that POI can arouse in

1–3. Vital, op. cit., pp. 94–95. For the history of one such recent attempt, see Anthony Sampson, *The Sovereign State: The Secret History of ITT* (Hodder and Stoughton, 1973).

developing countries. It must be emphasised that these fears of vulnerability are essentially a *state of mind* of the leaders of developing countries, which are likely to differ from country to country, depending in large part upon the factors in each case which are likely to be conducive to the success of politically motivated economic pressure or coercion.

The likely conditions for the effectiveness of economic pressure, and hence the likelihood of its deployment are summarised by Vital as '(a) the overall importance of the sector of the economy under attack; (b) the availability of alternatives; (c) the importance of the political issues at stake; (d) the relations between government and governed; (e) the tenacity with which each party pursues its course'.[1]

In translating these conditions into the specific situations and likely fear 'levels' of particular developing countries vis-à-vis foreign investors and their parent governments, the following general considerations would be relevant. First, the perceived past relationship with foreign investors and their parent governments would obviously be an important factor conditioning the current states of mind of host country leaders. As Diaz Alejandro has emphasised in his discussion of POI in Latin America, the past strongly conditions current attitudes.[2] Though the economist's training ('bygones are bygones') tends to be a-historical, history is a powerful influence on men's actions, and we neglect it at our peril. Second, the fear of a particular country's foreign investment will depend largely upon the power relationship, on the

1. Vital, op. cit., p. 99.
2. C. F. Diaz Alejandro, 'Direct Foreign Investment in Latin America' in Kindleberger, ed., op. cit. He says, 'Original sins and past adolescent escapades plague many foreign investors now operating in Latin America. Cool Latin American bargaining is hampered by memories of that not so distant past. The key point is that much DFI involved not just commercial bargaining, including bribery, but the implicit and explicit use of the political and military muscle of foreign governments to further their nationals' business interests', p. 320. The importance of the 'distance' of the past, as well as of the relative power ranking of the foreign country must be emphasised. Thus whilst British colonialism in the past had many of the above features noted by Diaz Alejandro, for many countries this past is by now fairly distant, and also the British lion is now perceived by most developing countries as being toothless. This would account in part for the relatively lower level of fear of U.K. POI, as compared with that from the U.S.A. in most of the ex-U.K. colonies.

concentration of that country's foreign investment, as well as its share of the total capital stock in the host country. On all three counts, we would expect (as is the case) that fear of U.S. foreign investment in Latin America would be particularly virulent.[1] Third, the deeds and words of the powerful foreign parent country, would also (*ceteris paribus*) tend to exacerbate or mitigate the host country's fears. Here again the words and deeds of the U.S. government, particularly in its relations with Latin America are likely to accentuate the host country's fears.[2]

These fears of the loss of political sovereignty are further buttressed by other fears about the non-economic effects of the operation of POI. Many of these fears, which we discuss below, are moreover not confined to developing countries, and seem to be common fears of all nation states when confronting the multinational corporation. These fears too concern the loss of sovereignty. But whereas the fears we have discussed so far were those of losing sovereignty as a result of pressures put by another nation state in the interests of its own nationals, this second set of fears relates to the loss

1. As we saw in part I, POI is heavily concentrated in Latin America, and most of this POI is by U.S. companies, whilst the U.S. is obviously seen to be (as it is) the most powerful external power by Latin Americans. Thus Diaz Alejandro states: 'Italian investors enjoy in Latin America greater popularity than those from the United States. History and the Hickenlooper amendment remind Latin America that investors from hegemonic powers are too often tempted to convert economic disputes into political ones when dealing with politically weak countries, and that foreign countries are tempted to use the economic power of its overseas investors to further their policy goals', p. 320.
2. For deeds, there are the 1965 invasion of the Dominican republic, the recent disclosures of CIA involvement in the fall of Mossadegh in Iran, and the disclosures of the whole ITT affair with Chile. For words the following statement by John Connally, then Secretary of the Treasury, before a U.S. Congress committee discussing the U.S. energy shortage, should suffice. He recommended that the United States give more support to American corporations that are threatened with expropriation of their property in foreign countries. In such situations, Mr. Connally said, Washington should put itself in the position of saying to other governments, 'You don't negotiate just with American business enterprise. You negotiate with the United States Government. I think we have to come to that type of posture,' the Secretary added. 'Otherwise, American business will be helpless in dealing with foreign governments around the world', (*New York Times*, April 19th, 1972). Whilst the recent 'Watergate' and linked disclosures of the translation into fact of the wildest fantasies of the thriller writers, in the operations of the White House 'plumbers', would give even the least paranoic host country some food for thought.

of sovereignty and control over the domestic economy through the 'normal' operations of the multinational corporation. It is the *multi*national nature of these corporations and the flexibility this gives them which is the basic source of these fears, just as the inherent inequality of nation states was the basic source of the first set of fears.

The problems arise from the divergence in the goals of the nation state and the multinational firms. Whereas the former is interested in maximising the welfare of its nationals, the international firm seeks, on the whole, to maximise its global profits, though there may be internal conflicts of interest in some cases within the corporation between the head office and the national subsidiaries. Moreover, whereas national corporations are largely subject to the jurisdiction and legal/moral sanctions of their national governments when the pursuit of their interests is considered to be at odds with national goals, the multinational corporation, given its worldwide activities, can often escape the nominal jurisdiction of each of the national governments under which its subsidiaries operate.

There are three main aspects of the flexibility of the international corporations which seem to upset nation states. The first concerns the practice of transfer pricing,[1] which we have discussed briefly in Chapter II.9. The second concerns their alleged ability to affect a country's foreign exchange rate as a result of the vast pool of foreign currencies which they deal in and hold. Thus they can through short-term flow of funds (financed by the appropriate leads and lags in international payments and receipts, and through 'normal' hedging operations) force countries to change their foreign exchange rate. Whether or not this is desirable from an economic point of view (and on the whole the arguments for it being desirable seem to me more persuasive), this supposed

1. For a theoretical discussion of transfer pricing, see L. W. Copithorne, 'International Corporate Transfer Pricing and Government Policy', *Canadian Journal of Economics*, August 1971. For empirical evidence see C. V. Vaitsos, 'Transfer of Resources and Preservation of Monopoly Rents', Development Advisory Service, Harvard, 1970; S. Lall, 'Determinants and Implications of Transfer Pricing by International Firms', *Bulletin of the Oxford Institute of Economics and Statistics*, 1973; Vernon, op. cit.

power to force reluctant exchange rate changes on national governments clearly exacerbates the fears of national governments which on the whole tend to look upon exchange rate changes as an important national policy instrument and hence an important aspect of their national sovereignty.[1] Thirdly there is the undisputed fact that most countries and certainly developing countries are competitors for the favour of international companies, whose locational decisions can thereby profoundly influence the relative fortunes of these various countries. These locational decisions can concern new investments, as much as the rationalisation of past investment decisions (e.g. if a plant has to be shut down should the one in country X rather than in country Y be shut down).[2] This factor not only profoundly affects the relative bargaining power of host developing countries vis à vis the foreign investor, but can also be a source of fears about the loss of national power and sovereignty.[3]

Finally, there are the fears of cultural penetration, and the gradual erosion of a national identity if a predominant part of the national economy is controlled by one particular foreign country's POI. These fears are to be found not only in developing countries but also in developed ones (e.g. Canada, France and Japan). Again it is easy to dismiss these fears as being chauvinistic and xenophobic, but that would be to assume a world-wide homogeneity of moral and political beliefs which, despite the universal lip-service paid to certain ideals (liberty, democracy, the brotherhood of Man, etc.), by no means exists at present. This point, moreover, underlines the complexity of the problem of appraising the validity of many of these political fears, and the dangers of the application of a set of parochial (explicit or implicit) value premises. For, as should be evident from our discussion, many of these fears are 'subjective', and depend upon each country's image of itself and others as well as upon its own goals and values and those attributed to others. The task of

---

1. and 2. See Louis Turner, *Politics and the Multinational Company* (Fabian Research Series 279, 1969).
3. Though in the case of various extractive industries (like oil), the boot would now seem to be firmly on the other foot!

evaluation therefore involves all the deep problems in moral and political philosophy connected with power, justice, equity, and the proper 'world order'. It is beyond the scope of this book to discuss these very important issues. Nevertheless to the extent that these fears exist and are a powerful source of tension between host countries and foreign investors, they cannot (and in the real world will not) be ignored. It is therefore necessary to discuss ways in which they can be mitigated.

In conclusion a possible criticism of our discussion of host country fears should be taken into account, namely our neglect of the problems and issues posed in the literature of imperialism, neo-colonialism et al. The reason for this neglect, is that this literature is not, in my view, of much help in understanding the nature of the political fears of host countries when faced by foreign investors, for it seems to be concerned on the one hand with tedious and essentially scholastic disputes about the definition of imperialism, whether various current relationships between countries are (or are not) imperialist or neo-colonialist, and on the other with discussions of the causes of imperialism — past and present.[1] Whilst these discussions are of historical and ideological interest, they do not illuminate current fears of POI. Given the emotive connotation of the words 'imperialism' and 'colonialism', and the necessarily partial explanations provided of the complex, multi-faceted and highly

---

1. The 'classical' writings on the subject are J. A. Hobson, *Imperialism* (New York 1902); V. I. Lenin, *Imperialism* (1917); Schumpeter, *Imperialism* (Blackwell, Oxford, 1951). D. K. Fieldhouse, ' "Imperialism": An Historiographical Revision', *Economic History Review*, 1961. Gallagher and Robinson, 'The Imperialism of Free Trade', *Economic History Review*, 1953, and Robinson and Gallagher, *Africa and the Victorians* (Macmillan 1961), are historical critiques of the Hobson—Lenin thesis. Hugh Stretton, *The Political Sciences* (Routledge, 1969), presents an illuminating discussion of the various theories of imperialism, whilst Boulding and Mukherjee, eds., op. cit., and Owen and Sutcliffe, eds., *Studies in the Theory of Imperialism* (Longmans 1972), are useful collections of past and current writings on imperialism and neo-imperialism. Also see Baran and Sweezy, 'Notes on the theory of Imperialism' in *Problems of Economic Dynamics and Planning: Essays in Honour of Michael Kalecki* (Pergamon, Oxford, 1966); A. Lindbeck, *The Political Economy of the New Left* (Harper and Row, New York, 1971), and the Symposium on this book in *Quarterly Journal of Economics*, Nov. 1972.

variegated historical record of these phenomena, it is easy to react in an extreme form (either of acceptance or rejection) to the claims that the contemporary relationships between the rich and poor nations are neo-colonialist or neo-imperialist. As a result the arguably legitimate fears of political vulnerability and coercion (which as we have tried to argue are essentially rooted in the unavoidable inequality of states) are either grossly exaggerated or facilely dismissed. As the essential facts of inequalities of power, and the possible link between direct subversion and economic pressure are not in dispute, and as it is these factors which account, in large part, for host country fears of a possible violation of their political sovereignty, it seems best to discuss these aspects directly, without bringing in the possible red herring of the 'imperialism' controversy. Moreover in discussing ways of allaying these political fears the 'imperialism' literature is likely to lead to extreme conclusions. Caricaturing somewhat, one side would maintain that nothing needs to be done about POI, because there is no essential link between it and 'imperialism'; whilst the other side would claim that nothing *can* be done about POI till the world-wide capitalist system is smashed, as imperialism and POI are linked and both are a necessary feature of such a system, so that the best host developing countries can do is to shut themselves up against the whole evil capitalist world.[1] However as we have argued in this Chapter neither of these conclusions seems very sensible, and it is to ways in which these fears might be allayed that we turn in the next chapter.

V.2 REMEDIES

The remedies which have been suggested[2] to deal with a host country's fears of loss of political sovereignty, cover both main sources of these fears identified in the last chapter,

1. It is however likely to be extremely valuable to gain an understanding of the psychology of the colonialists and the colonised. But here the novelist's skills are likely to be much more valuable than political pamphleteers. See for instance the works of the novelist V. S. Naipaul.
2. Vernon, *Sovereignty at Bay* (Basic Books, New York, 1971), provides an excellent account of these remedies, and this chapter owes a great deal to this magisterial work.

namely fears of pressure by another nation state in the interests of its foreign investors and/or the use of its foreign investors to subserve its own national interests; secondly fears of loss of sovereignty in national fiscal, monetary, exchange rate and employment policies as a result of the lack of national control over the multinational firm's 'normal' operations.

One remedy which has been suggested for alleviating host country fears of foreign coercion, is the so-called Calvo clause. This has been persistently advanced by Latin American countries (being named after the Argentinian minister who first devised it). Under this clause any foreign subsidiary would be denied all legal rights if it sought the support of a foreign government in any dispute with its host government. This doctrine is clearly unpalatable to foreign investors, and there is likely to be justification for their fears, unless there is in conjunction with such a clause some agreed basis for international adjudication for international business disputes.

The next set of remedies are various proposals for planned divestiture of foreign investors over a given time period.[1] The divestiture could be total or partial (into some form of joint venture). Vernon sets out a formidable set of objections against these proposals the gist of which seems to be that they could be economically harmful to the host country in terms of inhibiting both the volume and quality of POI flows to these countries. However, as he admits, 'the existence of the arrangements could serve some of the political and psychological needs of the host country by blunting the government's sense of being irrevocably blocked from controlling a major facility in its own economy'.[2] As these fears of foreign control are likely to increase with the concentration of POI in the particular host country's capital stock, divestiture might be a useful short-run method of alleviating these fears. Given the concentration of POI in Latin America, and the consequent fear of loss of national sovereignty in this

1. A. O. Hirschman, 'How to Divest in Latin America, and Why', *Princeton Essays in International Finance*, no. 76 (Princeton, 1969).
2. Vernon, op. cit., p. 269.

region, divestiture would seem to me to make much sense, particularly as in the absence of alternative and immediate ways of alleviating these fears even more extreme forms of restrictions on POI in this region may be contemplated. Planned divestiture in Latin America may therefore represent the lesser of two evils, even from the viewpoint of the foreign investor.

The third set of remedies concern some form of international agreement on the regulation of international business including their surveillance through some form of international organisation. In this context the secrecy surrounding the accounting practices of most multinational firms, must be first attacked.[1] More open and meaningful accounts would also be a safeguard against the obvious abuses like 'transfer' pricing. Moreover this is one area, where the interests of most governments are likely to coincide, and hence international agreement may be more likely. Various other fears concerning the 'normal' operations of the multinationals could perhaps also be tackled in this piecemeal way. For instance host country fears about the multinational company's power to shift its location and hence affect the international distribution of the gains from its investments, could to some extent be mitigated by some form of built-in adjustment assistance whose financing the multinationals could share with the host country, in order to ease any 'employment' problems caused by the withdrawal (or running down) of foreign investment in the host country.

The natural extension of such piecemeal reform could be the establishment of some sort of multilateral Commission for Regulating International Business (CRIB), to which the international firms would be accountable, and which would keep the multinationals' operations under surveillance in line with some agreed multilateral principles.[2] Though the establishment of a CRIB may seem Utopian at the moment, in the long run it may be the only way, as Vernon points out,[3] to prevent the internecine conflict between nation states and

---

1. See Sampson, op. cit., for an account of ITT's accounting system.
2. See Vernon, op. cit., p. 284.
3. Ibid., p. 282.

multinational corporations, which could occur increasingly in the future. However the establishment of CRIB will involve a good degree of self-abnegation on the part of all nation-states. For the powerful it will involve the renunciation of their power to use their international corporations as a tool of their foreign policy,[1] and from the weak it will require the acceptance of some form of international ground rules for allowing foreign corporations to operate equitably within their territories, as well as of the international adjudication of any business disputes they may have with foreign investors. However once *all* nation-states realise that in facing the multinational corporation, they are facing an organisation which is not subject to the control of any one of them,[2] the will to undertake such multilateral co-operation may not long be absent.

This is not to minimise the problems involved (political, diplomatic, legal and moral) in reaching an agreement to set up CRIB, and even more importantly in devising its charter and ground rules. For, again as Vernon has pertinently noted, 'what nations shortly will discover when they turn to a concerted approach is that the heart of the problem is its least tractable part: how to ensure that the fruits of such enterprises' operations are distributed among such nations in some "equitable" way'.[3] However, just as within each nation state (be it developed or developing) the problems of equity are coming to the fore as the single most important problem of political economy in the 1970s, the day may not be too distant when in an increasingly overcrowded and inter-

1. As Vernon puts it, it will mean that 'governments − particularly the U.S. government' − will have 'to distinguish their national interests from the interests of their multinational enterprises rather more explicitly than they have in the past', Vernon, 'Future of the Multinational Enterprise', in Kindleberger, ed., op. cit., p. 395.
2. Thus the Dow Chemical Company's Chairman, Carl A. Gerstacker was quoted as having said in 1972, 'I have long dreamed of buying an island owned by no nation, and of establishing World Headquarters of the Dow Company on the truly neutral ground of such an island, beholden to no nation or society' (quoted in Leonard Woodcock, 'Force Social Responsibility on International Companies', *New York Times*, Jan. 7, 1973).
3. Vernon, 'Future . . .', in Kindleberger, ed., op. cit., p. 397.

dependent world the nettle of international equity too will have to be firmly grasped.

Recently the UN, ECSOC, at its 53rd session decided to set up an expert group 'to study the role of multinational corporations and their impact on the development process, especially in developing countries, as well as the implications of the role of these corporations for international relations. The group was asked to formulate conclusions which might possibly be used by Governments in making their sovereign decisions regarding national policy. It was asked to make recommendations for appropriate international action.'[1] This marks the beginning of what could turn out to be the process of setting up a CRIB. But it will be important that in the ensuing discussions and — we hope — eventual negotiations the LDCs are brought in at an early stage.

However if the developing countries are not to be hopelessly divided amongst themselves on the essential principles which should govern CRIB, it will be necessary for them to find some way of resolving their own regional and interregional conflicts of national interest. Thus for instance they will have to agree on some common set of principles about the incentives offered to foreign investors, as well as on a formula for pro-ration of the consolidated profits of multinational companies (if an alternative and international form of taxation of multinational corporations is considered desirable).[2] As the particular principles adopted will have differential effects on the relative gains of different developing countries which will remain competitors (on the whole) for POI, the possibility of conflicts of interest within the Third World is very acute. As these countries have so far

1. United Nations Press Release ECOSOC/559, 28 July 1972.
2. This has been suggested cautiously in Vernon, 'Sovereignty . . .', in Kindleberger, ed., op. cit., p. 276. He argues on the basis of analogy with the corporate tax formula of several states in the U.S.A. that 'the operations of the individual subsidiaries of multinational enterprises are inescapably interrelated; the profits assigned to each of them are unavoidably arbitrary. Therefore . . . the assessment of tax liability in any jurisdiction should be based on the pro-ration of the consolidated profit of the multinational enterprise as a whole, according to an agreed pro-ration formula'.

not been notably successful in resolving their own conflicts of interests even in the sphere of foreign trade (even on a commodity or regional basis),[1] the future prospects of their doing so in the sphere of POI do not seem very bright.

Similarly, if there is to be international acceptance of the Calvo doctrine (as in my view there should be), developing countries will have to accept some form of international adjudication of their business disputes with foreign investors, on some commonly agreed set of principles and by an impartial international adjudicating body. More importantly, they will have to convince the parent countries of foreign investors that they will abide by these adjudications. If developing countries prove to be incapable of developing a well thought-out and united stand on these fundamental problems, they are likely to be used one against the other, and collectively be left out in the cold (as they have been in the past) in any future reconstruction of the world economic system. In that case the suggestion by Vernon[2] that as a start a CRIB should be confined to the advanced nations may well be the only feasible one, and though this would then inevitably be another rich men's club, developing countries might well have themselves to blame, in large measure, for the outcome. Wise statesmanship on the part of developing countries to resolve their currently conflicting national economic interests (which is a formidable task) would thus appear to be a *sine qua non* of their real participation in shaping the world economic order, in which the establishment of a truly international CRIB might play an important part in reconciling the two seemingly divergent faces of international business.

Meanwhile, in the world system as it is at present,

---

1. The chequered history of commodity agreements is a case in point. Also the recent experience of UNCTAD III does not augur well for the Third World's equal participation in any future reconstruction of the world economic order. See Sidney Dell, 'An Appraisal of UNCTAD III', *World Development*, Vol. 1, No. 5, May 1973. However, against this we must set the 1971 establishment of the Andean Pact between Colombia, Ecuador, Chile, Peru and Bolivia, to co-ordinate their policies towards foreign investment. In the immediate future, such regional groupings may be more feasible than the sort of global agreements discussed in the text.
2. Vernon, 'Sovereignty . . .', in Kindleberger, op. cit., p. 280.

developing countries will have to live with their non-economic fears as best they can, if they are to make use of POI as an aid to their development. But at the very least they must ascertain that *there are* positive social gains to them from the operation of POI. The type of economic appraisal advocated and applied in the earlier parts of this book must therefore form an integral part of their processes for appraising foreign investment.

Bibliography

P. Ady, ed. *Private Foreign Investment and the Developing World* (Praeger, 1971).

K. J. Arrow, *Aspects of the Theory of Risk-Bearing* (Yrjo Johansson Lectures, Helsinki, 1965).

K. J. Arrow and R. C. Lind, 'Uncertainty and the Evaluation of Public Investment Decisions', *American Economic Review*, June 1970.

E. Bacha and L. Taylor, 'Foreign Exchange Shadow Prices: A Critical Review of Current Theory', *Quarterly Journal of Economics*, May 1971.

R. E. Baldwin, 'Equilibrium in International Trade', *Quarterly Journal of Economics*, 1948.

P. Baran and P. Sweezy, 'Notes on the Theory of Imperialism' in *Problems of Economic Dynamics and Planning: Essays in Honour of Michael Kalecki* (Pergamon, 1966).

J. Baranson, *Manufacturing Problems in India* (Syracuse, 1967).

G. S. Becker, *Human Capital* (Columbia, 1964).

J. Bhagwati, 'Immiserising Growth: A Geometrical Note', *Review of Economic Studies*, June 1958.

J. Bhagwati and S. Chakravarty, 'Contributions to Indian Economic Analysis: A Survey', *American Economic Review*, Supplement, 1970.

K. Boulding and T. Mukherjee, *Economic Imperialism* (Michigan, 1972).

M. Brown and J. S. de Cani, 'Technological Choice and the Distribution of Income', *International Economic Review*, Sept. 1963.

R. E. Caves, 'International Corporations: The Industrial Economics of Foreign Investment', *Economica*, February 1971.

A. Chakravarti, 'The Social Profitability of Training Unskilled Workers in the Public Sector in India', *Oxford Economic Papers*, March 1972.

L. W. Copithorne, 'International Corporate Transfer Pricing and Government Policy', *Canadian Journal of Economics*, August 1971.

W. M. Corden, 'The Balance of Payments Effects of Foreign Investment: Some Theory', (mimeo), OECD/UNCTAD, 1970.

J. Cramer, 'Notes on the Population of Kenya' (mimeo), (Nairobi, 1971).

V. M. Dandekar and N. Rath, *Poverty in India*, (Ford Foundation, Delhi, 1970).

R. Datt and K. Sundharam, *Indian Economy*, (Delhi, 1971).

S. Dell, 'An Appraisal of UNCTAD III', *World Development*, May 1973.

P. A. Diamond, 'Effective Protection of the East African Transfer Taxes', *East African Economic Review*, 1968.

276

P. A. Diamond, 'On the Economics of Tourism', *East African Economic Review*, 1969.

P. A. Diamond and J. A. Mirrlees, 'Optimal Taxation and Public Production', Parts I and II, *American Economic Review*, March and June 1971.

J. Dunning, ed. *The Multinational Enterprise* (Allen and Unwin, 1971).

M. Feldstein and J. S. Flemming, 'The Problem of Time-stream Evaluation: Present Value versus Internal Rate of Return Rules', *Bulletin Oxford University Institute of Economics and Statistics* February 1964.

W. Fellner, 'Operational Utility; the Theoretical Background and a Measurement' in Fellner, et. al., *Ten Economic Studies in the Tradition of Irving Fisher* (John Wiley, 1967).

J. S. Fforde, *An International Trade in Managerial Skills* (Blackwell, 1957).

D. K. Fieldhouse, '"Imperialism": An Historiographical Revision', *Economic History Review*, 1961.

J. Gallagher and R. Robinson, 'The Imperialism of Free Trade', *Economic History Review*, 1953.

D. Ghai, 'Analytic Aspects of an Income Policy for Kenya' (mimeo), (Nairobi, 1967).

D. Ghai, 'Incomes Policy in Kenya: Needs, Criteria and Machinery', (mimeo), (Nairobi, 1968).

D. Ghai, 'Priorities in Economic Research in Kenya over the Second Plan Period 1970–4', (mimeo), (Nairobi, 1970).

B. Hansen, *Long and Short-Term Planning in Underdeveloped Countries* (De Vries Lectures, North-Holland, Amsterdam, 1967).

J. R. Harris and M. P. Todaro, 'Wages, Industrial Employment and Labour Productivity: the Kenyan Experience', *East African Economic Review*, 1969.

J. R. Harris and M. P. Todaro, 'Migration, Unemployment and Development: a Two Sector Analysis', *American Economic Review*, 1970.

G. Helliner, 'Manufactured Exports and Multinational Firms: their Impact Upon Economic Development' (mimeo) April 1972.

J. F. Helliwell, *Public Policies and Private Investment* (OUP, 1968).

S. Hirsch, *Location of Industry and International Competitiveness* (OUP, 1967).

A. O. Hirschman, 'How to Divest in Latin America and Why', *Essays in International Finance*, No. 76 (Princeton, 1969).

A. O. Hirschman, *The Strategy of Economic Development* (Yale, 1958).

A. O. Hirschman, *Development Projects Observed*, (Brookings, 1967).

J. A. Hobson, *Imperialism* (New York, 1902).

G. C. Huffbauer, *Synthetic Materials and the Theory of International Trade* (Duckworth, 1965).

G. C. Huffbauer and F. M. Adler, *Overseas Manufacturing Investment and the Balance of Payments* (US Treasury Dept., Washington DC, 1968).

Government of India, *Pocketbook of Economic Information 1971.*
Government of India, *Economic Survey 1970–71* (Delhi, 1971).
Government of India, *Report of the Committee on Distribution of Income and Levels of Living,* (Delhi, 1964).
Government of India, *Pocketbook of Labour Statistics* (Delhi, 1971).
H. G. Johnson, 'The Efficiency and Welfare Implications of the International Corporation' in Kindleberger, ed. *The International Corporation.*
R. W. Jones, 'International Capital Movements and the Theory of Tariffs and Trade', *Quarterly Journal of Economics,*February 1967.
D. Jorgenson, 'Capital Theory and Investment Behaviour', *American Economic Review,* May 1963.
N. O. Jorgenson, 'ICDC: Its Purpose and Performance', IDS Discussion Papers No. 47, Nairobi, 1967.
M. Kemp, *The Pure Theory of International Trade and Investment* (Prentice-Hall, 1969).
Republic of Kenya, *Kenya Economic Survey 1971.*
Republic of Kenya, *Development Plan 1970–4* (Nairobi, 1969).
M. Kidron, *Foreign Investment in India* (OUP, 1965).
M. Kidron, 'Indo-Foreign Financial Collaboration in the Private Sector' (mimeo), Seminar on Foreign Collaboration of the Centre of Advanced Studies in Economics, 1965.
C. Kindleberger, *American Business Abroad* (Yale, 1969).
C. Kindleberger, *Power and Money* (Macmillan, 1970).
C. Kindleberger, ed. *The International Corporation* (MIT, 1970).
D. Lal, 'When is Foreign Borrowing Desirable?', *Bulletin Oxford University Institute of Economics and Statistics,* August 1971.
D. Lal, *Wells and Welfare* (OECD Development Centre, Paris, 1972).
D. Lal, 'Disutility of Effort, Migration and the Shadow Wage Rate', *Oxford Economic Papers,* March 1973.
D. Lal, 'Adjustments for Trade Distortions in Project Analysis', *Journal of Development Studies* October 1974 .
D. Lal, 'On Estimating Income Distribution Weights for Project Analysis', *IBRD Economic Staff Working Papers* No. 130, March 1972, revised June 1973.
D. Lal, *Methods of Project Analysis – A Review,* (World Bank Occasional Papers, Johns Hopkins, Baltimore, 1974).
D. Lal, *Men or Machines* (ILO, Geneva) (forthcoming).
S. Lall, 'Determinants and Implications of Transfer Pricing by International Firms', *Bulletin of the Oxford University Institute of Economics and Statistics,* August 1973.
V. I. Lenin, *Imperialism* (1917).
A. Lindbeck, *The Political Economy of the New Left* (Harper and Row, New York, 1971). Also see the symposium on this book in *Quarterly Journal of Economics,* November 1972.
I. M. D. Little, 'On Measuring the Value of Private Direct Overseas Investment' in G. Ranis, ed. *The Gap Between Rich and Poor Nations.*

I. M. D. Little and J. A. Mirrlees, *Manual of Industrial Project Analysis in Developing Countries, Vol. II; Social Cost Benefit Analysis* (OECD Dev. Centre, 1969).

I. M. D. Little and J. A. Mirrlees, *Project Appraisal and Planning for Developing Countries* (Heinemann, 1974).

I. M. D. Little and D. G. Tipping, *A Social Cost Benefit Analysis of the Kulai Oil Palm Estate* (OECD Development Centre, Paris, 1972).

G. D. A. MacDougall, 'The Benefits and Costs of Private Investment from Abroad: a Theoretical Approach', *The Economic Record*, 1960.

P. Marris and A. Somerset, *African Businessmen: a Study of Entrepreneurship and Development in Kenya* (London, 1971).

A. Mazumdar, 'Overseas Investment and Indian Taxation' in Ady, ed. *Private Foreign Investment and the Developing World.*

J. S. Meade, *Trade and Welfare* (Oxford University Press, 1955).

J. Mincer, 'The Distribution of Labour Incomes', *Journal of Economic Literatures*, 1970.

F. Mitchell, 'The Value of Tourism in East Africa', *East African Economic Review*, 1969.

F. Mitchell, 'Costs and Benefits of Tourism in Kenya', *East African Economic Review*, June 1970.

NCAER: *Foreign Technology and Investment* (Delhi, 1971).

NCAER: *Survey of Urban Income and Saving* (Delhi, 1962).

NEDC: *Investment Appraisal* (HMSO, London, 1967).

L. Needleman, S. Lall, R. Lacey, and J. Seagrave, 'Balance of Payments Effects of Private Foreign Investment', UNCTAD, T.D./B/C/379 Add 2.

ODI and SID, *Britain's Role in the Second Development Decade* (London, 1972).

OECD: *Development Assistance Review* (various years) (OECD, Paris).

OECD: 'Guide to the Methods Used in Cost-Benefit Studies of Industrial Projects in India' (mimeo), OECD Development Centre, Paris, 1970.

R. Owen and R. Sutcliffe, eds. *Studies in the Theory of Imperialism* (Longmans, 1972).

L. H. Pack and M. P. Todaro, 'Technological Transfer, Labour Absorption and Economic Development' *Oxford Economic Papers*, 1969.

Pearson Commission: *Partners in Development* (Pall Mall Press. 1969).

G. Ranis, ed. *The Gap Between Rich and Poor Nations* (Macmillan, 1972).

W. B. Reddaway, *Effects of UK Direct Overseas Investment — An Interim Report* (Cambridge, 1967).

Reserve Bank of India, *Foreign Collaboration in Indian Industry* (Bombay, 1968).

G. L. Reuber, H. Crookell, M. Emerson, G. Gallais-Hamonno, *Private Foreign Investment in Development* (Clarendon Press, Oxford, 1973).

H. J. Robinson, 'The Motivation and Flow of Private Foreign Investment', International Development Centre, Stanford Research Institute, California, 1961.

R. Robinson and J. Gallagher, *Africa and the Victorians* (Macmillan, 1961).

N. Rosenberg, ed. *The Economics of Technological Change* (Penguin, 1971).

W. E. G. Salter, *Productivity and Technical Change* (Cambridge, 1966).

A. Sampson, *The Sovereign State: the Secret History of ITT* (Hodder and Stoughton, 1973).

J. Schumpeter, *Imperialism* (Blackwell, Oxford, 1951).

M. Fg. Scott, 'Shadow Wages for "Surplus" Labour in Mauritius' (mimeo), (Nuffield College, Oxford, 1972).

M. Fg. Scott, J. MacArthur and D. Newberry, *Project Appraisal in Practice* (Heinemann, forthcoming).

M. Fg. Scott, 'Note on the Estimation of Accounting Prices for some Non-Tradeable and Tradeable Goods and Services in Kenya' (mimeo) 1970, to be included in Scott, MacArthur, Newberry, *Project Appraisal in Practice*.

A. K. Sen, 'Cost-Benefit Analysis of Foreign Investment' OECD/UNCTAD (mimeo), 1970.

A. K. Sen, 'Cost-Benefit Analysis of Private Foreign Investment and the OECD—UNCTAD Meeting in Paris' (mimeo), 1971.

F. Seton, *Shadow Wages in the Chilean Economy* (OECD Development Centre, Paris, 1972).

A. Smith, *The Wealth of Nations* (Routledge).

P. N. Snowden, 'Preliminary Study on Company Savings in Kenya' (mimeo), Nairobi, 1971.

Spencer and Woroniak, ed. *The Transfer of Technology to Developing Countries* (Praeger, 1967).

N. H. Stern, *An Appraisal of Tea Production on Small Holdings in Kenya* (OECD Development Centre, 1972).

M. D. Steuer et. al., *The Impact of Foreign Direct Investment on the United Kingdom* (Dept. of Trade and Industry, HMSO, London, 1973).

P. Streeten, 'Costs and Benefits of Multinational Enterprises in Less Developed Countries' in Dunning, ed. *The Multinational Enterprise*.

P. Streeten, 'New Approaches to Private Overseas Investment' in Ady, ed. *Private Foreign Investment and the Developing World*.

H. Stretton, *The Political Sciences* (Routledge, 1969).

K. K. Subrahmaniam, *A Study of Private Foreign Investment in India since 1950* (Bombay University, 1967).

K. K. Subrahmaniam, 'Market Structure and R&D Activity — a Case Study of the Chemical Industry' *Economic and Political Weekly*, Bombay, August 1971.

R. B. Sutcliffe, *Industry and Underdevelopment* (Addison-Wesley, 1971).

Symposium on the Little-Mirrlees Manual, *Bulletin of the Oxford University Institute of Economics and Statistics*, February 1972.

L. Turner, *Politics and the Multinational Company* (Fabian Research Series, 279, 1969).

UNIDO, *Guidelines for Project Evaluation* by A. K. Sen, S. Marglin, and P. Dasgupta (United Nations, New York, 1972).

C. V. Vaitsos, 'Transfer of Resources and Preservation of Monopoly Rents', Development Advisory Service, Harvard, 1970.

R. Vernon, *Sovereignty at Bay* (Basic Books, New York, 1971).

R, Vernon, 'International Investment and International Trade in the Product Cycle' *Quarterly Journal of Economics*, 1966.

R. Vernon, 'United States Enterprise in Less Developed Countries: Evaluation of Cost and Benefit' in G. Ranis, ed. *The Gap Between Rich and Poor Nations*.

R. Vernon, ed. *The Technology Factor In International Trade* (NBER, 1970).

D. Vital, *The Inequality of States* (Oxford, 1967).

B. Ward et. al., *The Widening Gap: Development in the 1970's* (Columbia, 1970).

Index